S0-CIH-606

Sunil Gavaskar is undoubtedly one of the finest cricketers India has produced, and she has produced a formidable array. Author of *Sunny Days,* a bestseller and a cricket classic, Gavaskar is one of the few sportmen who keeps writing and writes beautifully. In *Idols* he pays tribute to thirty-one of his contemporaries all over the cricket world. The stars that he writes about are not only the sportslovers' idols, they are also figures who Gavaskar himself admires for their verve, technique and style. And also grace—for cricket is a gentleman's sport.

In Gavaskar's parade of idols are included such stalwarts as Gary Sobers, Rohan Kanhai, Imran Khan, Zaheer Abbas, Glenn Turner, Greg Chappell, Ian Chappell, Jeff Thomson, Bishan Singh Bedi, G.R. Viswanath, Derek Underwood, Alan Knott, to name some.

Sunil Manohar Gavaskar (b.1949) was born and brought up in Bombay, where he attended St Xavier's High School and St Xavier's College. He inherited his interest in cricket from his parents and uncle and justified their high hopes in him when in 1961, at the age of twelve, he distinguished himself in Schools' Tournaments.

The College XI, the Irani Cup and the Ranji Trophy paved the way for his selection in Test Cricket and in 1971 Gavaskar made his debut in the West Indies, where his run average was the high figure of 154.8. So brilliant was his game that the West Indians composed a calypso in his honour whose refrain was 'We couldn't out Gavaskar at all'.

Gavaskar has played Test Cricket for India all over the world, besides playing regularly for Irani Cup, Duleep Trophy and Ranji Trophy. Now within a century of the great Bradman's record, Gavaskar remains one of cricket's greatest gentlemen. Readers of *Sunny Days* will remember how often, and how generously, he praises other cricketers and how modest he is about his own achievements.

He is now the Editor of *Indian Cricketer* and regularly writes several sports columns.

Idols

SUNIL GAVASKAR

Rupa & Co.

CALCUTTA ALLAHABAD BOMBAY DELHI

1983

First published in Rupa Paperback 1983
Fourth impression 1983

Published by

Rupa & Co

15 Bankim Chatterjee Street, Calcutta-700073
94 South Malaka, Allahabad-211001
102 Prasad Chambers, Opera House, Bombay-400004
3831 Pataudi House Road, Daryaganj, New Delhi-110002

Printed by
Rekha Printers Pvt. Ltd.
A-102/1, Okhla Industrial Estate,
Phase-II, New Delhi-110020.

PRICE : Rs. 20.00

Dedicated to
the many cricketing Idols
who are not in this book.

ACKNOWLEDGEMENTS

The author and publishers are grateful to the following for permission to reproduce copyright photographs:
The Statesman, *Indian Express*, *Times of India*, *Sportsweek* and specially *S. Karmakar* for cover photograph. In some instances the copyright owner is not known and it is hoped that any ommissions will be excused.

CONTENTS :

LIST OF ILLUSTRATIONS

Ian Botham — Big, beefy and the best all-rounder in the world.

Ian Chappell — Growling, fighting Aussie who led from the front.

Imran Khan — Super athlete and the heartthrob of millions of girls all over the, world.

Between pages 160 and 161

Javed Miandad — Great improviser, a provocater of bowlers, fielders, batsmen and umpires.

Jeff Thomson — Pace like lightning.

John Snow — England's hit man of the early 70's.

Kapil Dev — The most natural cricketer in the world.

Mohinder Amarnath — Courage, thy name is 'Jimmy'.

P.K. Shivalkar — Honest trier who missed out.

Rajinder Goel — Simply unlucky.

Richard Hadlee — New Zealand's man of steel, super all-rounder.

Between pages 224 and 225

Rodney Marsh — Gutsy player who overcame initial problems to be acknowledged as the best of his kind.

Rohan Kanhai — Friend, philosopher and guide.

S. Venkatraghavan — The patient Indian.

Sir Gary Sobers — The greatest.

Syed Kirmani — Keeper of India's fortunes.

Viv Richards — Does anybody bat better than he does today?

Zaheer Abbas — The big hundred specialist.

Sir Donald Bradman — Idol of idols

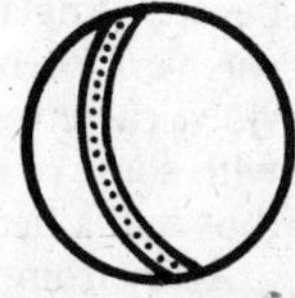

PREFACE

I wrote *Sunny Days* in 1976 when I had over four months off from cricket. There was very little to do and the Bombay monsoon season being what it is there was hardly any physical activity. So to keep myself busy I started writing my experiences in cricket till then. Fortunately I had written up my first tour in 1971 in a diary form and thus it was fairly easy to recall events and chronicle them. I realised that it was presumptuous of me to call the book an "autobiography" because I had hardly played cricket. And that was certainly not the age when one writes an autobiography. Yet I let myself be persuaded and *Sunny Days* was published.

It created ripples because some of the views I had expressed were, to put it mildly, quite strong. At that stage I was the media's blue-eyed boy and there was almost unanimous approval of some of views I held. This of course helped the book and it quickly climbed the charts of the bestsellers. I understand that even today it sells and I do not deceive myself that it is my style of writing that is helping the sale of the book. I know fully well that it's the controversial contents of the book that's making people buy it. The success of the book has certainly inspired me to write this one.

My publishers, particularly R.K. Mehra, have been after me to write a sequel to *Sunny Days*, but somehow I am reluctant to do so yet.

1981 was also a similar kind of monsoon season and I again had plenty of time to spare. I made a trip to England not only for a holiday but also to see the England players play Australia and bring back some video cassettes of the Tests. This was because England was due to come over in the winter and I was very keen to see that India emerged victorious. Those video cassettes helped a lot because I sat and watched them with some of my colleagues and some senior cricketers. We thus had a better idea of what to expect and what to do.

Apart from that, in order to keep my mind on cricket, I began to write articles on my own World XI. These were to be published in a sports weekly but another colleague of mine started a column on similar lines. Only, he wrote about Indian cricketers.

The idea thus got shelved and when R.K. Mehra again pressed me during the Delhi Test against England to write a sequel to *Sunny Days* I told him that I had written about my World XI instead and asked whether he was interested in publishing that as a book. He agreed and so I had to expand the eleven to more to make it into a book and hence plenty of cricketers came into it.

The book is essentially about players whom I have not only played with and against but also about the players whom I have spent time with off the field and so know a bit more than other cricketers who I have only played with. I have thus had not only professional but also a bit of personal rapport with them.

This does not mean that I have no rapport, personal or professional, with the cricketers not mentioned in the book. There are plenty of top cricketers not included in this book. To name a few, Michael Holding, Joel Garner, Gordon Greenidge, Alvin Kallicharan, Malcolm Marshall from the West Indies; Bob Willis, David Gower, Bob Taylor, Graham Gooch from England; Mushtaq Mohammed, Sarfraz Nawaz, Wasim Bari from Pakistan; Allan Border, Kim Hughes,

Rodney Hogg, Ian Redpath, Graham McKenzie from Australia, and from our very own India, Ajit Wadekar, 'Tiger' Pataudi, Farokh Engineer, Eknath Solkar, Dilip Vengsarkar, Ashok Mankad, Sandeep Patil and Anshuman Gaekwad.

The book had to be limited in size and regretfully those mentioned above were among those who could not be written about. It does not in any way reflect on the tremendous contribution they have made and are making to their country's cricket. I just did not have enough material on them, cricket and otherwise, to include them and also because most of those included have been idols of mine at some stage or the other, and I have followed their cricket with more than ordinary interest.

In writing this book I have had invaluable help from Sharad Kotnis who transferred what I had spoken on tape to paper and added vital statistics and figures which I did not remember. In spite of his busy schedule, looking after a weekly sports magazine, he found time and energy after office hours to listen to my tapes and transcribe them. To him go my sincere thanks.

Thanks are also due to the publishers for being patient with me as the book has taken almost two years to write. To the photographers too whose photos have been used in the book my grateful thanks but most of all I would like to thank all those wonderful cricketers who have, by their personalities on and off the field, made my cricketing career such an enjoyable, memorable and exciting one so far.

20th October, 1983 — Sunil Gavaskar

1

Alan Knott

Alan Knott is the finest wicketkeeper I have seen. He came into the England side in 1968-69 when he was picked as the understudy to Jim Parks for the tour of the West Indies. Midway through the tour, he came into the side and played two determined innings which saved England from defeat. Thereafter, he had been a regular member of the side until the Packer affair and has an incredible record in Tests, both as a wicket-keeper and a batsman behind him.

I first saw Alan Knott in 1971 when the Indian team toured England and the match against Kent was played at Canterbury. Knott kept wickets brilliantly and took balls, going down the leg side, with so much ease and that too in his right hand that it was more than obvious that here was a wicket-keeper of extraordinary quality.

His batting was always dangerous and though he did not score many runs in that game against the Indians, we knew that he was a very dangerous player, coming at No. 7 and capable of turning the match with his totally unorthodox batting.

In Tests that summer, he kept wickets brilliantly, hardly conceding any byes and he was in such a livewire form that the rest of the team were inspired by his performance. That was the time when spinners were more in use and his 'keeping to the spinners' was of the highest order. I still remember the catch he took in the Oval Test to dismiss Dilip Sardesai off Underwood. It was an edge and the ball would have normally gone away between the wicket-keeper and the first slip, but Knott was quick enough to reach his right hand out and catch that snick. The ball would not have carried to a slip fielder. That dismissal was crucial because Sardesai was batting beautifully and looked in control of the situation.

Of course, for the quick bowlers, he was absolutely magnificent. His diving was superb and the effortless triumphant way in which he came up with the ball in his gloves was to be seen to be believed. This infectious joy spread quickly to the rest of the team as soon as the wicket had fallen and he would be the first to rush to the bowler to congratulate him on capturing a wicket.

In 1974 he took two catches, one to dismiss Brijesh Patel in the Lord's Test and the other to dismiss Ashok Mankad, diving both the times between the first and the second slips and picking up the ball which was going to fall short of the slip fielders. Somebody like Knott behind the wickets meant that England actually had a sharp edge to it and that nothing would be missed. In fact, when Knott is keeping wickets, the first slip would stand a little wider and the leg slip also the same way. Some of the finest leg glances would be covered by Knott's agility.

His batting at most times was unorthodox, although he played straight most of the time. It was only when the spinners came on the scene that he used his reflexes and eyesight and played shots which many a top-ranked batsman would not even dream of. His shots were not in the M.C.C. coaching book and, certainly, cannot be advised to the young aspirants trying to learn the art of batting. These were all typical Knott shots and they came through because he had great ability and confidence in his batting. His sweeping was precise and he would sweep the ball from outside the off-stump anywhere between mid-wicket and the finest of the fine-leg. Similarly, short balls from pacemen would be regularly cut over the slips' heads for four runs. In a way, this was more frustrating to the quick bowlers because to be cut over the slips' heads regularly is very, very annoying, as most of the fast bowlers would testify.

Later on after having played fast bowlers on the Packer circuit, he changed his grip and he was able to fend off the short, rising deliveries and play them down instead of sending them up in the air. This meant that he practically lost the drive from his batting armoury and had to rely mainly on cuts and deflections to score most of the runs. He was always a good cutter and with his ability to push and run singles, he was seldom kept in check and only bowlers like Bishen Bedi and Chandrasekhar could bowl to him and earn a lot of respect and this eventually led to his famous sweep shots from anywhere, even outside the off-stump. To score over 4,000 Test runs is ample proof of his batting ability and that too against the best bowlers in the world.

When he came to India with the England team in 1976, the England team had perhaps decided as part of their strategy to appeal for anything and everything and go on running to the umpires. To a great extent, they succeeded in the first two Tests when, for every strong appeal, they found the umpires responding in their favour. Alan Knott was one of the players who led the appeals and he used to throw the ball in the air even if the batsman had missed it by the width of a foot or two. This happened in Delhi where Underwood was turning the ball appreciably. After this had happened more than once and I turned to Knotty and said, "Well, I hope you will be able to finish what you have started, because if we boys start appealing, you have no chance." Thereafter, Knotty was a little less exuberant in his appeals though the rest of the slip fielders, including Fletcher, Underwood and Tony Greig, continued to appeal.

However, their strength in appealing had gone down considerably since Knott was not that willing a partner in their tactics. But then, the wicket-keepers all over the world have a tendency to appeal because that's the way the bowlers all over the world want them to do so. The bowlers believe that if there is no support from the wicket-keeper in appealing, the umpires generally tend to ignore the appeal. If a wicket-keeper chips in with the appeal, then the umpires give it a lot of consideration. But that does not mean that Knott was a cheat. He was one of the nicest blokes you can ever come across. Off the field, he was always smiling, always willing to exchange a word with you and to the wicket-keepers all over the world, he was always available for any tips on their technique, on physical fitness or on any other matter concerning wicket-keepers.

He was a physical fitness nut and that could be seen by the number of exercises he did even while waiting for the bowler to go back to his bowling mark. These exercises, he explained, were necessary to loosen up hip joints which were rather stiff. He was a health fanatic also and very carefully chose his diet. For example, when he came on his first tour of India in 1972-73, he brought along with him a lot of canned food. He decided to eat plenty of fruits and did not take anything else. When he was signing autographs, he reportedly used his own pen and did not use pens offered by the cricket fans. I do not know how far this is true, but it goes on to show how careful he was about his health. It may look as if it was a little far-fetched, but then he had to look after his health and see that nothing endangered his professional career. I remember sitting with him at a lunch table in New York when we had gone to America for the Rest of the World match against the All Americans. I was simply amazed at how carefully he chose his food and how meticulously he chewed every morsel, almost according to doctor's orders, and took such a long time in finishing his meal. But then he has shown time and again that he is one of the fittest persons playing cricket in the world and he thus enjoys the game to the fullest.

He is still the best wicket-keeper in the world till today and will remain so for some time. Now that he has decided not to be available for any future England tours, England will be poorer to that extent. Because not only is he a great wicket-keeper, he is also a fairly good batsman at No. 7 that England needs to take them out of many a tight situation, which they often find themselves in.

Like most sportsmen in England he has gone into the sporting goods business and it is mainly to develop this that he has opted out of winter tours for England. I am given to understand that this business is doing rather well which is not really surprising. Alan Knott is not just good behind the wicket but has proved equally efficient behind the counter.

2

Andy Roberts

The customs and immigration official at St. Kitt's Airport shouted out loudly, "Hey man, 'Sardi' man. Come over here." Dilip Sardesai, after his double hundred in the first Test, strode over very confidently towards this official. And the official shook his hand and pumped it vigorously congratulating 'Sardi man' on his double hundred. But then, with a wicked look in his eyes he said, "Now you watch out for this Roberts fella. He gonna knock your head off."

To which, Dilip, cocky as ever, replied, "Well, I don't know if he's going to knock my head over because I'm not playing in this game. But you better tell that to this little fella behind me."

There I was, wide-eyed, taking everything in with awe on my first trip. The customs and immigration official had a look at me, saw a person who had just barely begun to shave and did not know what touring was all about and thought 'right' So as I came to his counter he asked me my name and then asked me what I did. When I said I was the opening batsman he burst into a typical West Indian laugh in which the whole body gets bent forward, backward, sideways and the hands slap the thighs vigorously.

He then proceeded to tell me, "This fella, Andy Roberts, he faster than Wes Hall, man. He the best fast bowler West Indies ever had. He got two bouncers like missiles that come at your head and knock it down. You better watch that head of yours, man. Because this fella Roberts, he already hit so many people on the head in Antigua. In cricket nobody wanna face him."

Well, that I thought was a very warm welcome, indeed, in Antigua. When the match started there wasn't any disappointment about Roberts' speed because we won the toss and went in to bat. And sure enough, when Roberts bowled, the ball hit your bat faster than at any other time.

Andy Roberts wasn't very successful in that game. But then he's come a long way since. In that game, my memory of Andy Roberts is just the fact that he was trying to bowl too short and trying to frighten you more with his speed than trying to get you out. The transformation from the erratic and inaccurate bowler to one of the most deadly and accurate bowlers was complete in barely a couple of years. He had also learnt that the short ball should be used more as a surprise weapon rather than trying to frighten Test batsmen.

I think that Andy is the finest fast bowler I have ever faced. Perhaps, because I have played longer innings against him than I have played against Dennis Lillee. And therefore, having not played long innings against Lillee it's difficult to compare the two though universally Dennis is acknowledged as the best fast bowler of our generation. I'm not disputing that fact, I'm just saying that because I did not play a long innings against Dennis Lillee I could not judge the variation that Lillee had in his repertoire like I could when Andy bowled against me.

I will never forget how Andy, when I was well past a hundred, the ball, a tattered 60 overs old, brought so many balls back from way outside the off stump, literally cutting them viciously over the middle stump. He followed that with two perfectly pitched leg cutters in the next over and one marvelled at the versatility of this man.

I had heard a great deal about the Calypso record made by Lord Relator about our 1971 tour to the West Indies but I had never actually heard the numbers in that record. Andy Roberts was the first one who got me the cassette when we played Hampshire in 1974. He was then playing for Hampshire in the county championships and by the time we had arrived he had already become a feared fast bowler. His accuracy,by then, was absolutely frightening and his speed was unbelievable even on the sluggish English wickets.

He had knocked no less a person than Colin Cowdrey out with his bouncer and Cowdrey, even when he was past 30, was still a very good judge of the short ball.

Well, Andy came up to me in the lunch time and wanted me to listen to that tape because I had told him in the morning that I had not heard that tape at all. He let me carry it back to the hotel to listen to it and so that the rest of the blokes could also listen to. Andy, in those days, used to have his tape recorder with him regularly like most of the West Indian players who all love music and carry their own music and musical equipment along with them on tours. Andy was no different, his love was West Indian music, the throbbing, pulsating music that makes your feet tap. Also, one could say the same thing about Andy's bowling because it was so good that it was the batsman whose feet not tapped but danced a different rhythm altogether, a rhythm more to try and see that the ball did not hit them on the body.

Andy had already played his first Test against England the previous winter in the West Indies and though he wasn't among the wickets he impressed one and all with his lively speed and his willingness to bowl long spells.

Hampshire had signed him up at that stage and that season in England in 1974 really sharpened his bowling talents. That's where he learnt accuracy and along with his speed, accuracy was his forte and it was very, very seldom thereafter that Andy bowled a ball which you didn't have to play. He made you play almost all the deliveries. 95 per cent of the deliveries he sent down you had to play and that was the greatness of Andy Roberts.

He came down to India already with a reputation made in county cricket. In his first season he had captured over a hundred wickets and so when he came down to India people were really looking forward to Andy Roberts' speed. They were not disappointed because Andy really bowled quick and struck like a tornado in the Madras Test when he captured seven wickets and generally was a very, very difficult bowler to face.

The thing about Andy was that he had bouncers of different speeds. There was the bouncer that came not as quick as one expected and which one could not only avoid easily but even score runs off it. And there was the other bouncer with hardly any apparent change of action or any urgency in the run-up, but which really came at you like a rocket and one barely had time to get out of its way leave aside contemplating an attacking shot of that ball.

This coupled with a very good outswinger when the ball was new and when it had lost its hardness and shine the ability to bring the ball back were the strong points of Andy Roberts. The only thing one could say about Andy was that he did not have a very good yorker — not as good a yorker as

Michael Holding or Jeff Thompson or Joel Garner has — and that was perhaps his drawback because after he bowled those two quick bouncers the batsman would be expecting another good one and if he had as good a yorker as these three above players have, his striking rate would have been even more tremendous.

Be that as it may, Andy Roberts carried the tour of India before him. He captured 32 wickets which was more than what Wes Hall and the others had done when they came on tour to India and that too on wickets which were generally unresponsive to his speed. The only wicket which helped him a little bit was the Madras wicket which has traditionally been a harder wicket than most in India and therefore gives the bowlers, particularly in the earlier stages of the match a fair amount of help.

Yet, Andy had 32 wickets and that spoke of his accuracy and his ability to get wickets. He would come back in the late stage of the day and still bowl devastatingly quick as he had done in the first session of play.

I missed out on three of the five Test matches due to the injury on my finger which was broken twice in two months but I was around for most of the Test matches and saw Andy bowl everywhere except in the Calcutta Test.

In the first Test at Bangalore on a rain-affected track he made the ball fizz around and made life uncomfortable for all our players and similarly in Delhi on a wicket which had been affected by rain and the game was surprisingly started half an hour before lunch when the game could well have been started after lunch, Andy just ran through us and made life very uncomfortable for us again.

In Calcutta he shattered us by taking a wicket off the first delivery of the match when he had Sudhir Naik caught behind by Derek Murray. And he just kept on coming on and getting wickets almost at will. I think Andy Roberts' bowling in that series, the batting of Clive Lloyd and Viswanath were the highlights of the series. The duel between Andy and Vishwanath at Chepauk on bouncy track where Vishy scored 97 of the best runs one could ever see was a delight. The only way Andy could keep Vishy quiet was to bowl a bouncer, and Vishy would then duck under it. That was also the only way Andy Roberts could see that Vishy did not get a run off the last ball when Vishy with only the last three batsmen to support him was trying to keep the strike by taking a run off the last ball.

Clive Lloyd had two fielders, one deep point and one deep third man, yet Vishy managed to bisect both these fielders regularly with his square cuts.

Both those performances were the outstanding performances of the match — the seven wickets that Andy took and Vishy's 97 not out — and were truly memorable efforts which people who were fortunate to witness will always remember.

Thereafter, Andy got a little sick of playing continuous cricket. He was playing cricket during the English summer and when that was over he was playing Test cricket for the West Indies or playing on a tour somewhere. That took the competitive edge off him and in England where county captains used him more as a stock bowler rather than a strike bowler, he just seemed to have lost his rhythm and there were only very few matches in which he came up with the old speed although he had it all there and he produced it regularly whenever the West Indies were playing.

The 1975-76 Australia — West Indies series which was billed as the World Championship series had outstanding quick bowlers from both sides — Lillee, Thompson, Gilmour for Australia; Roberts, Holding, Julien on the West Indian side. That was a series in which Andy really bowled well,

Michael Holding was just coming on at that time and perhaps a year later the tables could have been turned on the Australians, so quickly did Michael Holding develop into a front line fast bowler.

Andy, till then — till the arrival of Croft, till the arrival of Holding, till the arrival of Garner—was shouldering the burden of being the main wicket-taker of the West Indies very manfully, though even that began to tell on him because pressure does tell on every player and Andy was no exception.

The burden of county cricket and the burden of bowling flat out for the West Indies took its toll and he quit county cricket for Hampshire midway through their season although he came back and played midweek games for Leicestershire in the county championships.

In 1976 when we played the series against the West Indies in the West Indies they had just arrived from Australia having lost the series and were in no mood to take things lightly against us. Roberts and Holding ran through us in the first Test. Although Holford took the main wickets in the first innings, it was Roberts and Holding who were dangerous. Roberts, right from the first over, was firing away on all cylinders and some of his deliveries were awkward to say the least. Similarly, when the next Test at Trinidad was played, Andy was the main person who was causing all our batsmen all the trouble although we managed to run up a score of over 400. One could never relax against him because he was always trying something. From that short run-up of his, he generated extreme pace. The little hop before delivery, the falling away of the left shoulder and then the arm coming down was exciting to watch. There were quite a few players in India who tried to copy Andy Roberts' run-up and action, but sadly for India, not with much success.

After that Test Andy was rested because the West Indies team was due to have a full tour of England immediately after we left and so they wanted to rest their main strike bowler and get him fit for the tour to follow. That tour, of course, was dominated more by Michael Holding, but Andy Roberts also got the wickets. Andy fell just one short of Holding's performance. Holding got 28 wickets and Andy got 27 wickets.

Out of Holding's 28 wickets 14 were taken in the last Test at the Oval which was a remarkable performance on that flat wicket. But Andy was the guy who had the Englishmen in trouble right through the series because he kept on chipping in with his three wickets and always those were vital wickets.

Thereafter, all the West Indian players joined World Series Cricket and Andy was therefore lost to Test cricket for a couple of years. One must realise that in the West Indies cricket is hardly a paying profession and therefore most of the West Indian cricketers come down to England to play county cricket or league cricket and if they get an offer they go down to Australia and play cricket in Australia. It's the only way that they can make their money and one must also remember that while the going is good it's the best time to make money. Therefore, Andy was no exception when Kerry Packer came forward with his offer and along with the entire West Indies side he signed up for World Series Cricket.

They had many exciting matches over there and always the WSC West Indies side versus the WSC Australian side was a match which was very well fought, very competitive and though it was not, and it is not being, recognised by the authorities, as Tests, those were matches which were very, very keenly contested. And nobody who played those games will ever believe that they were exhibition matches or matches which were played in a light-hearted way.

After that Andy Roberts began to go on the decline though it would be a harsh word to use as far as the fast bowler is concerned because Andy had the reserves to come back. Although he could not now generate the same kind of pace, he was intelligent enough to add variation to his bowling and with his regular accuracy he was always a difficult bowler to play.

By this time he had become a fairly respectable batsman and who could, at No. 9, add useful runs for the West Indies. In fact, when many a match was thought to have slipped out of the West Indies' hands, Andy with his batting came in very handy and scored runs for the West Indies team. When the England team was there in 1980 he hit Botham for four sixes in one over, all clouted over mid wicket, and reached his 50 in no time. Andy had got a couple of useful scores in Test cricket and it was Andy Roberts who, in 1980, again in the summer in England won the first Test of that series very narrowly for and West Indies when the West Indies won that Test with just two wickets to spare.

It was Andy Roberts who played very sensibly. He came down and instead of plodding around when the ball was moving he decided that attack was the best policy. That's what he did-everytime Botham pitched the ball up he just carted him over mid wicket for four runs. That's how he saw that there was hardly any pressure and with that kind of batting he won the Test for the West Indies when the West Indies looked to have made things very difficult for themselves by rather indifferent batting in the morning. And they should really thank Andy Roberts for the way he turned the match for them and won the match which looked lost.

As a fielder he is a good, safe fielder in the deep with a very powerful arm though not as good a return as Keith Boyce had. But still, batsmen dared not take the second run when the ball went to him at deep fine leg or deep third man where he used to field normally.

As a person he is very quiet and did not speak too much and was more immersed in his music than in conversation. If you went and spoke to him all that he would do was nod. His eyes used to get a little hooded when he did that and one didn't really know the Andy Roberts as much as one tried to make conversation with him. This was a bit of a pity because I think that led to him being misunderstood by a lot of players but I don't think Andy was ever an arrogant person. I think he was one of the nicest blokes who came around, just played his cricket and did not want to enter into any controversies or make a nuisance of himself.

I well remember how when my wife and I were going out during the 1979 World Cup — all the teams were in the same hotel — we saw four big people walking ahead of us. They were walking so slowly and so casually that one would not have given them a second look. But we knew who they were and my wife said, "Look, how innocent, quiet and harmless these four look, don't they? But give them a ball in their hands and they are really very dangerous."

Well, those four people ahead of us were Andy Roberts, Michael Holding, Joel Garner and Colin Croft. Theirs is an attack which has become the most feared attack in world cricket today and the leader of the pack is Andy Roberts.

Asif Iqbal

One of Pakistan's greatest cricketers and one of the most attractive batsmen in the world was Asif Iqbal. After the retirement of Gary Sobers in 1973, he was the undisputed best No. 6 batsman in the world. He came to the rescue of Pakistan on a number of occasions when they were down in the dumps. His batting is something which is only found in fairy tales. His first defiant rescue act came in 1967 when Pakistan were in danger of an innings defeat. The England players had checked out of their hotels and it was expected that the match would be over soon. But Asif Iqbal and Intikhab Alam had other ideas. And they added 190 runs for the eighth wicket out of which Asif scored 146 runs. These runs were scored at almost a run a minute and Asif Iqbal was finally out jumping out to a ball, missing it and Allan Knott doing the rest. So elated was Collin Cowdrey, the England captain, with Asif that he was offered a county contract with Kent, the then county champions, and Asif accepted it. In 1980-81 Asif was appointed the Kent captain.

Asif began his early cricket in Hyderabad (India) along with Jaisimha, Abbas Ali Baig and others and when his family decided to migrate to Pakistan, Asif went there and started his cricket. He was quickly noticed by his performances and in those days he was only known as a medium-pace bowler. Soon he was selected to play for Pakistan but mainly as a new ball bowler. He has some important victims to his credit and he began to take batting a lot more seriously and concentrated on becoming an all rounder. In those days even Majid Khan used to open bowling for Pakistan, before an injury laid him low and made him concentrate on batting.

Gradually, Asif developed into a batsman and his batting continued to flower, with the result that he rarely bowled later on in his career but, when he bowled, he was not to be taken lightly. From the early seventies for almost a decade, the Pakistan batting line-up was the strongest. Asif Iqbal was the man who in the lower order saw to it that an early collapse was taken care of. He always came to the rescue of Pakistan when the chips were down and when his team required nothing less than a hundred from him. He has got ten Test centuries which is ample testimony to his batting abilities and he has scored more than three thousand runs. Apart from that he was the quickest runner between the wickets and as a fielder he was brilliant anywhere but particularly in covers. Pakistan has produced some of the most brilliant fielders in this region and Asif had to move away to mid-off or in the slips where too he distinguished himself. He was able to guide the bowler with necessary encouragement from these positions. In 1976-77 Asif was the main scorer in Australia with two centuries and he batted with determination and concentration when Lillee was threatening to run through the side. It was because of one of these centuries that Pakistan were able to win at

Sydney and then Imran bowled his devastating spell to do the rest.

Thereafter the West Indies tour that followed was not so successful for Asif. But he redeemed the prestige of Pakistan with a brilliant hundred in the last Test. At the end of this Test, he announced his retirement because he wanted to give youngsters a chance and also because he thought that there was no real hope for playing against India. However, when the Indian tour of Pakistan was announced for 1978, Asif came back from retirement because it was his cherished dream to play against India, the country of his birth. Before that, like all leading Pakistani cricketers, he had joined the World Series Cricket and he had become its most active participant and its coordinator. He was also instrumental in getting a lot of Pakistani cricketers signed by the WSC. In 1978, he scored a hundred in his first appearance against India in the second innings till he was bowled by Surinder Amarnath. But his most cherished moments in that series were when he and Zaheer Abbas clinched victory in the second Test against India and one could see the jubilation on Asif's face as he came to the pavilion waving his bat. The next Test saw Javed and Asif snatch victory from a just about hopeless position. They started the fireworks and then Imran came on the scene to scatter the attack and win the match for Pakistan. Asif and Javed picked runs almost at will by their clever running between the wickets. Asif, who gave Javed about 12 to 13 years in age, was running almost as fast as Javed. That was a tribute to his skill, his fitness, his determination to succeed.

It was during this series that he approached some of us to play in the World Series Cricket and was damned by just about everybody for having done so. But being a co-ordinator for the WSC, it was his duty to get as many leading players for the WSC and he was only doing his bit professionally to recruit talent and it was left to the individual approached to accept or reject the offer. To damn Asif Iqbal for that was totally uncalled for. He had discussions with most of us and then the managing director Lynton Taylor, flew in from London to talk with the boys in the presence of Asif Iqbal, who was there to allay any fears and answer any queries. The fact was that none of the Indian players joined because the World Series Cricket ceased to exist from 1979. The Indian cricketers had decided that they would join only after 1979. But Asif's role in that was something the people in India have not forgotten. Therefore, he had achieved a reputation of being too commercial minded. This in itself is not a bad thing. Asif realises that few in this world look after a sportsman after his days are over. How many of the people who come to watch, or who write about it, come to the help of a sportsman when he is in need indeed? That is why Asif realised that, if anything had to be done in this respect, it has to be done in the active playing days.

In 1979-80, he was a surprise choice as captain for the tour of India because many people felt that Mushtaq, who had done a good job as captain in the 1978 series, should have been the choice. Asif Iqbal continued the captaincy in the 1979 Prudential World Cup and then came to India as captain with the team. In the Prudential Cup Asif was not at his best and the Pakistan team, a strong line-up, put up a valiant fight against the West Indies before losing. When Asif came to India, the Pakistan team was rated as almost the equal of the West Indies team. That they did not do well in our country was mainly due to the fantastic effort of Kapil Dev. He produced extra bursts of speed to demolish their batting. Our meetings to chalk out the overall weaknesses of the Pakistani batsmen, importantly the bowlers bowling to a plan, the bowlers bowling with determination; all led to India emerging victorious in that series. Asif had a score of fifty in the first Test, following it with another fifty-plus in the second Test and then almost went into decline. He was always a dangerous player and going at No. 6, he had the opportunity to study the attack and play his innings. So many times when we were right on top, he took the advantage away from us by his attacking batting or often forcing the withdrawal of a particular bowler from the firing line. But, somehow, he did not produce the big effort of a hundred that was required of him. He seemed to be particularly upset when Dilip Doshi was brought on to bowl and later on he said that anyone who takes that long to bowl an over, being a spinner, must be fired. We used that advantage to better use as everytime Asif came, Dilip was brought on to bowl and he gave us the impression that he wanted to hit Dilip out of the ground almost every delivery.

With that kind of psychological advantage, Asif never recovered his poise thereafter. And although had his bits of efforts, he could never produce a match-winning knock.

As a captain, he was a superb diplomat off the field with his natural charm and all round ability to get his boys together. On the field, however, one got the impression that there were quite a few disgruntled people in the Pakistan side who did not like the way Asif was leading. But then these were basically Asif's problems and I am sure he solved them in his own manner and style. In the fifth Test that disgruntled attitude was absent and there seemed to be a new resolve in the Pakistan side. Asif retired after the Calcutta Test and it was a retirement he probably would remember because 80,000 people gave him a standing ovation. He was run out and what a way to go on your farewell appearance for one who was reputed to be the fastest runner between wickets! Let me add here that he was run out because he slipped while turning to return to his crease and was therefore left stranded.

Asif, thereafter, has concentrated on his business activities. Playing for Kent in the County Championships though he was out much of the time in 1980 because of injury. he was one of the lynchpins of the Kent side and always a very popular man all round Kent and in England. Lately, he has been in the forefront of the Cricketers Benefit Fund Series under the stewardship of Abdul Rehman Bukhatir and he is the one who is coordinating the efforts among the Indian and Pakistani players. These matches continue to be a success and benefit all cricketers from the sub-continent. At the moment, every year, one current and one former cricketer from each country has a benefit in the UAE and Asif has a major role in getting this off the ground and therefore it is beneficial to a lot of cricketers and will benefit a plenty more in the years to come. He is one of those cricketers who will make good administrators after their playing days are over. And I hope that his cricketing experience is put to good use by the concerned authorities in Pakistan. He is a dear friend now particularly after the 1979-80 series when we were rival captains and I have a lot of regards for this ever-smiling cricketer, who has rendered yeomen service to cricket and particularly to Pakistan cricket.

4

Bishan Singh Bedi

The greatest left-arm bowler I have seen is Bishan Singh Bedi. Certainly, Sir Gary Sobers was more versatile because he could bowl left-arm pace, he could swing the ball, he could bowl cutters with the old ball, he could bowl left-arm unorthodox spin and he could bowl chinaman and googlies. In that respect, Sir Gary Sobers was perhaps the most versatile of them all. But quite simply, the greatest left-arm bowler was Bishan Bedi.

Bedi first came into prominence in 1966, playing in Delhi against the West Indies team for the President's Eleven. It was during this match that a national selector saw him and was very much impressed. He then urged the then chairman of the selection committee to include Bedi in the 14 to play in the second Test against the West Indies at Calcutta which was going to start on the New Year's Day in 1967. The team for this Test had already been selected, but the chairman decided to include Bishan Bedi on the advice of his colleague and when Tiger Pataudi saw him in the nets, he too was convinced that this young Sikh had all the makings of a Test bowler. And Bishan Singh Bedi has proved it to the hilt by becoming India's highest wicket-taker, with 267 wickets at a very impressive average in a career that spanned 13 years.

There at Calcutta on the New Year's Day, 1967, a career was launched, a career that gave immense delight to those who were commenting on the lost art of spin bowling; which gave immense delight to the connoisseurs of the game and which caused plenty of havoc to batsmen all over the world.

That particular Test match was not highly successful for Bishan but it was enough to convince the selectors that this youngster not only had the potential to become a world beater but also had the temperament to be pitchforked into a Test match without any notice and still come out without giving any evidence or signs of nervousness.

The next match at Madras would probably have been won by India had Rusi Surti taken a catch at backward short leg off the bowling of Bishan when the great Sobers had just scored a few runs. Sobers, in partnership with Charlie Griffith, went on to save the match and thus India had to wait for another four years before registering a victory over the West Indies. In 1971, even in this victory Test, Bishan played his part and with his impeccable line and length, saw to it that a stranglehold, which had been achieved after Abid Ali had given an early breakthrough, was never really released.

Immediately after the 1967 West Indies tour of India, the Indian team went to England and Bishan was in the side. He was an instant success with the media there because the boys in the Fleet Street were only too delighted to write about a man who came on the ground in different turbans for different sessions of the game and one who was able to bring for them memories of Wilfred Rhodes and Hedley Verity and other great English bowlers of the past. In those days, of course, Bishan used to wear the turban and not the patka which most Sikhs now adorn while playing various sports and I am pretty certain that the turban must not have been all that comfortable while bowling, although it must have surely helped to keep the cold away.

On the 1967 tour of England the weather did play an important part and there were lots of matches which were washed out and there were plenty of days when the sun never came out at all. Nonetheless, after the beating that India received, the team was off to Australia and again Bishan was in the team. He was not a great success on this trip though off the field he met an Australian girl who was in a couple of years to become his wife.

It was in New Zealand after the Australian tour that Bishan came into his own and along with Bapu Nadkarni formed a partnership that was deadly enough to keep the batsmen under control while Prasanna made inroads into the batting line-up, bowling his off-spinners at the other end. This was the first time that the Indian team won a series abroad beating New Zealand by a 2-1 margin and thus a new spin combination was formed on that tour.

When the New Zealanders were playing their first Test match in Bombay in 1969, all eyes were on the Sikh. He hadn't been among the wickets in the first innings and the cricket lovers of Bombay were wondering as to what was so outstanding about this left-arm bowler and why was he preferred to Bapu Nadkarni in 1967. Bishan showed them precisely of what stuff he was made in the second innings when he captured six New Zealand wickets to take India to a comfortable victory. That was Bombay's first sight of Bishan who they were going to admire not only as a cricketer but also as a character on the field. Characters on the field in cricket are a very rare commodity. It is players like Bishan,

Derek Randall, Tony Greig and Sandeep Patil, to name just a few, who spring to mind and are the ones who not only give the crowd value for money by their cricketing ability but also by their very presence and their ability to communicate with the crowd and make the crowd feel involved in the Test match or any other match in which they are playing.

Ever since that period when Bishan took six wickets and led India to victory, he has been a very popular figure with the Bombay crowds. True, the Bombay crowds have given him a bit of a stick. He being a Sikh, has added to that, but then Bishan has very sportingly taken it all and perhaps that is one of the reasons why he is so much popular than other cricketers who do not seem to be able to take it.

Later that season Bishan recorded his best figures when he took seven wickets in the Calcutta Test against the Australians. Ian Chappell played a superlative innings of 99 on a wicket that was truly helping the spinners. But apart from him, there was very little resistance to Bishan and he finished with seven wickets in that particular innings. This performance came immediately after his marriage and naturally he was teased a great deal not only by the team members but also by others who seemed to be unanimous in their opinion that the marriage had helped him get a better grip on the ball. India lost that series to Australia because of their superior pace bowling and the fact that India's middle order had not come to terms with itself and also because India had not solved the opening batsman problem. This meant that the Australians could strike early and keep the pressure on the later batsmen. Bishan, Pras and Venkat performed admirably and they were helped by the induction of some youngsters in the side, like Viswanath, Eknath Solkar and Ashok Mankad who made their debut in the series and went on to serve India for a long time thereafter.

The next series that the Indians played was against the West Indies. That was the first time that I met Bishan when we were having a training camp at Bombay prior to our departure. What impressed me about him at that time was his willingness to bowl endlessly to all the batsmen and after that still find energy to go round for a training run. This is something which marks Bishan out from the other spin bowlers of the era. Because, while the other spin bowlers were perfectly happy to rely on their talent and ability, Bishan worked hard at it. Bishan never took things for granted. He trained hard and one could always see he was trying to put in an effort. Probably, he needed to train harder than the others because he had a body which was more susceptible to stresses and strains and many times later on in his career, he suffered from muscle injuries that handicapped him to a great extent.

Bishan on that trip was again a force to reckon with and the West Indians truly loved what they saw. Here was a bowler coming from just a few yards away weaving magic spells and making great players like Sobers and Kanhai look like novices at times. Sobers, of course, came into his own later on in the series when he slammed three consecutive centuries but unfortunately for the West Indies, Kanhai never showed the form that he had shown in the first Test when he scored a brilliant 150 not out to save the West Indies. Part of it was due to the fact that the Indian spinners got into a magnificent rhythm which meant that the West Indies were really hard put to score runs. Not too many world class spinners were around at that time but the few that were there, were fortunately playing for India, Bishan being the prime example.

Bishan kept on teasing and bowling at a tantalising length and Venkat was the one who ran away with wickets because he very intelligently capitalised on the fact, with Bishan bowling his left-arm spinners, going away from the right-handers most of the time, the ball coming in to the batsmen was the ball the batsmen chose to attack. Thus, Venkat kept very tight control over his direction and ended up getting the wickets. This was, of course, intelligent bowling.

Much of the credit was given to the spinners for having got ourselves into the position from where we could afford to dominate the West Indian bowlers. One did not get to know Bishan on this trip because this being my first tour with the Indian team, I was wide-eyed about everything and dutifully went around looking at tourist spots etc. However, a surprise, not just a surprise but a great honour, was done at the end of the tour during the last Test after I had scored a hundred in the second innings following a hundred in the first innings, Bishan decided to name his son, who was born during that Test, after me. Bishan's son was thus christened "Gavasinder Singh" and that was a tremendous honour for me, particularly because I was on my first tour. I didn't even know the man as such and he had paid his tribute in his own unique way and a tribute coming from one of the greatest spinners of the world is something that I really cherish and I am proud of.

The tour to England that followed was even more of a trial for Chandra, who was recalled to the Indian team, than Bishan. Bishan, with his flight and beautiful action, captivated the hearts of the English critics and spectators, resulting in his being offered a contract by Northamptonshire to play in the county championship. Towards the end of that tour, three of us—Bishan, Engineer and myself—were invited to be part of the Rest of the World side. He had earlier gone to Australia because his wife was from Australia and thus we met him at Melbourne when the team assembled there. Bishan's magic moment on that tour was when he clean-bowled both the Chappell brothers in the Sydney 'Test'. Ian, coming out to drive, was beaten in the flight and was bowled. Greg played the first ball he received down the wrong line and the ball turned sufficiently around the edge to knock his bails off. This was great bowling and enabled us to come in the match very strongly. In the last Test, it was again Bishan and Intikhab who spun the Australians out and bowled us to victory. This was the tour when one came to know more about Bishan because on the earlier tours to the West Indies and England, he was with his own circle of friends and thus it was not possible to get to know him at all apart from the playing days when he was in the dressing room.

On the 1972 tour of Australia, one could meet in the evenings and Bishan spent a great deal of time with the Pakistani players and us and thus one came to know him a little more. Of course, in Melbourne, he had very little time for us because his wife came from that place.

The following year when the England team came to India, Bishan completed his 100 wickets and that too in front of his Delhi (home) crowd, and it was a great moment because capturing one's first 100 wickets is a proud moment. Chandra, Pras and, of course, Venkat were there to take us to a very comfortable victory and thus Ajit Wadekar, the captain of the side, was able to complete a hat-trick of victories in the first three series in which he led the side. These victories were welcomed by an enthusiastic response from the cricket loving people of India but the joy was shortlived and soon forgotten when the Indian team lost to England very, very badly in the 1974 summer. That was a wet and windy summer and most uncomfortable to play cricket. That was a tour which should be best forgotten because there were plenty of incidents on the tour which did not at all bring credit to the Indian team and did not reflect on the plus side of the Indian team.

Ajit Wadekar lost his place in the West Zone and announced his retirement and thus the way was paved for Mansur Ali Khan Pataudi to stage a comeback and lead the side against the West Indies. Bishan was in good form and Pras and Chandra bowled very well to bring India back into the series after having lost the first two Tests. It was during this particular year that the controversies surrounding Bishan came to surface. He was dropped from the first Test against the West Indies on the ground that he had breached his tour contract. He had given an interview on British TV and the then Board President gave a directive to the selection committee not to consider him for the first Test. However, Bishan could not be dropped from the second Test, not because the second Test was to be played in Delhi, but because a bowler of Bishan's calibre could not be easily found and though Rajinder Goel was selected in the 14, he was not eventually selected in the final eleven and he missed the only opportunity of playing in a Test.

It was Bishan who kept such a talented bowler like Goel out of the Test side and it is the misfortune of Indian cricket that two outstanding left-arm spinners like Goel and Shivalkar were unable to play Test for India. This was due to the fact that Bishan was just that little bit better than the two bowlers. He had more variety than either Goel or Shivalkar. Goel and Shivalkar were absolutely unplayable on wickets that afforded a little bit of help and were very difficult to score off on good batting tracks. Bishan's strong point was that on good batting wickets also he was able to get the batsmen out because he had more variety, his loop, his armer, were bowled with such guile that they happened to trouble the batsmen all the time.

By the time this series ended, Tiger Pataudi announced his retirement and a new captain had to be appointed for the World Cup in 1975. The selectors chose Venkat because of his experience and for being a regular participant in the one-day matches and county championship for Derbyshire. But when the team was picked to go to New Zealand and the West Indies in 1976, Bishan was an automatic choice for the captaincy. He was fortunate to have a very good side, a side which comprised cricketers who were in top form, a side full of youngsters and a lot of experience. The series against New Zealand was drawn 1-1 and the series against West Indies saw India make a record score of 406 in the third Test to win the Test and level the series score with one to go.

It was during the last Test match at Sabina Park that Bishan got into another controversy when he declared India's innings closed with only five wickets down. Bishan's reasoning was very simple. He had three batsmen who were unable to bat with injuries and with only himself and Chandra left to bat he saw no point in continuing the innings. His own batting calibre as well as that of Chandra was well known and the two would not have been able to score many runs, since India were only 13 ahead at that time. Perhaps, what was wrong on his part was not coming out to field as the West Indians could have scored those runs in just one or two overs. Thus, Bishan got himself involved in another bit of controversy.

When the England team came in 1976 there was yet another bigger controversy when he accused John Lever of having used vaseline to keep the shine on the ball. This in effect is the reason mentioned in many quarters for his losing his contract with Northamptonshire in the county championship. The disappointing thing was that in spite of

Bishan's great service to the country, not many people came forward to support him when the allegation was made. Whatever may be the truth or otherwise of the allegation, the same should have been examined thoroughly and Bishan should not have been blamed completely for his part in the episode. The English cricketers over the years have been used to pressurising the umpires, sometimes bluntly, to win matches by using every trick in the book and so Bishan's allegation should not have gone without support at that stage.

Bishan then led the side to Australia in 1977-78 which turned out to be a classic series much alike the 1974-75 series against the West Indies when all the five Test matches were decisive. It was Bishan's excellent bowling in the first two Test matches that got the Indians so close to victory. Somehow, we fell at the last hurdle when the victory was in our grasp. It must have been very disappointing for Bishan for he bowled very well yet the victories eluded him in the first two Tests. India came back strongly to win the next two Tests only to lose the last one at Adelaide.

In 1978 we went to Pakistan and this was the series where our quartet of spinners were hit out of Test cricket, although Bishan and Chandra made a comeback and Venkat four years later. Zaheer Abbas, Asif Iqbal, Javed Miandad and Mushtaq Mohammad played very well on those perfect batting pitches. There was very little that the spinners could do and we lost the series 2-0. Many still claim that it was the one over that Bishan bowled in the Karachi Test when Imran Khan took 19 runs, including two huge sixes, that cost India the match and Bishan the captaincy. Because as soon as the team landed in India, Bishan was told he had been given the sack.

By the time the West Indies arrived in India in 1978-79,

Bishan had lost that little bit of extra nip and perhaps the hammering that he received in Pakistan had hastened his slide downhill. He was not the same bowler that he was before. And it was amply proved when a second string West Indian team could score runs against him without being unduly perturbed by his spin. Bishan's strong point was that he deceived the batsmen in the air but the ball after pitching still went off the pitch quickly enough not to let the batsman change his mind on the shot. However, in that series against the West Indies, it was this particular characteristic of Bishan which was missing and even if he could beat the batsmen, in the air he could still go backward and change his shot at the last moment. This is what hastened Bishan's exit from Test scene.

It was my unpleasant duty as the captain of the Indian cricket team to break the news to him that he was dropped from the side for the fourth Test against the West Indies at Madras. I suggested in the selection committee meeting that somebody should accompany me, preferably the chairman of the selection committee, to break the news to him for cricketing reasons. For the kind of service he had rendered to Indian cricket, it was proper courtesy to tell him on our own rather than him being told by a third party. So Ghulam Ahmed, who was then the secretary of the Board, and myself went to his room to break the news. Bishan was lying down having a rub with a masseur. He took the news sportingly and said that these things do happen and he had quite expected it. He wished the team luck for the next series. This was very magnanimous on his part and we left the room in a very sad mood to continue with the selection committee deliberations.

He made a comeback when he was picked in the side to go to England in 1979 but he was not very successful and the wickets that he picked were those of tailenders when they were going for declarations and were under instructions to hit out against the spinners. Kapil Dev was the most successful bowler on that tour and Bishan and Venkat used to get tailend wickets.

Bishan lost his place in the Test side and has not played Test cricket again, although he ended as India's highest-ever wicket-taker with 267 wickets. It was by any stretch of imagination a fantastic performance to have been able to play that many Tests and get that many wickets because it works out to be a tremendous average. Not many bowlers can maintain that kind of average and Bishan has done it. He has shown to the world what a great spinner he was. There have been many left-arm spinners but none good enough to replace Bishan, although Dilip Doshi in his first three or four seasons was outstanding and captured many wickets. But he was more of a defensive bowler while Bishan was always an attacking one.

Bishan as a person has been a very forthright man, a man not afraid to speak his mind and let the others know exactly what he thought of them and so I do not believe when people suggest that it was he who had got an article written insinuating that it was I who was responsible for getting him chopped from the Indian team. This is far from truth for the simple reason that if Bishan thought that it was I who was responsible for it, he would have told me on my face and not made someone else write about it though that other person might be his greatest 'chamcha'. Bishan is not a person to fire a gun from someone else's shoulder. Another person might have tried that.

I have been privileged to play with Bishan and I am proud of his performance for the Indian cricket team. He took Indian cricket to a height which would not have been possible and he instilled in each member of the team confidence in his ability. This was his greatest contribution as a captain. He made the players aware of their ability and made them feel inferior to no one. It was he who was instrumental in getting the Cricketers Association of India launched during his tenure as captain and, though Bishan did not want to be actively associated with it in any official capacity, he was always there behind the scene encouraging and giving valuable advice to the cricketers.

He is now a member of the selection committee and the secretary of the Delhi and District Cricket Association. Thus, he shoulders great responsibility. As a former cricketer, he has shown that cricketers do make good and able administrators and as a selection committee member he has even a greater responsibility towards seeing that the heights that the Indian cricket team has achieved since winning the World Cup will be maintained

Bishan is perfectly capable of achieving all this but in doing so he might hurt a few people because of his forthrightness. People like Bishan do not come very often in one's lifetime and it was not just an honour and privilege but a great pleasure to have sampled the friendship of Bishan during his active playing career and now when he is serving cricket in a different category altogether.

5

B.S. Chandrasekhar

The close-in fielders made the batsman tense, a shiver going down his spine as he took guard and as the crowd of almost eighty thousand howled "booo...wled" to a man as the bowler ran up to bowl, the batsman became pale. The bowler was B.S. Chandrasekhar and everytime he bowled in Calcutta, the Calcutta crowd would give him this terrific support. I dare say that the crowds of Calcutta have got him a few wickets by simply making the batsman nervous by their rhythmic shouts of "booo...wled" as he ran up to bowl.

Calcutta is one place where it is great fun to be successful, because the stadium itself can accommodate hundred thousand people and when hundred thousand supporters are backing you, it is an almost top of the world feeling. That's why to score runs and get wickets, one must do it in Calcutta to really savour the appreciation of the huge crowd that converges on to the stadium. Chandra is Calcutta's favourite player and seldom has he let them down.

Chandra's debut was in 1964 against England, the team

that Mike Smith had got over and with his fastish leg-breaks and googlies Chandra was the bowler who was very difficult to read and not so easy to score runs off.

Later on in the same season, when the Australians visited India for a short trip, the ball with which he bowled Peter Burge in the second innings is memorable. It pitched about leg and middle stumps and turned enough to bowl his off-stump as the batsman came forward for defence. Earlier on in the first innings, he had lached on to a terrific catch when Peter Burge had swept at a ball from Bapu Nadkarni and the ball was travelling at a speed of 90 miles per hour. Chandra was near the square-leg umpire and he struck out both his hands to the right and came out with a real blinder.

As Chandra got confidence, and he realised that, he was making a permanent place for himself in the Indian side, the world began to sit up and take notice of this bowler, whom they called a 'freak' bowler. In fact, there was nothing 'freaky' about him at all, the only thing was that his right arm was affected by polio and with which he really could not do much except bowl. He would throw with his left hand and use his left hand for most occasions.

Chandra, thus, worked in tandem with Venkataraghavan when the New Zealanders came in 1965, the year before the Indian team was to face the West Indians in 1966. That was the battle eagerly awaited because people wanted to find out how far Chandra would be successful against great players like Sobers, Kanhai, Butcher and Nurse. Chandra bowled superlatively and was always a bowler whom the West Indians respected. They tried to hit him off the ground but did not succeed and, therefore, decided to play as he came, rather than plan anything against Chandra. To plan anything against Chandra was, in fact, to invite disaster. Chandra's bowling was something which you really could not predict.

The 1967 tour of England by his standards was not a

successful one for him and the reason could be that Chandra found it difficult to grip the ball in the English cold weather. 1967 was a miserable summer and as a result he tended to bowl too short and bowl loose deliveries more often than before.

Thereafter followed a lean period in Chandra's career because midway through the Australian tour in 1967-68, he was sent back home due to an injury and though there were doubts raised as to why he was really sent back. The questions were not really answered because Chandra is not a man for a controversy and would not provide the media with any material.

He went into a bit of decline after that for the simple reason that he suffered a scooter accident which meant that when the New Zealanders and the Australians.came in 1969, he was not fit enough to be playing against them. Many people had then written Chandra off, because with Bedi, Prasanna and Venkataraghavan holding the fort as spinners in the Indian side, they felt that there was no need for Chandra in the side. Chandra missed the 1971 tour of the West Indies, but the selectors showed rare wisdom and insight in selecting him for the tour of England later that year. And what he did at the Oval is now history. After that Chandra has seldom looked back, in fact, in the 1972-73 series at home against England, he lowered the mark set by Vinoo Mankad for the highest number of wickets against England in the series by capturing 35 wickets. His favourite batsman seemed to be Keith Fletcher whom he could dismiss almost at will. When Keith Fletcher was finally able to unravel Chandra's mystery, he slammed a brilliant innings and then followed it up with a century in Bombay.

The 1974 trip to England was again not so successful for Chandra. The summer was cold and he had the same problem of gripping the ball and then an injury added to his miseries. He broke his thumb and was not able to take part midway through the second Test and also missed the third Test.

However, he was fit once again when the West Indians came down that winter and amongst his prized scalps was Vivian Richards playing his first Test match — he got him out in both the innings. But Viv Richards came back with vengeance in the second Test at Delhi scoring 192 not out and thereafter, although Viv was not as successful as expected, he had somehow managed to get out of the grip of Chandra.

In New Zealand and West Indies in 1976, Chandra was not his usual devastating self, bowling some tremendous spells but generally looking off colour. The problem perhaps was that he was bowling long spells and his arm used to be tired and thus he took a lot of stick and once Chandra took stick, he seemed to lose his confidence in his bowling. Confidence was his big asset and if he lost that, he was a bowler not to be feared of. In fact, one could pick runs with relative ease.

After this tour, which wasn't all that great by his standards, but where, he had the great Viv Richards in many a difficulty Chandra concentrated on the home season in India and he bowled remarkably well against the New Zealanders and then the Englishmen. The Englishmen, and particularly Tony Greig, had found a new way to play him by standing upright. This put Chandra off to a great extent because as Chandra ran in to bowl, Greig would suddenly stand up, which, Chandra thought then, was Greig withdrawing from the crease. With his concentration being affected, Chandra was not able to bowl with the same venom as he had bowled earlier in the first Test. Also the practice of some English players to swear at him while taking a run upset Chandra who was not the one to retaliate. He was getting upset slowly and he thus lost his concentration and was not the same bowler that he was against the New Zealanders.

The trip to Australia in 1977-78 saw both Bishan and Chandra bowl excellently. Australia had lost many players to the World Series Cricket. Bobby Simpson had been recalled to lead the side and he was the one man whom Chandra troubled the most. Simpson's habit of going on the back foot and trying to work the ball away on the leg side found him often in front of the wicket but due to the kindness of the Australian umpires, Simpson continued to bat and thus got out of many an awkward situation the Australian team found itself in.

Bishan got about 31 wickets, but Chandra was not very much behind with 29 wickets in that series. Both of them bowled absolutely tops and it was a great sight and delight to be able to field in the close-in positions and watch the confrontation between them and the Aussies batsmen. Nobody seemed to have any clue to their guiles excepting Peter Toohey and Bobby Simpson, to some extent.

The following season was India's visit to Pakistan after 18 long years and it was the series that had the eyes of the sub-continent. The series, in fact, turned out to be one that should be easily forgotten for our spinners, because they got absolutely nothing over there on those wickets, accepting plenty of runs against their names for their labours. Zaheer Abbas was in irresistible form and with Javed Miandad chipping in two 100's and everybody scoring runs, it was embarrassing to read the figures of the three great bowlers. The Pakistanis are exceptionally adept at playing the spinners by using their feet, by dancing down the wicket and even not being afraid to loft, they demoralised the spinners and the figures that you read against the names of Prasanna, Chandra and Bedi were the figures you read against the names of ordinary spin bowlers. Not that they had lost their ability, but they had met players who were not afraid to go down the track and in the process, the effectiveness of our spinners was considerably reduced.

Midway through the series that followed against the West Indies in 1978-79, Chandra found himself out of the Indian side. But forced himself back in the side for the last Test and also found a place in the Indian team that went to England in 1979. However, in the first Test, Chandra was not supposed to play because he had an ankle injury. On the morning of the match, Bedi reported unfit with a stiff neck. Then the selection committee requested Chandra to go ahead and play. He was not hundred per cent fit at all and on the plumb Edgbaston wicket, he just could not get the turn and the nip off the wicket at all and ended up with no wickets, while England piled up a huge total of 600 runs. There was no disgrace in not getting a wicket for the only bowler who was amongst the wickets was young Kapil Dev. None of the others got any wicket as England declared with five wickets down.

That was the last Test Chandra played because in 1979-80, he was not picked against the Australians and nor was he picked against the Pakistanis and thereafter he was never considered for any matches.

Chandra retired in 1981 and was awarded a benefit and whatever he got by way of his benefit somehow was not really commensurate with the efforts he had put for India, despite his handicap. Still the benefit was the sign of affection that the people had for Chandra. He was totally an uncontroversial man, a man who went about his own ways without getting involved in the pros and cons of discussing cricket and was quite happy to be by himself. He was often misunderstood for keeping aloof. He was a very, very simple person, a very likeable man and a person who you could rely upon to be your friend. I had been fortunate to share rooms with him. I shared a room with him when he bowled us to victory in 1971 and it was always he who got up early in the morning, made a cup of tea and gave it across to me. Also at times, when I was not batting well, he was around to give me confidence, to speak just those couple of words and knowing Chandra, those words were always sincerely meant and were great for you to regain confidence in your own ability.

Chandra was a great fan of Mukesh, the singer. To start with, this led to their meeting and becoming very, very good friends and it was a big blow to Chandra when Mukesh expired suddenly when on a concert trip in America. Chandra, who hates flying, then flew down to Bombay for his funeral. He used to call me 'Sun' and it was a name he used with affection and I am privileged to be his friend. I still look forward to going to Bangalore and every time I go, it's great fun to be able to sit with this greatest of spinners and chat of the old times.

6

Clive Lloyd

When the West Indian team to India in 1966 was announced the Indian cricket loving public were excited because the West Indian team has always been a team which has played attractive cricket wherever it has gone. The team's record in India had been tremendous, it had yet to lose a Test match to India and had carried everything before it in the earlier series.

People were discussing what kind of mayhem Rohan Kanhai, Gary Sobers, Conrad Hunt, Seymour Nurse were going to cause to the Indian bowlers. And also, the topic of discussion lingered on what Charlie Griffith, Wesley Hall and Lester King would do to our batsmen.

As usual in the West Indies there were one or two new comers about whom nobody had much idea and they were expected to be used to play in the first class games where the big stars could take a break from the tensions of Test cricket. Nobody had even thought that at the end of the tour that a young man wearing glasses and who walked with his neck seemingly ahead of the rest of his body with his shoulders hunched together and who was greased-lightning in the field — would be the hero of the tour before it began? The young man's name was Clive Lloyd and he really carried everything before him in the series that was played.

Before the first Test started Lloyd had done nothing outstanding and it was expected that he would be in the reserves. But an injury to Seymour Nurse meant that Lloyd was asked to play along with stalwarts like Hunt, Kanhai, Sobers, Griffith, Hall and Lance Gibbs. This young man was also a cousin of Lance Gibbs and so, perhaps, was fortunate that his cousin was there on hand to give him any advice or to ease his tension a bit. Not that he needed it after his first innings in Test cricket.

Bapu Nadkarni holds the record for the most maidens bowled, and for that remarkable bowling analysis of 29 overs, 26 maidens, 3 runs and no wicket. Yet, I've never seen Bapu Nadkarni annihilated, as Clive Lloyd annihilated him in the Bombay Test. On a wicket which was a dream wicket for the batsman to bat on where the ball came on very nicely onto the bat, Lloyd just plonked his foot down and hammered everything. He was lucky that before he could get the hand of Chandrasekhar a mix up enabled him to get a life when he was only nine. But he never looked back thereafter, and his 82 was awesome in the manner in which the ball thudded into the boundary fence. The power that he generated from that loose, easy pick up of his was unbelievable. People who had seen Clyde Walcott belt the ball off the back foot and thought that there could be nobody who could hit the ball harder than Walcott off the back foot, had to think again after demonstration by Clive Lloyd.

Poor Bapu Nadkarni. His career was set back after that assault on him, though to be fair, one must say that none of the Indian bowlers escaped Lloyd's assault. Everybody was dealt equally harshly perhaps with the exception of Chandrasekhar. And then, apart from his batting, the crowd just wondered at the man's agility on the field. It was simply incredible. The number of times he picked up and threw the stumps down on the run or on the turn were numerous and the crowd went wild trying to cheer this young man. He had stolen the limelight completely away from the established stars like Sobers, Kanhai, Hall, Griffith.

In the second innings too, he played his part with an unbeaten 78 which helped Gary Sobers finish off the match in a frenzy because Gary wanted to go to the races in Bombay. What looked like a target which would take well past tea time to attain, Sobers and Lloyd just hammered around, tapped a few singles and cruised to it even before tea so that Gary could go and attend the races.

The youngster with 82 and 78 not out in his first Test had certainly arrived and everybody in the world sat up to take notice of this young man. The only person who may have been dejected was Seymour Nurse because it was his place in the side which was in danger with the arrival of this giant from Guyana.

Lloyd carried on the good work in the second and third Tests as well and apart from his explosive batting, his quick-silver fielding, another facet of this cricketer, was evident to the Indian cricket loving public, and that was his ability to bowl leg spinners. In the Calcutta Test he bowled Chandu Borde who scored centuries in the first and third Tests but failed in the Calcutta Test. He bowled him round his legs, trying to sweep and managed to get even more turn than Lance Gibbs on that track.

I don't know why Clive stopped bowling his leg spinners, but he stopped it for a while and reverted to medium pacers.

Maybe he got a little bit of pasting in the Lancashire league with his leg spinners and thought it better to resort to his seamer style which he uses today though he doesn't bowl as much as he used to.

Thereafter, one followed his career with interest because one felt an affinity towards the man since he had made his debut in India and done it in such a brilliant fashion.

He had a fairly useful tour of Pakistan after the Indian tour and then in his first Test at home against the English team he scored a hundred. He didn't do extraordinarily well thereafter, though he followed it up with a hundred in his first appearance against Australia when the West Indies went there in 1967-68. There the Australians seemed to have noticed some weakness and they exploited that weakness to see that Clive Lloyd didn't trouble them too much after that but Lloyd was destined for greater things. He practised hard, thought about his weaknesses — the very thinking which has got him the captaincy of the West Indies: a job which he has done extremely successfully over the last ten years.

Seymour Nurse retired from Test cricket after the 1968-69 tour of Australia and New Zealand and that meant that Clive Lloyd was assured of a place in the side and needn't have worried about losing his place. Thereafter, Lloyd went steadily from strength to strength, he was always a person whose wicket the opposition was after, whose bowling was treated with respect and when the ball went to him the batsman thought not once or twice but thrice before embarking on a run. His reputation as a fielder perhaps got him more publicity than the sheer power of his batting and this was in a way unfortunate because his batting was always very dangerous for the opposition.

When the Indian team went to West Indies in 1971 Lloyd

was under a bit of a cloud because he hadn't had a very successful series previously and there were murmurs going around that if he didn't do well in the first couple of Test matches his place would go to Kallicharran or Lawrence Rowe among the younger players who were knocking on the doors of Test cricket. Well, that didn't happen because though Lloyd didn't get a hundred against us he certainly got his share of runs, he got his 40s and 50s fairly regularly and so although he wasn't spectacular success, he was quite consistent and that's what was needed in the series where most of the West Indian batsmen didn't seem to do themselves any justice against an Indian spin attack which was just coming into its own before being rated as the best spin attack in the world.

In the first Test Lloyd was run out in a mix up and that happened again in the second innings and also in the Test at Guyana where he collided with Gary Sobers and had to be assisted off the field after being run out just when he looked in sight of his hundred.

The last Test in Port of Spain was the one where the West Indians were desperate to try and even the score but that was not to be. Having been set a target in the second which they could have achieved if Kanhai and Sobers had survived along with Lloyd, they lost Sobers and Kanhai quickly which left Lloyd to do the holding up operation instead of the attacking operation which he loved so much.

In any case that innings of 64 of his was the innings which saved West Indies from losing that Test which at one stage they looked they would win. This was a very responsible innings and although we were defensive to start with Ajit Wadekar quickly switched to attack when he sensed victory and it was only Lloyd with his long front foot coming down the track on a wicket which was beginning to turn that prevented our spinners from running through the side. The

West Indians barely survived by the skin of their teeth being 8 wickets down and many runs away from the victory target when the last of the mandatory overs was bowled.

That winter due to the withdrawal of the invitation to the South African team a Rest of the World team was formed and Clive Lloyd also happened to be a part of that trip. The two members of the side which really made that trip memorable were Clive Lloyd and Richard Hutton. Both had a tremendous sense of humour and while Richard said everything with a straight face, Lloyd, the moment he cracked a joke, would double up into laughter with his entire body shaking thereby infecting everybody around and everybody else would start laughing as well.

In the first Test at Brisbane Lloyd didn't have to do too much but in the second Test he found Lillee's pace a bit difficult to handle like most of us did and that was the last of the Tests he played in Australia before the unfortunate accident took place which put a question mark on his future as a cricketer. Fortunately, he came out of it and cricket lovers all over the world are thankful that he has continued to play cricket and was saved from serious injury. What happened was that Ashley Mallet drove a ball uppishly from Intikhab Alam in the game against South Australia at the Adelaide Oval and Lloyd jumped up to his right to take the catch at extra cover, but as he fell down he lost his balance and fell on his back rather awkwardly and the ball slipped out from his fingers which he had earlier held onto and thereby gave Ashley Mallet a life. We were surprised when he wouldn't get up after his fall. Most of us thought that it was simply out of disappointment that he missed the catch that he wasn't getting up It was only when Tony Greig who was at cover point noticed the agony on Clive's face that the seriousness of the injury was diagnosed. He couldn't move his arms and he was partially paralysed and therefore a stretcher had to be brought on to cart him away to the hospital. X-Rays and examinations at the hospital revealed a spinal injury and the doctors said that if a bone which had protruded had gone in another half an inch or three-quarters of an inch, Clive would have been a paralegic for the rest of his life. In any case, with the nature of his injury being serious he was out of the running for the side and had to stay back in Adelaide while the rest of the team went ahead to continue the programme. But the spirit in the side was so good that we rang up Clive regularly in his hospital to cheer him up. Not that Lloyd needed any cheering but we thought it was our duty in view of the serious injury that Lloyd had suffered.

For Christmas the side had even composed a song and we decided to sing it over the telephone from Melbourne to Lloyd in Adelaide and we had all geared up with our throats lubricated properly, having rehearsed for some time before the call was put through. We were all waiting anxiously for Clive Lloyd to come on to the phone only to be not just disappointed but simply amazed when told that Lloyd was not in the hospital but had gone out on a date! Well, we don't know if the date was for certain, but for a man who was as badly injured just a week ago and who one feared would have to spend the rest of his life in a wheel chair if that bone had gone in a little further, we were simply amazed to find that that man had got better so fast. We were, of course, delighted that "Hubert," as everybody calls him, had recovered so quickly though we knew that he wouldn't be participating any more on the tour. We missed him because his sense of humour was very infectious. He always kept the spirit in the side up with a timely remark, a timely joke, and he always had a very pleasant outlook to life which was evidently reflected in the way he played his cricket.

The thing I remember most about Clive is the way he was always eager to talk cricketing problems with you and to try and help you out with what he thought was going wrong with you. During that time in Australia when things were not going too well with me, I talked to a lot of people and amongst the people I can think of who were most sincere in their help were Rohan Kanhai and Clive Lloyd. They tried their best to tell me, because they had seen me play in the West Indies in 1971 and also while we were in England they had watched me on television in the Test matches when India played England and so they were in a better position to tell me what was going wrong with my batting. I am grateful to both of them for the interest they took and what they told me about how to get over that weak moment in my career.

During that tour we invariably would end up having breakfast together because Lloyd and Farokh would be having breakfast and I would join them and it was fun along with these two blokes with their non-stop array of jokes flying in–between and it was difficult to swallow your breakfast simply because they made you laugh so much.

I also remember one remark of Lloyd when he was asked by the waiter in Australia whether he would like any milk in his coffee. And he said: "Yes, please, I'm not racial." That set the waiter back a little bit though I must say that perhaps racial overtones in Australia are perhaps the least one can encounter anywhere in the world where one had gone and played cricket.

Another incident from that trip which is memorable is the firing that the receptionist of our hotel in Melbourne gave to Clive for trying to fool with her daughter. It so happened that the daughter and the mother shared the duty of the reception desk and during the time when the mother was away one of the team members tried to fool around with the daughter and this was reported to the mother by one of the staff who reported that it was 'one curly-haired man' who was fooling around with her daughter. The obvious one to pick was Clive Lloyd because the mother perhaps thought that Gary Sobers would never resort to such a thing and Clive Lloyd was the only other curly-haired fellow in the side. Lloyd thought that it was me, but I pointed out to him that I didn't have curly hair but I had wavy hair and both of us, for the next one week, were trying to tell each other that it was the other one who was fooling around with the receptionist's daughter.

This was even more funny because it happened when Clive was recuperating and had come to Melbourne before he flew off to join his family. And therefore, he was obviously in no position to have been mischievous and the firing was therefore totally uncalled for.

It was good to hear that he made his come-back in a couple of months against the New Zealanders and cracked a brilliant hundred against them in the Guyana Test. This was because players of the ability of Lloyd don't come too often on to the Test cricket scene and so his recovery, although it would cause a lot of problems to the Indian cricket team when it played against the West Indies, was welcome. One should look at it from a broader point of view more than a narrow point of view and, therefore, most cricket lovers, including Indian cricket lovers, were happy that Clive Lloyd had recovered completely from that injury of his and was back to Test cricket.

One met Lloyd thereafter in 1974 when he was playing for Lancashire in the county championships and as usual, Lloyd was great fun and it was nice to spend some time with him. I've always enjoyed Lloyd's company for one thing, he never talks cricket unless you want to talk cricket, which means that you can get away without having your ears filled with more cricket talk as most cricketers tend to do nothing else but talk cricket. There are plenty of topics that Clive can talk on, he's a good conversationalist and always with that underlying humour of his one can see the funny side of just about everything that he talks on.

During that tour of England in 1974 it was anticipated that Lloyd would be the captain of the team to India if Rohan Kanhai was not available. It turned out that Rohan Kanhai was available but the selection committee had decided at that stage to do away with Rohan and look for fresh blood and the step they took was to appoint Clive Lloyd as the captain of the team to tour India.

That team consisted of a lot of youngsters and Lloyd himself was one of the stars along with Lance Gibbs and one of the most explosive newcomers, Andy Roberts, who had done so well in the English county championship at that stage. Lloyd's team came down to India and was tremendously popular wherever it went. Not only did they play a brand of cricket which was typically West Indian, full of aggressive shots, full of aggressive bowling and with brilliant fielding all through, but the team's behaviour off the field was impeccable and it was due to the captain, Clive Lloyd, who did so much to mould the side into a fighting unit.

They got a bit of a shock when, after having won the first two Tests in a canter, they were knocked back in the third and fourth Tests on wickets which were not the best of wickets and due solely to Viswanath's brilliant innings in both these Test matches. Vishy literally counter-attacked the West Indian pace attack and therefore set his side's totals from which our spinners could work their magic over the impatient West Indian batsmen. During that time one noticed that if things weren't going too well for the West Indian team they tended to panic and try to hit their way out of trouble instead of playing a more patient role. Lloyd failed in both these Tests and that perhaps is an indicator as to why the team lost, because they did not have somebody of the calm and experience of Lloyd to stay around and guide the rest of the inexperienced players during the tough periods of batting.

When the fifth Test came up at the newly laid Wankhede Stadium there were doubts raised about the quality of the wicket before even the Test started. The West Indian manager took photographs of the wicket and there was general doubt expressed not just about whether the wicket would last for three days but whether the stadium would stay up during the Test. The stadium had been completed in a rush in less than a year's time and therefore there were doubts as to how strong the structure was. Well, on both counts, those who were worried were proved wrong because not only the wicket lasted — and would have lasted for another ten days — but the stadium has now lasted for nearly ten years without even looking in any danger whatsoever.

During that Test the West Indians piled up 604 runs out of which Clive scored a massive 242 not out and perhaps could have gone on and on and scored innumerable amount of runs had he not decided to take the side's interest into account and declared so as to try and get us out twice in the Test match.

Unfortunately his plans were set back a little bit when there was a hold-up of play after tea on the second day when the police beat up an enthusiast who had come on to the field to congratulate Lloyd for having scored 200 runs. Lloyd became the first person to score a double century at the Wankhede Stadium, though the honour to get the first century at the Wankhede Stadium went to the West Indian opener, Roy Fredericks, who slammed a brilliant hundred in no time and thereby laid the stage for the attack of Lloyd to follow.

In that innings Lloyd was simply magnificent. He just flogged the bowling about and twice hit Bedi deep into the Garware Stand. By this time it was common knowledge that Clive Lloyd used a bat which was almost three pounds in weight, perhaps the heaviest one ever used, and with six or seven grips around the handle which really made it a thick handle. Lots of things have been written about Clive's bat — the weight, the balance, etc. But I can't think of a better bat than this one Clive had used because the sound when the ball is hit is so sweet that it was taken for granted that it was four runs. On many occasions Lloyd did not have to exert any power at all but he merely seemed to caress the ball particularly when he played the shots on the on side and the ball thudded into the boundary post at the Wankhede Stadium.

It was truly an un unforgettable innings which was spoilt only by that one incident when the police had to face the wrath of the crowd for beating up an enthusiast and there was no play possible in spite of repeated appeals by a lot of VIPs. that the game should not be interrupted. Lloyd's team won that Test although over a thousand runs were scored before the first innings was completed. But then Lloyd and Viv Richards went into the attack in the second innings and hammered our attack away and set us a target which was stiff, and while we could have survived it was Vanburn Holder's magnificent bowling that saw that we were skittled away and lost that Test and therefore the series by a margin of 3-2.

At the end of that series Clive Lloyd had established himself as the captain of the West Indies team for years to come. It was apparent that the side respected him not only as a captain but as a player and they were prepared to do anything that Lloyd asked. There were lot of times when he asked Andy Roberts to bowl a couple of more overs in the heat of Madras and in Bombay and Roberts never refused to bowl for Lloyd. That goes to show how much of respect he had from the team, how much the team respected his ability and his views and his judgment and therefore the West Indian team was in the process of being moulded into one of the strongest outfits ever to be seen from that part of the world

That old truth, that a captain is only as good as the performance of the rest of teammates, was aptly proved the following summer when the West Indies was thrashed 5-1 by the Australians in Australia in the series which was billed as the World Championship for Test cricket. The tour had been arranged after the Australian Board withdrew the invitation to the South African team, and so the West Indian tour was arranged very hurriedly.

Before that tour, however, the first World Cup was held in England and it was Clive Lloyd who won the first ever World Cup for the West Indies team with a brilliant hundred in the finals which was played in front of a packed house at Lord's. When the West Indian captain came in to bat things were not looking very bright for his team and it was greatly due to the magic of Rohan Kanhai, the influence and the experience which Rohan had on the bowling, that Lloyd could get into his stride and slam that brilliant hundred. That hundred was really the one that turned the tables, because he slammed the Aussie pace bowlers all over the field and this was something which the English crowds were stunned to witness because just a few months before their team had been destroyed by Lillee and Thompson in the Ashes series in Australia.

Lloyd then led the side astutely making very clever

bowling changes to see that the advantage that his century had got to his team was never let away and although it was a thriller to the end and the Australians lost by 17 runs only, it was apparent that the West Indians were the champion side. When Clive hoisted the cup, after receiving it from Prince Phillip, high over the head, the West Indian population in the crowd went berserk and all kind of noise was heard — the typical West Indian music, the banging, the screaming, the shouting, the jostling, the laughing which is so typical West Indian was evident in as staid a place as Lord's. I'm sure Lord's has never really recovered from that and it's a good thing because participation by the spectators is so important for the players to give off their best, though the participation, if it becomes a little too much in the form of intrusions on the field, can upset players more than anything else that they encounter in their playing career.

So the West Indians, having beaten the Australians by a narrow margin, were looked upon as the world champions. Having received the title of world champions of limited overs cricket it was but natural that when thev went over to Australia later on in the year that the Test series would be labelled as the world championship and in reality that would have been true because the West Indians and the Australians were the strongest sides in the world at that stage and they really looked as if they would produce sparkling cricket.

Well, there was a lot of attractive cricket and a lot of sparkling cricket was played but the West Indians, in trying to play too much of sparkling cricket, lost that series and by the sorry margin of five against one.

Australia at that stage were captained by Greg Chappell who had taken over from his brother Ian who retired after the tour of England in 1975, and Chappell celebrated his appointment as captain by hitting a century in each innings of his first Test. He thereafter left his stamp on the series by scoring over 700 runs in the series and with his authoritative batting completely dominated the series. The West Indians had problems, they could never find a suitable opening partner for Roy Fredericks and although Fredericks himself played a brilliant innings of 169 in Perth, he was never as consistent as the West Indians would have liked. Eventually, Viv Richards was pushed in to fill the slot of the opening batsman and he did a magnificent job and it was as an opening batsman that Viv's upward stride as the world's best batsman started.

But this particular series was a blow to Clive Lloyd and when they returned to the West Indies they had to play the Indian team. Talking to them one got the impression that Lillee and Thompson must have been frighteningly quick. For the West Indians to admit that Thompson was grease-lightning means really something because they themselves have genuine pace bowlers in every nook and corner of their islands. Holding was establishing himself as one of the finest fast bowlers the world had seen, Andy Roberts was reaching his peak and Bernard Julien was there to offer variety by way of his left hand swing.

It was therefore that the West Indians took the field in the first Test against the Indians at Barbados with murder in their eyes because they had to beat India in a very convincing manner to rub off the shame which had fallen upon them after their defeat by the Australians by that margin. And they did that, in a very convincing manner beating us in the first Test in which Lloyd came back to form with a brilliant hundred. It was a superb innings full of brilliant shots and as usual it was an innings which did not take too much time but was just played in a very short while.

Viv Richards came in and made a hundred and it was the beginning of a very high scoring time for him and he never really looked back after that innings against us. Lloyd was very happy to have won that Test in three days. At that time the Indian team was really down in the dumps because we had lost two consecutive Tests, the third and the last one in New Zealand and then as soon as we landed in the West Indies, the first Test in merely three days. Morale at that time in the Indian team was pretty low and what we needed was some good thinking and plenty of determination to see that the series just did not go downhill. That determination came to the fore in the second Test which we almost won and this was where Clive Lloyd got a little jumpy. Only Viv Richards was scoring runs and the rest of the team was not contributing runs as it should have. It was at this stage that Lloyd began to get a little nervous about the performance of his side and also because there was talk going round that he should be replaced as captain.

The second Test was saved barely by the skin of their teeth by the West Indians. For the West Indians, the Port of Spain venue against the Indians has not been a very lucky venue for them. The wicket hasn't been quite what their pacers would like, on the first day it has always been unpredictable and there is more turn on it than on any other West Indian wicket. Therefore, the West Indians weren't exactly very happy with their performance and more so because Bishan had refused a runner for Viv Richards during the second innings when Viv had pulled a leg muscle and was not in a position to run. This angered Clive Lloyd and there was a big discussion on the rule with the umpires and between Clive and Bishan, and eventually Bishan was told that he was right though Bishan very graciously allowed Richards to come in at the fall of the next wicket. But the damage had been done because Clive was not the same again. He resented what Bishan had done in the first place because he thought that was not done in cricket. The West Indians, just about having survived that one, were to play in Guyana and with that game against the island having been washed out and the rains hardly looking like stopping, the match was transferred to Trinidad which is a bigger ground with bigger capacity. Lloyd had a frown on his face when he came to know that.

It is now history that we recorded 400 runs in the second innings to record the biggest total in the second innings for a victory and thereby levelled the series one all. Lloyd was very upset at this though it was hardly any fault of his that his bowlers could not get us out in a day and a half. I think it was just that we batted better than at anytime in the series and every one of us seemed to have clicked at the same time.

Not many would have given us a chance to last out the day leave aside scoring the runs required to win. But that's what we did and Clive was very upset about it. No captain likes to lose, and Clive was no exception. Therefore, when the Kingston Test came about Clive wanted to take advantage of the early life and the early moisture in the wicket and sent us in to bat. His bowlers did not bowl as well as they should have bowled and at the end of the tea session we had put on almost a hundred runs without being separated. Before that, however, in a sheer move of desperation, Lloyd thought that the bowlers should come round the wicket and have us fending off the short deliveries. While this was a good tactical ploy it got out of hand when the bowlers got carried away and started bouncing the ball almost every delivery round our heads.

No batsman, not even the West Indian batsman, would like this kind of bowling because that is hardly cricket and besides the hook shot is not the only shot in the game, though the West Indian crowd likes to see the ball whiz past the ears or the ball hooked off the fast bowlers.

That was a Test which saw a lot of injuries and eventually the West Indians won that having been required to score only a few runs to win. That was perhaps a bitter note on which to end the series and while what happened on the field was unfortunate, let there be no mistake that relationships between the players of both the teams were always very cordial. And for this, credit is due to Clive Lloyd who, in spite of all the tensions of having to play a home series and being under pressure till the last Test, kept his sense of humour and handled the side well and was always very friendly and very approachable even for the opposition.

Thereafter, it has been one long victory march for Clive Lloyd and his band excepting the series in New Zealand which they lost 1-0 two years ago and which was also a very bitter series due to the fact that the West Indians were not very happy with the New Zealand umpiring and there were shows of defiance by their players.

Under Clive, the team has gone from strength to strength. It has got plenty of great players, the best batsman in the world today, Viv Richards, and the most fearsome fast bowling attack of Croft, Holding, Roberts and Garner with Marshall and Clarke waiting in the wings to take over when one of their people gets injured or retires. They've got a very good opening pair in Greenidge and Haynes though the spinner hasn't played a very prominent role in the West Indian bowling attack over the last few years. Otherwise it has been a very complete West Indian side. Perhaps the only problem has been that they haven't had a regular wicketkeeper, Derek Murray has been there and then afterwards David Murray has been there, but both of them have not been of very high standard or they have been required to merely take the ball standing back. But Clive has built a tremendous spirit in this side, the members in this side respect him a great deal and one can see that he's very popular with them. With his easy-going attitude, off the field, and with his sense of humour it is very easy to see why people like him. Also, it is easy to understand that with his attacking cricket on the field why he's such a favourite of the crowds.

He has only recently become the father of a boy and when I talked to him in England last year he seemed very relieved about the fact because he had two daughters earlier on. In 1976 I got the news that I had become the father of a boy and just before the Barbados Test Suresh Suraiya and Ravi Chaturvedi who had come down from India had brought along an album of pictures of Rohan who was born while I was away in New Zealand. While I was looking at the pictures at a party Clive came up to me and wanted to know what I was looking at. When I told him he just shrugged his shoulders and said: "Well you know how to do it the right way, don't you?" This was said because he had two daughters and I had got a son and he wanted a son.

When I met him last in England I congratulated him on the birth of a son to which his reply was typically Clive. He said: "Well, at last I got the right turn of the screw!"

That's Clive Lloyd for you — not just a great cricketer and a great captain, but a person who has always looked at the funnier side of life and given so much enjoyment to cricket lovers all over the world.

I get a little disappointed when people talk that Clive is going to quit because the cricket world needs players like Clive Lloyd more than anytime, now that the world of cricket is going through many crises which seem to crop up out of nowhere. Clive, I just hope you keep on playing. We need you — we the cricketers and the cricket lovers need you more than you can think.

7

Dennis Lillee

Dennis Lillee is the greatest fast bowler in cricket's history. Old-timers will surely dispute this statement. They would talk about other fast bowlers and Fred Truman may object to that as well but look at Lillee's record. In just 65 Tests, he has taken 335 wickets and when you take into consideration the fact that he missed out Test cricket for three seasons due to his association with the World Series Cricket, and his absence from many Tests due to his recurring back injuries, then he must have surely missed out on 70 to 100 wickets, which would have taken his tally of wickets to 400 by now. You can thus gauge the class of this speedster. That would have been an all-time record which would have taken a long time to overhaul. Even now he could achieve this mark, but he is obviously coming to the end of his career and he will leave behind his stamp as the greatest fast bowler the world has seen.

Our first sight of Lillee was in 1971 in Brisbane and we had heard about his being a slippery customer. I was taking strike and Lillee thundered in to bowl—he has in recent years modified that run-up—he kept up the movement of his arms. He now runs to the barest minimum. At that time his arms would move about, pump vigorously and that must have caused additional strain on his back which was to give him recurring trouble later on.

Well, there he was bowling the first ball of the over to me and I steered it to the left of gully for a boundary The next ball was short and I cut it across past gully for another boundary. Throughout that World Eleven series, he troubled me. In the first innings after I had made 22, an inswinger from him kept a little low and nicked in between my bat and pad and bowled me. It was in the second innings of that 'Test' that I decided to have second thoughts on hooking short balls. Till that time, I used to go for the hook whenever a fast bowler pitched short, because that was a challenge and I wanted to accept it. In the second innings which was of no consequence, because the match was petering out into a tame draw, we were given just 90 minutes in the post-tea session to chase an impossible target after Ian Chappell had scored a century in each innings and declared his side's innings.

This was the time to get some batting practice, some confidence against the Australian fast bowlers. Lillee came in and pitched the ball short, I went for the hook, I was in perfect position to hook the ball, but as I brought my bat down to hit the ball, it had already thudded in Rodney Marsh's gloves. If that wasn't the quickest delivery I have ever seen, then I haven't seen too many quick deliveries. It was at this stage that I decided that it is safer to get under the delivery pitched short or sway inside or outside the line of the ball. That was the year when Lillee was the fastest bowler in the world as he was to prove in the next 'Test'

The Australians were all out by the end of the first day's play and our innings was to start the next day. The wicket looked good, a typical Perth wicket, hard, bouncy and obviously the new ball would have caused problems. It was important that the opening batsmen, Engineer and myself, get a good start so that the strokeplayers, Lloyd,

Sobers and Kanhai, could capitalise on it. Ackerman was already out of the side with an ankle injury. The fourth ball of the first over was a shortish delivery and as I tried to defend it, the ball brushed the glove and Marsh took an easy catch. That was the start of the slide, because in just 100 minutes, the entire side was knocked out for a paltry 59 runs and players of the calibre of Sobers and Lloyd perished just the same way, defending the ball off their chins and only managing to edge it to the wicketkeeper or to the slips. As if that was not enough, in the ten minutes we had to bat before the lunch interval, we lost another wicket when Engineer lofted a catch to Paul Sheahan in the covers. So Lillee had taken nine wickets in that session and the greatest fast bowler to be in the world had really arrived.

In the fifth 'Test' he couldn't play due to an injury, but in the fourth 'Test', he had given enough indication of the kind of menace he was going to cause to the leading batsmen in the world. Someone like Gary Sobers was out to him twice, the first ball, defending the ball off the chin to be caught behind. And I am sure in the 100-plus innings that Gary has played, he had never been out in this manner, defending the ball off his chin in such an abject manner. Every time Lillee pitched short, Gary was in a position to hook it, but Lillee had that little bit of extra pace that forced the great man on the defence.

When Lillee went to England in 1972, he bowled some of the quickest stuff one had seen for a long, long time. Those who watched the Manchester Test believe that his spell was quite frightening. It was only bad batting that cost Australians the match. But it was Massie's bowling at Lord's which brought the Australians back in the series and level it at two wins each. Lillee finished that series with 31 wickets and his reputation at that stage was second to none. Even in this series, he was showing himself to be a great competitor, aggressive, to the point of being offensive and he was not afraid to exchange a word or two with the batsman and let him know exactly what he thought about his ability.

But then there was a setback when he went to the West Indies in 1973. He found to his dismay that he was getting pain in the back and he was not able to pound in and bend his back as he would have liked. It was diagnosed as stress fracture in the vertebra and which meant at that stage that Lillee's cricketing career was almost finished. But those who thought so did not reckon with his fighting spirit. He underwent strenuous physical tests, hard exercises and really slogged and sweated to get back in the peak of condition.

So when the 1974 season began, in Australia, doubts were expressed about Lillee's ability to bowl with the same kind of speed. In the first Sheffield Shield match, he did not impress and did not get wickets and to a battery of TV cameras and the rest of the media, he just looked an average medium pacer. But the Australian selectors knew that the Englishmen would be under psychological pressure and disadvantage if Lillee was included in the first Test. So Lillee and another young fast bowler, Jeff Thomson, were picked to have a go at the Englishmen.

It was obvious that Lillee had been playing a game with the TV and media by not bowling at his regular pace and perhaps his most sensible explanation was that he was building himself up to full pace gradually so as not to damage his back once again. To many Lillee appeared little slow but it was due to the fact that Thomson was quicker than Lillee and in fact was so quick that bowling against the wind, he looked quicker than Lillee. By the end of the fifth Test, they had together annihilated the Englishmen and their batsmen were shell-shocked, to say the least, with the exception of Tony Greig who went on gustily taunting the fearsome duo and getting away with it. The Englishmen and particularly their press accused Lillee and Thomson of being bouncer-happy and it was only Ian Chappell's comments that Peter Lever and Bob Willis, who had started it off, silenced them off to some extent. Ian Chappell proved the point that it was they who

Alan Knott — Fitness fanatic, who made wicket-keeping look so easy.

Andy Roberts — The quietest fast bowler in the world.

Asif Iqbal — Swift runner between the wickets; one of the charmers on the field.

Bishan Bedi — Floats like a butterfly, stings like a bee.

B.S. Chandrashekhar — "Wicked" taking arm of India.

Clive Lloyd — Supercat. Cricket's real gentleman.

Dennis Lillee — The greatest fast bowler of all time.

Derek Underwood — 'Deadly' on the field, perfect gentleman off it.

started the bouncer war, knowing fully well that Australia had the better artillery.

There was this very humorous story about David Lloyd who was writing a letter to his mother and he started off saying, "Dear Mom, today I played a ball pitched in my half of the wicket." That goes on to show that neither Lillee nor Thomson bowled most well-pitched up deliveries. But I would like to believe that with their extra pace and particularly when they play the Englishmen, they always fry to add a yard or two to their pace and they managed to get that extra steep bounce from just short of a length which was perhaps imagined by the Englishmen as short deliveries.

So the duo came to England in 1975 and their activities were followed with great interest. The media was fully after them, ignoring the rest of the Australian players. That was the year of the inaugural World Cup competition and, contrary to expectations, the Australians reached the final and just when everyone had given up hopes of them making a recovery in the final against the West Indies, it was Lillee and Thomson who made the recovery possible with a last wicket partnership that brought the Australians within 17 runs of the target before a misunderstanding caused Thomson to be run out.

This fighting spirit was evident in the four-Test series that followed during which for the first time one saw in England wickets which were whitish in appearance and devoid of any grass. The Indian team never had any good quick bowlers with the result that the wickets were thick with grass, obviously prepared to suit the attack of the Englishmen.

I was fortunate to watch the first Test and what one saw was unbelievable. Yet, Lillee managed to extract pace and bounce from the first few overs and then switched over to either cutting the ball or moving it off the wicket. Thomson, on the contrary, found it a bit difficult since he relied entirely on sheer speed and since the wicket was devoid of any grass, he could not get much bounce or movement off the pitch.

Lillee's greatness came to his rescue then and one saw why he was rated so high by everybody. By varying his pace and using the crease and cutting the ball off the wicket, Lillee exploited whatever the wicket had to offer and ran through half of the England side. Only a bold aggressive innings by Tony Greig and David Steel, who played with his front foot down the wicket, helped England to a respectable score. John Snow then ripped though the Australian side as he had done in 1970, but here again Lillee showed tremendous fighting spirit and smashed everybody including John Snow to knock off 73 runs which is his highest score in Test cricket. He seemed to be really enjoying himself and played on the front foot knowing well that no one would pitch short stuff against him.

However, the Australians did not do well and also looked pretty ineffective in the next Test, and when it was well poised, it was spoiled by vandals digging up the wicket and spraying it with oil. What would have been the finest last day's play in the Test was thus ruined.

The Oval Test also provided a docile track and there was not much that Lillee could do, but at the end of that series, he had come down a peg from his standing, but by no means he was disgraced. He was hostile, sincere in his efforts but the wickets did not help him.

When the West Indians came to Australia in 1975-76, Lillee had kept himself in trim, ready to have a go at them. Both teams had a battery of fast bowlers and the series was awaited with baited breath by the knowledgeables. Despite having a fairly good, well-balanced side, Lillee and Thomson destroyed the West Indians and won the series 5-1. Most of the West Indian batsmen were caught on the bigger Australian grounds while hooking the short-pitched deliveries. They could not resist the temptation of hooking and fell an easy prey to the wiles of the duo.

The following season, a short series against Pakistan was drawn due to the magnificent bowling of Imran

Khan in the Sydney Test when he took 12 wickets and which prompted the Australian skipper, Greg Chappell, to say that, at times, he bowled as quick as Lillee. At that time it was the highest praise that could have been showered on a bowler and it goes to show that even in 1976, Lillee was considered the greatest fast bowler in the world.

Next year, there was the Centenary Test between England and Australia. It was dramatic right from the start. Rick McCosker's jaw was broken by a rising delivery from Bob Willis when he tried to hook and ended up by pulling the ball on his jaw, in the process, hitting the wicket and getting out as well. This Test will be remembered for two reasons. Derek Randall's brilliant innings of 174 and the magnificent bowling of Dennis Lillee on a wicket which helped the bowlers on the first day but was easier as the match progressed. He captured ten wickets in this game and was quite simply the major difference between the two sides, which were till then evenly matched. It was Lillee's bowling that swung the match in Australia's favour.

At one stage, it looked as if England were going to pile up the highest ever fourth innings score in a Test match. That they ended up only 45 runs short, is proof enough of the closeness of the match. By coincidence the margin of victory in the first-ever Test between the two countries in 1975 was also 45 runs. It was Lillee who claimed Alan Knott leg before to give Australia the victory in 1977.

This was followed by a series in England in 1977. The euphoria of winning the Centenary Test was sweeping through Australia because Lillee had demolished the Pommies single-handedly but it was soon forgotten when Lillee announced that he would not be able to tour England because his back was causing him trouble once again. This announcement produced shock waves throughout the cricketing world. Lillee's partner Thomson too was a doubtful starter having fractured a collar bone earlier in the season. Thomson was not too sure of giving off his best. Lillee decided to rest his back as much as possible with a view to make himself available in a fuly-fit condition when the Australian season started. With their main strikeforce not available, the Australian selectors were in a quandary.

Thomson passed the fitness test and went on the tour much to the relief of everyone but he was not a success on that tour. As the team prepared to go to England came the news that the majority of the Australian players had signed with the W.S.C. cricket. It was a very busy season for Australia in 1977, with the Centenary Test, the emergence of the W.S.C. cricket and then the England tour. Off the field activities were more in news rather than cricket and cricketers. Many people jumped to the conclusion that Lillee was resting to keep himself fit for the Packer series. These people did not know Dennis Lillee at all. Because he would never withdraw from a cricket match and particularly where Australia was concerned unless he was really unfit. It was rather unfortunate for him that just before this tour of England the announcement about the W.S.C. signing up star cricketers from the cricketing world for the W.S.C. series was made.

With the International Cricket Conference deciding to ban cricketers participating in the Packer series from official Test cricket series, Lillee was out of Test cricket for three years till a compromise was reached between the Australian Cricket Board and the W.S.C. management in 1979. He missed quite a few Tests during this period and if he had played those Tests he would have had 400 Test wickets to his name instead of 335 wickets which he is having today. This would have been really possible because the fifty-odd wickets he took in the World Series Cricket during those years were of some of the world's best batsmen from England, West Indies and other countries. Perhaps he is right in his thinking that he has already 400 Test wickets to his bag, but since these matches were not official, one cannot agree with that. But he is still capable of achieving the 400-wicket mark, if he keeps going for a few more years.

The 1979 season in Australia, which was revamped after the W.S.C. compromise formula was accepted by the authorities, was very gruelling and busy. Australia lost all three Tests against the West Indies and won all three against England, thus all six matches were decisive. Lillee's performance in these six Tests was once again outstanding. Against the West Indians, he troubled every batsman except Vivian Richards who was in terrific form that season with his lowest score in five Test innings being 70. Lillee was in his element against the old enemy, England, and was firing on all cylinders and in the last Test at Melbourne, which was not a very good track for fast bowlers, his cutters were described by the English captain, Mike Brearley, as the best piece of fast bowling he had even seen. To induce a great judge of fast bowling like Geoff Boycott to shoulder arms and then knock his off stump back was a great achievement. And Lillee just did that much to Boycott's annoyance and discomfiture.

After that, Australia visited England for the solitary Centenary Test. And here too Lillee made his presence felt though not with the same degree of success he is known to.

The following season he made his first appearance against India Down Under. It is a pity that Lillee, who made his debut in Tests in 1970, had to wait for ten long years to play against India. When India toured Australia in 1977-78 and when Australia returned the visit in 1979, Lillee was with the W.S.C. and was not selected in the Australian side. So this was the series which was eagerly looked forward to by both the sides and perhaps by Lillee himself.

We first met him in the one-day game at Melbourne. He was bowling to me and his first ball was short but it had enough bounce. It hit me on the glove, then my ribs and went to deep fine leg for a single. As we crossed for that run, Lillee after his follow-through kept glaring at me, and I said to myself he is a dragon allright. In that series, Lillee, though a firebrand and fiery on the field, was the mildest of persons in our dressing rooms.

In the first Test, I won the toss and elected to bat, a decision which was criticised by critics who did not even bother to go to the wicket and imagined moisture and dampness. Given the choice I would do the same thing again since we might be able to do better. In the first hour I was out, being caught behind for a 'duck', and Chetan and Dilip were playing, Lillee, Thomson and Pascoe with care and a degree of comfort though the ball was moving around on the Sydney track, which is normally a hard track much like the one we have in Madras.

It was in the second hour that wickets began to fall and it was mainly due to careless batting rather than good bowling by the Australians and that got us back for 204 and Australia followed it up with a 400-plus score. In the second innings also we scored 204 and it beats me how people can criticise that we would have done well to bat second in this Test when we could not score more runs than the first innings even in the second knock.

It is now an established fact that the Indians never seem to do well in the first Test when they tour other countries and wait to gauge the strength of the opposition and their bowling. It is always after the first Test that they come into their own. So most of the time on tours the Indians have lost the first Test and performed badly or have not played to their full abilities. And so it was in this Test.

The second Test was remarkable because we scored 400 runs after chasing a 500-plus total. This was mainly due to Sandeep Patil's brilliant innings of 174 and a fine 97 by Chetan Chauhan and it was only that man Lillee who deprived Chetan of his first century in Test cricket. He beat him with a cleverly concealed slow leg-cutter.

And then, of course, our memorable victory at

Melbourne but before that there was that unfortunate incident where I wanted to take the side off the field along with Chetan which would have meant that the Test would have been won by Australia as we were still short of the target. But the background of that incident needs to be told to the readers to give them a clearer picture.

I was batting well and for the first time in the series that I was middling the ball well and looked like getting a few runs when a ball from Lillee kept low and as I played it with the inside edge of the bat went on to hit the pad. After that a typical Lillee appeal for leg before follwed as he danced down the track, eventually winning the appeal. At this stage, I must say that the umpiring of Mr. Whitehead had disappointed us for he gave a lot of decisions that went against us. It was getting to a stage where the teammates were saying that I must do something about it. Or else it won't be good for Indian cricket. For example the previous day when Allan Border was bowled while trying to sweep Shivlal Yadav, the umpires had to confer with each other to give that decision.

Then Kirmani had told me that if the umpire had given Border not out he would have walked off. And I remember having talked to him that, well, whatever may be the decision, we have to abide by it. But perhaps that word 'walk out' was imprinted in the back of my mind so the next day when Lillee's appeal was upheld I was furious against the umpire for having given that decision.

When the umpire did not reverse his decision a lot of anger was boiling within me but still the idea of walking off did not strike me. When I walked past Chetan I heard friend Lillee utter one of his profanities which was a very delayed action from Lillee and it was then I lost my balance of mind and told Chetan to walk off with me.

That is one of the most regrettable incidents in my life. Whatever may be the provocation and whatever may be the reason, there was no justification for my action and I realise now that I did not behave as a captain and sportsman should. I take all the blame and responsibility for my action and I think that Lillee in his own way forced me to take that action by uttering those word I was walking back to the dressing room and the most that could have happened would have been that the bench where I was sitting would have come under the impact of my bat or the locker where I kept my clothes and kit would have been knocked about. I do not fully blame Lillee because whatever may be the provocation, I should have kept my cool and allowed the anger to die down. I should have shown my disappointment in the dressing room and not on the field of play. That was Lillee on the field.

Then there was Dennis Lillee shaking our hands and wishing us well after the Test was over and hoping to come to India some day. I remember at a dinner where some Indian and Australian players were invited. Also present were Sir Don Bradman and Lady Bradman. There were Dennis Lillee and Doug Walters, Karsan Ghavri, Viswanath, Kapil Dev and myself. Kapil asked Dennis why he abused so much on the cricket field and to which Dennis replied that "it's because I am a fast bowler and when I bowl a bad ball or see the batsman edge without result my frustrations come out in open. Because there is so much effort to be put in fast bowling than you medium-pacers do."

That sums up the man's attitude, the man's characteristics, and goes to show why he has become the greatest fast bowler in the world. He is a very, very tough competitor. He will not smile at you, give an inch, he always tries to get you out and whether he has a cricket ball in hand or a verbal missile, he never lets you in doubt as to his intentions to get you back to the pavilion as quickly as possible.

Off the field he is a perfect gentleman, a man who likes to be by himself. He would like to spend his time in one corner. He would like to be anonymous and does not like to be recognised and spends his time with family and dear friends. Yet, while Dennis Lillee is playing cricket, and getting the wickets by dozens, the anonymity which he seeks shall be elusive. And this is something which he has to bear with or else, as most batsmen would wish, stop getting wickets in Test cricket.

8

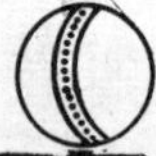

Derek Underwood

It is a pity that Derek Underwood did not complete his bag of three hundred wickets during the England team's winter tour of India and Sri Lanka in 1981-82. He is very close to that magic figure which only three bowlers have reached so far. It is not certain that he would be picked in the England team for the future Tests and so it is a pity that he may not join the ranks of those 300 plus wicket-takers in the history of the game.

On the previous tour of India in 1976, Underwood took 29 wickets. He was the most successful of the English bowlers, although it was the English pace bowlers who had done the most of the damage and capitalised in getting rid of the Indian middle-order batting during that series. On the last tour in 1981-82, Underwood was just a shadow of his self and though the old determination, the nagging accuracy, the old miserliness, as far as giving away the runs was considered, was still there, the vital nip off the wicket was often missing and, therefore, he was not as successful in India as one expected him to do as per his previous performances.

Derek Underwood is one of the nicest chaps you can ever come across. He wants to give the impression of being very tough on the field of play but his natural niceness prevents him from doing so and even though he might not like to exchange a word with others on the field lest that could relieve a little pressure or tension on a batsman, the nice part of him comes to the fore and he is always there with a greeting and it is always a pleasure to play against this great left-arm bowler. He runs a little further away than most of the left-arm spinners would do. Perhaps it is not really fair to level him as a spinner as he is so much quicker than a normal spinner. But then, similarly, Chandrasekhar could not be called a spinner because he was so much quicker than a normal leg spinner. But Underwood has been known as a spinner so we shall go by what the world knows him as and treat him as a spinner.

With a little longer run-up than other spinners and a diagonal run-up he bowls at a quickish pace and, on a wicket which is slightly soft or offers him a little bit of help, he is practically unplayable because at that pace there is hardly any chance for a batsman to use his feet against him and try and convert a good ball into a driveable ball. His accuracy is well known and more important is his ability to throw up a batsman's weakness as soon as he has seen him in action for a certain amount of time. With that legendary accuracy, he would pin a batsman down until he was fed up and try an attacking shot and got out. Because of Underwood's accuracy, a lot of other bowlers at the other end had got wickets. Having got tired with being tied down, they would try to break free at the other end and lose their wickets.

I first knew about a bowler called Underwood when a company came out with a miniature set of photographs of top cricketers in the world sometime in 1966 and there was a photograph of Underwood. After that time, whenever I followed the scores of County Cricket in England, the name Underwood caught the eye and after the photographs were published, I came to identify the exploits of this man called Underwood in the English county matches. He soon became a Test bowler and having played Tests he did not look back and has been a household name in the cricketing circles, since the time he made his debut. He has had his ups and downs and in the earlier part of his career he was not able to keep a regular place in the England squad. For example, Norman Gifford was preferred to him during 1971 and 1972 by Ray Illingworth for reasons only Illingworth would be able to give. Perhaps, it was that Gifford was an orthodox left-arm spinner, while Underwood needed a helpful track to get his wickets. But that is something of a reputation which he had acquired and which does not really do him justice. Underwood is perfectly capable of bowling well and get his wickets on most tracks and he does not actually need a helping track to get his wickets.

I have got out to him many times and I think the most regular way to get out to him was the caught and bowled variety, where he has decieved me with his flight, the result being my playing the shot too early for him to fasten on to the catch. I have been out to him, caught at forward short-leg, on a couple of occasions and on the opposite side at silly point as well. I think his best delivery to me was the one during the recent Calcutta Test when I played down the wrong line and was bowled by a ball that went straight through. The earlier two deliveries he had bowled just outside the leg stump so that when the third ball was about to be delivered, my left foot automatically went down in the direction of the leg stump and the ball which was pitched on the off-stump saw me going on the wrong line completely and hit back my off stump. That was very, very good bowling by Underwood because this ball was also delivered little slower than the earlier two deliveries. Apart from his normal pace, he has got a ball which comes in and is quicker than his normal delivery and this is the ball which has got him a lot of leg-before-wicket illusions as the batsmen have been completely beaten by the sheer speed of the ball and before their bat comes down are trapped leg before the wicket.

As a batsman too, he has been a stubborn customer and many times he has gone in as a night watchman and done a very commendable job of not only seeing the day through, but also taking the sting out of the attack when the play resumed the next day. He is very, very proud to be playing for England. Unfortunately, joining the Packer series meant missing three very important and vital series for England. God alone knows how many more wickets he would have taken, if he would have been around then. Certainly, he would have reached the 350-wicket mark if not more. One also remembers the ball he bowled in the 1974 Test to Viswanath when Vishy was looking good. It pitched on the leg stump and turned enough to knock back the off-stump. A gem of a delivery and it broke a promising partnership which was on at the moment and that virtually meant England got the breakthrough to go on and win that Test match.

The other delivery which is memorable is the one when he bowled Brijesh Patel in the Madras Test in 1976. Till that time, the ball had not turned much, though there was a lot of bounce Bob Willis was able to get off this wicket, but the spinners were not able to turn the ball much and this one from Underwood again pitched somewhere on the middle and the leg stumps, turned and went off with rocket-like speed to knock back Brijesh's off-stump. That was a delivery which would have foxed most of the batsmen in the world.

So quickly did it move after pitching and so big was the turn. As he turned round after being congratulated by the rest of the team, he remarked that a few more like this and "we would be in business". Well he certainly was in business in the second innings when the wicket had started turning appreciably and with the bounce having not lessened, he was almost unplayable. And India were knocked down for a paltry 83 which meant England not only won that Test but also the series. Well, I hope he gets a few more deliveries like that so that he can reach the magic figure of 300 Test wickets because no one deserves it more than this likeable, genuinely dedicated professional English cricketer.

9

E.A.S. Prasanna

Earapalli Prasanna played his first Test match in 1960-61 against the Englishmen, went to the West Indies in 1962 and then, after a gap of four years, he was back in the Indian side. This gap of four years was necessary for completing his engineering studies and obtain a degree. That was what his father had insisted.

In those days playing cricket was not as much of a monetary advantage as it is now. Of course, the glamour of being a Test cricketer was always there, but it was only in mid-seventies, particularly after Kerry Packer paraded his world's best cricketers in his series, that cricketers have been able to earn a decent living. Thus, Prasanna's father was correct in asking young Prasanna to continue with his studies so that his engineering degree would stand him in good stead along with his cricketing ability to get a good job.

It is very difficult to make a come-back into a Test side and particularly so after a lapse of four years. For that, one needs, apart from the resolve, ability, lots of fighting spirit, lots of guts, lots of hard work, determination and, of course, that element of luck. Pras, as he is lovingly called, had all these qualities and having acquired a taste of Test cricket earlier on, he was not going to give up easily.

Recalled against the mighty West Indians in the mini series in 1966-67, he spun a web round their batsmen and along with Bishan Bedi, who was making his debut in the series, made life pretty uncomfortable for the West Indies batsmen. That the West Indies still managed to win the series is a tribute to the depth of their batting and just goes on to show how strong they were that year.

They had just come from a very successful tour of England and with Gary Sobers in fine form and the up-and-coming Clive Lloyd around, the Indians had a tough time. Among those who came out with credit after this series was Prasanna. After this performance, he was a certainty for the tour of England in 1967 that was to follow the West Indies tour of India. Before that tour, however, one witnessed the duo of Chandrasekhar and Prasanna against Wadekar and Sardesai when Bombay met Mysore (now Karnataka) in the Ranji Trophy Championship. Ajit Wadekar was merciless in scoring 323 runs, while Sardesai scored a hundred, but the initial period when both Wadekar and Sardesai were trying to find their feet, was fascinating to watch. It was a great sight for a student like me who was trying to get into cricket. Two outstanding players of spin bowling and two outstanding spin bowlers were trying to get on top of each other. Pras was all his crafty self as he went on making it appear that he had an ace up his sleeve and was going to produce it during his next delivery and Ajit, grim, bending over his bat, concentrating very hard to see that Pras was not going to slip one between his bat and pad.

Dilip Sardesai was happier against Prasanna because Dilip

used his feet well. Whenever Pras tossed the ball up a shade more, Dilip was down the track and, taking advantage of the flight, scored some runs. Chandra, on the other hand, was a different bowler. His flight was unpredictable, his length too was unpredictable and so Dilip was not as keen to play Chandra. Ajit, on the other hand, played Chandra well because Chandra found it difficult bowling to left-handers, and Ajit was making full use of the short-pitched deliveries that Chandra used to bowl. The result was a massive partnership and it was as good a contest between the bat and the ball that one could have hoped to see.

Pras went off after some time complaining of a pulled muscle and it gave rise to idle gossip that Pras had chickened out. But Pras mostly had trouble with his leg muscles as his engineering job was such that he did not get enough time for training and exercising. Thus, he tended to put on a bit of weight and that, in fact, made it more difficult for him to be supple and agile. This was one of the things that let Pras down when Venkat was around because Venkat was trimmer and more agile. When two batsmen were completely dominating, Venkat would peg away and try to restrict the scoring with his tidy length. His superior physical fitness made him a bowler which most captains would have liked to have in their sides.

The tour of England in 1967, though not extremely successful for Pras, still helped him to establish his place in the side over Venkat and so when the tour of Australia and New Zealand came in 1967-68, Pras was able to get ahead in the side. That was Pras's most successful trip. He took 49 wickets in eight Tests, 25 in Australia and 24 in New Zealand. It was a remarkable performance and he had most of the Australian batsmen at sea. Many Australian batsmen rated Pras as the best off-spinner they had faced, rating him over someone like Lance Gibbs who had 300-plus wickets in Test cricket. When the Australian and New Zealand teams returned the visits in 1969, Pras was there, but this time it was Bishan Bedi who dominated the series with his left-arm spin and took the most wickets. They formed a deadly combination. Bishan, coming in easily, gliding in, while Pras coming in just a bit quicker but making the ball do exactly the opposite of what the left-armer did. And to top it all there was Chandrasekhar who would come on and bowl. And just when the batsmen thought that they were off the cunning flight of Bishan and Pras, they were confronted with Chandra who also was a spinner but a much quicker spinner than the other two. While these bowlers were on, life was not easy for batsmen and particularly in India where the wickets tended to help them almost from the word go. It set India's new ball bowlers a difficult task because unless a new ball bowler could bat like Abid Ali, it was always impossible for a new ball bowler to be picked for the Indian team.

When the Indian team went to the West Indies in 1971, Pras was in the team along with Venkataraghavan who by now had been made a vice-captain. The surprise omission was that of Chandrasekhar. Two other spinners in the team were Bishan Bedi and Salim Durrani. Durrani, of course, was more of an all-rounder. We had thus four bowlers who were all successful at Test level, plus we had also Eknath Solkar who could bowl a bit left-hand spin; and Ashok Mankad whose off-spin had picked up wickets for Bombay and West Zone in first-class matches. And to bowl with new ball were Abid, Govindraj and Solkar, who had started very recently to seam the ball. It was a fairly well-balanced side and the only question mark was how our batsmen would face the West Indies quickies on their tracks.

Apart from Sardesai, Jaisimha, Pras and Salim Durrani, no one had been to the West Indies before and so these were the men on whom Ajit Wadekar had to rely the most on this tour. I was fortunate to have players like Salim Durrani, Jaisimha and Prasanna to help me out. This was my first trip and before this tour, I had come across these players in the domestic first-class matches. I had made friends with them easily and I was fortunate to have encouragement from these players plus of course Ajit Wadekar. If I am not mistaken, Jai and Pras were roommates and I spent most of my evenings with them. It was usual for Vishy, Eknath and me to go to their rooms and listen to them and get some cricketing knowledge and education as well. It was in the first Test itself that Pras damaged his finger. He tried to stop a drive in his follow-through and the non-striker accidentally put his foot on his palm as Pras bent down to stop the ball. The non-striker was trying to get back to his crease. This accident meant that Pras was out of that Test and also the next one. That gave Venkat just the opening he needed. Venkat bowled well, took wickets and was always on the plus side with his close-to-the-wicket fielding. So Pras found himself sitting on the sidelines more than he would have thought off before the team took off.

Thereafter Pras was always under pressure, for one thing, Venkat being the vice-captain, his place was more or less secured. And so Pras was always struggling. He had not only to take wickets but had to take them in plenty and that set additional pressure on him. Thus Pras found himself out of the side and only when England came in 1972-73, that he was back in the side. The smile was back on his face.

The following season was one of ups and downs for Pras. But even during that lean period, he led Karnataka to their maiden triumph in the Ranji Trophy Championship. Karnataka beat Bombay convincingly at Bangalore in the semi-finals and then went on to beat Rajasthan in the final. The Karnataka team was undergoing a great transformation at that stage. The team has just begun to believe in its ability to take on allcomers. Pras was already a world class spinner. Chandra had stunned everybody with his devastating bowling. Viswanath was acknowledged as the best batsman India was going to have for the next ten years and Brijesh Patel and Syed Kirmani were coming up with plenty of promise and potential. With these players as his lieutenants, Pras had no difficulty in winning the Ranji Trophy.

Pras's greatest moment as a bowler, however, was yet to come. That was on the tour of New Zealand and the West Indies in 1976. In the first Test at Auckland, Pras spun them to their doom taking eight wickets and paving the way for India's victory. It was off-spin bowling at its best. The flight, the variety, the quicker ones were all there. But when Pras found a turning wicket, his greatest joy was not in getting the batsman caught off the inside edge at forward short-leg or backward short-leg, as the most off-spinners do, but the great off-spinner that he was, his greatest joy was to get the batsman out bowled trying to drive him through the covers and the ball sneaking in between the bat and the pad. The ball would pitch outside the off-stump, appearing to the batsman as a desirable half-volley and as the batsman went for it, found it just a little bit short for a drive, the ball would sneak in to bowl him. The other mode of dismissal that gave Prasanna the most thrill, particularly on a turning.track, was getting the batsman out caught and bowled. Players would go for the cover-drive only to find the ball turn and Prasanna waiting to snap up the return catch. These, to him,were the best methods of dismissal on a turning track. It showed that he was not just using the turning track to get the batsman out, but he was using his talent,his flight and guile. After the first Test against New Zealand in 1976, they saw to it that he didn't get any wickets without thick grass on the wicket. So Pras and other bowlers found it difficult to get going, Pras seemed to fade away somewhat after that and although he made another tour of Australia in 1977-78 and of Pakistan in 1978, he was not quite the same bowler he was before. By that time the new technique of the batsmen to play more with the pads rather than with the bats had been developed and that certainly frustrated Pras. It really was not cricket when batsmen tried to place the pad as the first line of defence and the bat as the second line. It was all against the technique of the game we were taught at school and Pras belonging to the old school wasn't able to quite adjust himself to that and so he went out of Test cricket.

And it was a big disappointment for us for it's not easy to lose first-class players like Pras.

Pras was not only a world class player but also first-class company off the field. We missed him running up to bowl to the batsman, beating him and then walking backwards, up to his bowling mark, with a smile on his face, which was probably another irritant to the batsman, particularly if Pras had beaten him and then jumped up throwing his hands on the top of his head and showing surprise at the survival of the batsman and then going backwards to his mark.

Another notable characteristic of Pras on the field was that everytime he got a wicket, he would run back to his old comrade-in-arms Bishan Bedi who would normally be at mid-off or mid-on positions, embrace him and both of them would have hearty laugh as if to show what a great joke they had played at the batsman. This was a very familiar sight, one which was a source of great joy for us.

This sense of enjoyment, this enjoyment of life was what Pras infected in all of us. It was great fun to be with Pras on tours as well as on the same side in domestic cricket. He was always smiling and looking at the brighter side of everything and whenever you needed advice he was always there to give it.

Pras did a splendid job for India, something he can be very proud of. He has an enviable record and it was sheer bad luck that prevented him from completing 200 wickets in Tests. In fact, he and Venkat with their off-spinners have set such a high standard that other off-spinners who are striving hard to get in the Indian team are finding it difficult to do so. The new aspirants are invariably compared to Venkat and Prasanna and are found wanting. In that sense their greatness has been a bit of disadvantage for the new offspinners who would much more certainly have loved to follow in the footsteps of spinners not as great as these. It is a gap which will take a long time to fill and even if it is filled, I have no doubt in my mind that there cannot be another bowler like Prasanna.

10

Geoffrey Boycott

No other Test cricketer, perhaps not even Sir Donald Bradman, nor Harold Larwood, has been so much in the news as Geoffrey Boycott. Ever since his arrival at the Test level, he has been in the news in some form or the other and his actions on the field and off the field has attracted the attention of the media. He's been a good copy for the press, radio and television.

What has been forgotten amidst the complex controversies Boycott has got into, is his ability to play near-perfect against all kinds of bowling and on all kinds of wickets. There cannot be a better technician than Geoff Boycott. People of old generation talk about Sir Len Hutton and his technique, they also talk about Wally Hammond, they also talk about, in India, about Vijay Merchant and his technique, but the technique of this man is simply unbelievable. The only problem seems to be that, while he has geared himself to meet every possible good ball delivered by a bowler, it is the bad ball that has got him out too often because he has not thought as to what he should do with the bad ball. And having preoccupied himself with the thought of shutting out bowlers and their good deliveries, whenever bad ball comes, he is not ready to take care of it and gets into trouble. Along with technique is his unflagging concentration and superb physical fitness. He seems to go on, on and on and his appetite for runs is increasing day by day, as he grows older.

On the recent tour of India, he showed complete dedication by trying to have a net even during the lunch interval when the rest of the team was having lunch. He even had nets during the tea interval of 20 minutes to have a little warm-up session. This is something which has been his constant source of strength because he seems to be merged into constant batting practice and nothing else seems to exist for him.

Boycott started off as a middle-order batsman and seeing his aptitude and dedication to play the moving ball, the captain of the Yorkshire team brought him up to open the innings. Thereafter, he set himself up to be as good an opening batsman if ever there was one and he practised, saw films of himself, talked to people who mattered and sought their advice, erased various chinks in his armour and built up a reputation of being not satisfied with anything less than a hundred.

His Test debut against the Australians was not outstanding but neither was it discouraging for him or for the England selectors. He batted solidly, gave support to the others and generally made it known that his was the wicket that the bowlers would have to earn and would never be gifted away. I can't recall Boycott having gifted away his wicket even when the chase for runs was on. Everytime a bowler got Boycott's wicket it was solidly and sweatfully earned.

Unfortunately, he has also been dogged by injuries. Which

means that he has missed out on a number of Tests. It is staggering to think what his total aggregate and average would be, if he would have been physically fit to play all those matches he missed out.

There have been three phases of his absence from Test cricket. Firstly due to injuries. Then there was his self-imposed exile, and, thirdly, when he was censured by the selectors for slow scoring and dropped from the next Test match as a disciplinary measure.

In a career spanning from 1968, he has played in over 100 Test matches. He has scored over 100 first-class centuries and holds the record for over 8,000 aggregate runs in Tests and holds records for a host of other things. He has also taken a few wickets with his medium-paced inswingers and has become a useful bowler in limited overs cricket. He has done a bit of bowling and helped in terminating many a good partnership when it has threatened to cross all proportions. But it is as a great batsman that Boycott is known.

People for ever will call him names. There are people who will never be able to ignore him either. You either love him or hate him. There is no in-between as far as Boycott is concerned. That's all about sums up the conflicting emotions this person creates in other people. I cannot think of a better opening batsman than Geoff Boycott. Though Barry Richards came very close to that with almost a copybook defence, he did not allow his defence to get the better of his attacking strokes. Defence was used only to tackle the good balls and when the bad balls came around, Barry Richards (sometimes even good balls) would hit. And his batting was always exhilarating to watch. But Geoff Boycott, perhaps, thinks the other way. He was trying to carry the England batting on his shoulders when their batting was not always sound and, in recent years, giving problems. Boycott had, therefore, decided to play the role of a sheet anchor. While the other young England players go there and play their shots, he always remained rooted there in support, seeing that no wickets fall from his end. This is perhaps a good attitude but he carries it too far and sometimes he gets bogged down with the result that sometimes a new batsman feels the pressure and that brings the bowlers on top. While Boycott, in earlier years, looked as if he could rotate the strike by taking well-placed singles, today he has lost that art of keeping the scoreboard moving.

There is so much you can learn from Boycott's game, right from the stance which is correct, sideways, facing the bowler, with the elbow pointing towards the bowler and the head still, not moving and very little preliminary movement. The feet are placed just the right distance apart to stand comfortably together not too close together, not too wide apart and the bat, though placed just around the right toe, still comes down straight, although it is picked up towards third man before the ball is delivered. When it comes down, it comes down straight which is the most important thing. While the bat comes down straight, the foot is almost in perfect position in the direction in which the ball is intended to be hit and, therefore, the body is, if the ball is to be hit on the off-side, kept rigidly sideways which is what this game is all about, being sideways in batting and sideways in bowling. He has kept to those rigid fundamentals and therefore even at the age of 40-plus he is a most difficult batsman to get out. However, he gives the impression that he is more of a bottom-hand player and this can be seen by the way the bottom-hand slides down the handle of the bat just before the bowler has delivered the ball, although when he takes stance the hands on the bat handle are very close to each other.

This is perhaps the reason why he is not such a good driver

of the ball and prefers to nudge and cut the ball away for his runs rather than drive them off the front foot. He is also predominantly a front-foot player.

When he bats, and particularly when he plays forward, the old saying, "smelling the ball", comes through very clearly. So low does Boycott play off the front foot, in fact, a little lower and he would be really "smelling the ball". One of the reasons why he has got a lot of injuries is the fact that he tends to go forward to everything that is bowled. Some of the more serious injuries he has received were because of this, for example when Graham Mackenzie broke his left wrist when he went forward and the ball kicked up from just short of a length.

He now wears a chest protector and also extra padding round his lower glove which gets rapped when he plays forward and low. There are more risks of his fingers getting injured when the bounce is little more than expected. Because of his backlift which is not very high, and since his hands do not come together on the bat handle, he is not one of the renowned hookers of the ball. But one must say that he is one of the best leavers of the short ball I have seen. He just lifts his head and allows the ball to pass on either side. He never seems to be in any way affected by the short ball. I have also seen him drop his wrists most magnificently when the ball climbs up suddenly and leave the ball alone. Also the way he has taken knocks on his shoulders from deliveries when he has been pinned down is something extraordinary and only a player with courage and correct technique would be able to do that. Most batsmen will try to fend it off and would be caught round the corner or gully. It is sheer luck if the ball falls harmlessly but Boycott seems to be leaving such balls easily and gets out of such situations.

The one stroke of his which always thrills me is the square-cut. Viswanath plays it magnificently but Boycott plays it with such an ease and correctness that it is a joy to watch him play it. The right foot moves parallel to the crease and just the right distance before the bat comes down with a heavy chopping action, the ball scuttling away to the third man boundary. Another shot of Boycott I would love to watch is the one he plays side-ways forward.

Another aspect of Boycott is the superb way he carries on the field. There is just the touch of arrogance about him as he walks. He is the cynosure of almost everybody's eyes. Knowing that the eyes of the spectators are on him he carries himself superbly on the field. He is always well dressed on the field. You will never find him in untidy and dirty outfits. He is always sqick and span and with just the right amount of crease on his trousers. His shirt is also immaculate and his whole appearance on the field is how it should be. The old saying comes to mind: If you are not a cricketer, at least look like one. Boycott is not only a great cricketer but he looks every inch a cricketer. This sense of dress he carries off the field and, for him, there is not the culture of jeans and other casual dress as it is so common with other cricketers now-a-days.

Boycott might not be everybody's idea of a perfect cricketer but he has many fans as can be seen from the various conflicts he has got into with the authorities and there are people who have gone with him, supported him, in their endeavours to fight the authorities, whether it was the Test and County Cricket Board, the Yorkshire Committee or the Yorkshire players.

People have called him selfish because he tends to look more towards his individual runs rather than the team runs. And that is the reason he is not reportedly liked by his teammates.

On the 1974 tour of England, he used to be a regular visitor to our dressing room and so also in 1979 when he was almost a daily visitor to our dressing room to get the autograph books and cricket bats signed by our players. During that time, he was a welcome visitor because he always had a joke or two to crack, either about his team or on the situation prevailing at that time. We thought that he was quite a likeable chap. In fact, even when he came down to India in 1981-82, he was more often to be found with our players at functions in the evenings and also during the day's play. This might be due to the reason that his teammates did not seem to have time for him with their differences in thoughts and different ways of life.

He was most welcome in our dressing room whenever he came but I am not too sure if he will be welcome in our dressing room now after his remarks of the conditions in India on the last tour after having forced to go back before the tour was over.

He has been a complex individual in many ways. In 1974, after Eknath Solkar got him a couple of times, he refused to participate in the last Test and the three Tests against Pakistan that followed. Then followed his refusal to go on the tour of Australia in 1974-75 and again two years later. He made his comeback in 1977 against the Australians at home, led by Greg Chappell. He had his own reasons but they did not go down well with his colleagues in the England team. Thereafter, he has been a regular member of the England side, as it should have been, as their best player and runs have been always around when the England team needed them most. He was also in the middle of a controversy with Yorkshire manager Ray Illingworth and before that when he was sacked as the captain of Yorkshire by the Yorkshire committee. Well, he seems to be involved with controversy after controversy and hardly had the Illingworth controversy died down, than he departed from India in circumstances which were unusual to say the least. He was playing golf when he should have been in the middle assisting the England team in the field at Calcutta. The management of the England team rightly thought so but the reasons they gave were that he was keeping indifferent health, which did not give a proper perspective of things.

Then he was a prime mover in getting a team to South Africa and it appears now that with this particular tour and with this particular act, Boycott's Test career has ended. He has the highest aggregate runs, plus-8,000, in Test cricket with about 21 centuries which is fantastic by any standards and it speaks highly about the talent of the man and his application and dedication towards batting.

11

Glenn Turner

The best batsman the New Zealanders have ever produced is undoubtedly Glenn Turner. His records in Tests prove that and also his scores in first-class cricket show that he has been one of the top run-getters in the world. The fact that he had the highest aggregate runs in 1970s and thereafter just goes on to show his appetite for runs.

It is a pity that because of differences with the New Zealand Cricket Council, he hasn't been able to play as many Test matches as his supporters would have liked him to play. It is also a pity that the New Zealand Cricket Council and the New Zealand team do not have his services. The New Zealand bowling strength is not much to shout about, apart from Richard Hadlee and the batting revolves round Geoff Howarth. New Zealand will be a far more formidable side than it is today if Glenn Turner plays for them regularly. Today, Turner has got more than hundred centuries to his credit in first-class cricket and in spite of requests, he refused to play in domestic cricket for New Zealand. He decided to have a complete break from cricket after a strenuous season in English county cricket.

The Indians first saw Glenn Turner in 1969 when the New Zealand team came here after its tour of England to play three Tests. Turner looked like a frail person and since then has not put on much weight though he no longer appears frail.

The first match of that tour was against the Combined Universities and it was my first match against a touring Test side. Turner did not get too many runs but he was instrumental in cutting short my first innings. I had played for over two hours and it was the first time I was facing pace bowlers of that quality and was wondering why I was getting the balls more on the gloves than the middle of the bat. For one thing, Richard Collinge was a big man and his balls bounced more than the others. Dayle Hadlee, Richard's elder brother, was genuinely quick before back trouble put him out of Test cricket. For a long while, I played the new ball and was hoping to get some runs against the New Zealand spinners who weren't so impressive. I tried to cut a short delivery from Brian Yuile and just managed to nick it, and Barry Milburn, who was the wicketkeeper, muffed up the catch. It bounced off his gloves and went to the gully fielder. The gully fielder was too close and he could just get his hands to the ball which was falling by his side when Glenn Turner who was in the first slip, dived across and literally caught the ball inches from the ground in his left hand. It was truly a remarkable catch and would rank even better than the catch Viv Richards took in 1974 to dismiss me against the West Indies.

The first Test was to be played at Ahmedabad but because of riots it was shifted to Bombay at the eleventh hour and India coasted to a comfortable victory with Bishan Bedi running through the New Zealand side. New Zealand won the next Test at Nagpur on a turning track and looked set to win the third at Hyderabad before the rains came in their way and spoiled their chances.

Glenn Turner did not do anything outstanding on that trip to India, though he had come with a reputation of being a difficult man to dislodge. He had carried his bat through the innings at Lord's when England won the game scoring 40-odd runs. Even in the first innings he had scored some runs while there was another New Zealand batting collapse. So his tour of India wasn't successful but, he went back to county cricket and slowly began to acquire a reputation of scoring hundreds. He was not satisfied with a hundred and went on to score double hundreds.

The 1972 tour of the West Indies by New Zealand was a personal triumph for Glenn Turner. He scored over 650 runs with two double centuries and once again carrying his bat through the innings. And with a personal best of 259. In another first-class game, he scored another double century and got over 1,000 runs on the tour. So Glenn Turner had arrived on the Test scene with a bang. He was now the man the most teams wanted to dismiss to get the other side out.

He continued getting thousands of runs in the county championship and when New Zealand went to England in the first half of the 1973 summer, he became one of those rare cricketers who scored a thousand runs before June. Not many players have performed this feat and the last one to perform it was Sir Don Bradman in 1938. He was the first New Zealander to do it and achieved it against Northamptonshire on the last day of May and that too with a square-driven boundary off his friend Bishan Bedi. Unfortunately, scoring a thousand runs before June had taken a heavy toll of his concentration and when the Tests started, Turner had only one innings of above 50 in six Test innings. The result was that there was too much pressure on the other batsmen to score runs, though the New Zealand batsmen rose to the task magnificently and almost won the first Test chasing a total of about 480 runs and failing by 30-odd runs.Thus New Zealand's successes in this series were limited and the main reason would most certainly be the failure of Glenn Turner to strike any sort of form in the Tests.

When the New Zealanders went home they had a series against Australia. Glenn was unfortunate to break a finger and did not participate in Tests. But when Australia returned the visit, Glenn was in magnificent form and scored a century in each innings of the first Test which New Zealand won and then was involved in a controversy with Ian Chappell. One of the New Zealanders had hit the ball over the infielders and the umpire, following the crowd's noise had signalled a six, but Glenn was at the non-striker's end and he was explaining to the umpire that it was not a six. Ian Chappell came running down from the slips, being very agitated that the umpire had signalled a six, and got in an argument with the umpire and Glenn Turner which resulted in Glenn saying that he would never share the same dressing room with Ian Chappell. The incident made headlines all over the world and this was just one more incident in Ian Chappell's colourful career.

In the 1975 Prudential Cup, he was instrumental in leading the New Zealand recovery against India and then piloting a victory. However, New Zealand lost to England in the semi-finals but did not disgrace themselves at all in the World Cup by performing creditably in all their matches.

In 1976, the Indian team went on a tour of New Zealand and drew the series. Glenn Turner was the captain of New Zealand and Bishan Bedi captained India. In the first Test, I led the side as Bishan pulled a muscle, just on the eve of the Test in a practice session. I was given the chance to lead the country for the first time in my career. I walked out to toss very nervously and when Glenn tossed the coin up and I called, it was an odd sight of both captains running after the coin because the coin rolled almost half the length of the pitch before coming to rest. I had lost the toss in my first Test as captain and that was something I regularly did during the rest ofmy career as captain in Tests. Glenn had no hesitation in batting. That Test was a memorable one for me because I got a hundred and we also won that Test.

Bishan was back in the side for the second Test and so we had to make a change in the side and we were confident that with Bishan in the side we would be sitting pretty. But Glenn had other ideas. We won the toss and decided to bat on a greenish wicket under overcast conditions. The ball was moving around alarmingly but having the kind of spinners in our side, the decision to bat first was made so that we could take advantage of any wear and tear of the wicket. Vishy played a brilliant innings and Glenn handled his side well, shuffling around his bowlers — Richard Hadlee, Dayle Hadlee and Richard Collinge — in an impressive manner. Richard Hadlee was playing his first Test of the series then. The attack was handled most astutely by Turner and when New Zealand batted, Glenn scored a hundred but he should have been run out when he was going for his hundredth run. There was no doubt about his class. He middled the ball right from the beginning. He kept the scoreboard moving in a very professional manner, tucking the ball neatly off his legs.

We saved that game due to another brilliant innings by Viswanath and we went into the third Test at Wellington with confidence that we could not lose the series. But the wicket at Wellington was something else. I have never seen so much grass on a wicket. The groundsman had not even bothered to prepare a wicket as such. Only light mowing was done and the wicket was left untended. And on that wicket, pace bowlers Richard Hadlee and Richard Collinge made the ball talk. Glenn was batting well once again. He was well on his way to another hundred when he stepped out to drive Bishan and was stumped for 64. We lost the Test and New Zealand squared the series.

Glenn must have been a happy man because he lost the first Test but came back to win the third. He led by personal example. He was well respected by the New Zealand players because he had his individual performances. He had the flair for leadership and he could extract the best out of his boys. He had a very good sense of humour and also he used to enjoy a joke at his expense.

I remember at Otago, when the sides were exchanged, Glenn gave Bishan a list with only the nicknames of the players. So it became difficult for Bishan to know who was who. But that was Glenn and the two captains got on very well. When both captains get on well, it is good for the game and the disgruntled elements in the side can be effectively curbed. The harmony between the two sides is always maintained. The fact that Glenn has married a Sikh girl from Bombay whom he had met on the 1969 tour of India, must have been one of the reasons for Glenn's close friendship with Bishan.

The New Zealanders returned the visit after the English summer in October that year (1976) and played three Tests. The weather was uncertain with threats of rain and the series went easily India's way. In Bombay, New Zealand collapsed in the second innings without any reason and India ran out easy winners. In the second Test, they barely managed to survive though Glenn scored a hundred and showed his displeasure at the decision as he thought the ball had gone off his boots. At this stage, after the New Zealand batsmen's gesture shown after getting out, the Indian boys were getting a little worked up at this open disapproval because earlier in the year on the New Zealand tour, they were not given the benefit of the doubt. So when the New Zealanders started making excuses about our umpiring our players naturally got upset about it. There were quite a few harsh, words exchanged between the players during that series. In the last Test, Chandra ran through the side and the series was won fairly easily by India by a margin of 2-0. Glenn, apart from scoring that century in the Kanpur Test, wasn't among runs. He was obviously the player, we had to dismiss to get through the core of the New Zealand batting and it was so true that everytime India got Glenn's wicket cheaply, the New Zealand batting collapsed.

Unfortunately, that series was not memorable because of the behaviour of the New Zealand players as regards umpiring in India and so it was disappointing.

After that Glenn did not play as often for New Zealand as one would expect because of his battle with the authorities as he being a professional player, wanted to have a little better terms for himself than the others. The other players were all amateurs and he was justified in asking more but the dispute got wide publicity and that was not a very pleasant thing. The two sides were not ready to budge a bit and so New Zealand lost the services of one of their outstanding batsmen, and as a result, the New Zealand side became weaker. The differences, however, were patched up and he agreed to play for New Zealand in the 1979 Prudential World Cup and was ready to advise the captain with his vast experience. New Zealand once again reached the semi-finals.

When the West Indies came to New Zealand in 1980, Glenn once again decided not to play in Tests and had accepted a TV offer to comment on the Tests. The New Zealand public did not like this idea at all. They would have loved to have him playing Tests in the middle rather than remaining in the background behind the scenes of action. Whatever it was, it was rather unfortunate because Glenn is a world class player and is one of the finest batsmen the world has seen. Ever since the limited overs cricket began, he adjusted to the situation and turned into an attacking batsman from being entirely a defence-oriented one. There have been instances in recent years when he has scored centuries before lunch on quite a few occasions. Technically, he has always been correct, the bat coming down in perfect line and the bat and the pad coming close together with perfect judgment to play swing although he has been guilty of playing and missing more than any other player of his class I have seen. But the determination is still there, the concentration is there in abundance and the greed for runs does not seem to be getting lesser. I hope he patches up his differences with the New Zealand Cricket Council and makes himself available to play Test cricket once again.

12

Greg Chappell

Australia were down in the dumps on the fast bouncy track of Perth against the formidable John Snow. This was also the first–ever Test match on the ground of the Western Australia Cricket Association and so the Australians were doubly keen to do well in this Test match. And at this juncture, in strode, a tall, pencil-slim, young player to commence his Test career. John Snow had made life miserable for the Australians in the first Test and here he was threatening destruction once again. Only Ian Redpath of the old reliable guard remained and, obviously, the young man walking to the wicket showed a little sign of nervousness. After having been immediately greeted with a bouncer, he then pushed the ball off his legs and started a career which has placed Gregory Stephen Chappell as only the second highest run-getter among the Australians so far, with only Sir Donald Bradman leading the field with almost 7,000 runs.

Before the day's play ended, the cricketing world knew that a future star had arrived on the Test scene. With Ian Redpath giving him company and encouragement, Greg Chappell scored a hundred and saved Australia from a disaster and what a hundred it was! It was full of strokes, hardly a trace of nervousness, and most importantly was the confidence with which he tackled John Snow.

John Snow had become something of an ogre in the minds of the Australian batsmen, but the display of this young batsman must have surely caused a lot of heart-searching in the minds of the earlier Australian batsmen and must have showed them that if a boy making his debut can deal with John Snow so imperiously, then so could they. Ian Redpath scored 170 runs and Greg Chappell joined the band of those select few who had scored a century on their debut in the first innings. That was in 1971.

Many people thought that Greg should have gone to India and South Africa in 1969-70. But it was a blessing in disguise that Greg did not have to make his debut in international cricket in conditions which were foreign to him. Not that his career story would have been different, but to make a debut in India would have been difficult, because the crowds here can unnerve most of the foreign players and one has to be a really hardened veteran in Test matches to ignore the noise and din of the vociferous crowds.

After the Indian leg of the tour, the Australians went to South Africa where they were given a right royal hammering. The South Africans were thirsty for Test cricket and when they got it they really grabbed it and won the series 4-0. In that series, a batsman as accomplished as Ian Chappell had failed miserably and so had Doug Walters, a man who had a tremendous Test record till then.

The omission of Greg from the tour of India and South Africa only acted as a spur to Greg to stake his claim when the season in Australia began. The tour of India and South Africa had exposed some of the Australian batsmen and there were obviously places in the team for the asking and Greg was well aware of that. With fine performances in the Sheffield Shield, he got into the Australian side and was brought into the second Test at Perth. For him it must have been a daunting prospect of following in the footsteps of his grandfather, Victor Richardson, and elder brother Ian Chappell, who was already being talked of as the future captain. But there was no stress of nervousness on the face of Greg Chappell as he went and launched his Test career.

The shrewd English professionals, however, marked his preference on the on side and completely blocked him in the other Tests to such an extent that he could only score one fifty in the series thereafter and one was beginning to think that his earlier century was a mere flash in the pan. The Australian selectors must have believed that Greg had a lot to do before he could establish himself in the Australian team because when the South African tour of Australia was cancelled, and the Rest of the World side came over, Greg Chappell did not find a place in the team for the first two 'Tests' or internationals as one would like to call them. In the first 'Test', one noticed Greg sitting in the sun in a deck chair, doing his twelfth man's duty, reading a novel. A thing like that, if it were to happen in India, would have created a furore which could have been unimaginable, but in countries like England and Australia, it is the cricketing talent that really counts and not what else the cricketer does.

In any case Greg was well aware of what was going on on the field and was alive to the needs of the Australian team when they were on the field. One could see a certain nonchalance about the person, one could also see the confidence with which he worked, the way he carried himself and he knew that his time was round the corner. By the way, now Greg Chappell grows a beard because the hot sun's rays apparently affect his skin which has now become sensitive. This obviously was a far cry from the young player who sat in the deck chair reading a thriller.

It was New Year's day in 1972 when the third 'Test' began. Australia were already one-up in the series having won the Perth Test. The Rest of the World were thirsting for revenge and the World XI had made a couple of changes in their batting line-up. Greg Chappell turned out to be highly successful because he scored a hundred and stopped the Australian side from collapsing. Against the spin attack of Bedi and Intikhab Alam and supported by Gary Sobers, he batted confidently and his 100 was classic. There were drives on either side of the wicket which in our team meeting the previous day, we could not believe he could play. The Englishmen, who had seen him the previous year, had said that he was predominantly an on-side player and, therefore, his one weakness could be to the ball pitched on and around the off-stump and leaving him. Frankly, this particular thing about the ball pitched on and around the off-stump and leaving the batsman being a chink in his armour amuses me because it is there in each and every batsman and if everyone could judge such balls perfectly then the bowlers would have packed up and gone home.

In any case, that weakness was not apparent or not exploited by our bowlers or perhaps Greg did not give them a chance. Most of the time he was at the crease, the spinners were on as it were they who had struck for us. Later on, when Peter Pollock, the great burly South African, was given the bowling, he was not shy to whistle a few down Greg's ears. But Greg came out of it with flying colours. The shot he played off Bishan Bedi dancing down the track and lofting it in the direction of the straight sightscreen was tremendous, because the wicket was turning and here was a man who came down the wicket and could play the shot with so much confidence. He wasn't afraid to use his feet to the spinners. But this effort of his was over-shadowed by that superlative 254 not out by Gary Sobers and a lot of enthusiasm was generated by Doug Walters' century in the second innings. Yet we knew when we sat down on the eve of the fourth 'Test' that we had more top-class players to reckon with and whom we would have to plot to get out very quickly.

In that match he came to bat after Ian Chappell was comprehensively bowled by Bishan Bedi. Having scored a century in the previous 'Test', he was full of confidence and looked around with that arrogance which has now come to be with him after batting all over the world. But he was bowled by the first delivery from Bishan, a gem of a ball which was well flighted and, as Greg came down, turned slightly and saw his off stump uprooted. I will never forget it, nor I am sure will Bishan Bedi or Greg Chappell. So we had both the Chappell brothers out in two deliveries and we were really on top at that stage. He avenged himself in the second innings when he got himself 197 and that too unbeaten. Towards the end of the innings, Dennis Lillee who had no great batting pretensions, at that stage of his career, was around and had given him staunch support by blocking a ball or two which Greg allowed him very shrewdly, while dominating the strike. This also showed that here was a man who thought about cricket and would surely lead the side one day. Eventually there was an over which Lillee had to face from Intikhab and Inti fed back Lillee with a quick top spinner and castled him. This left Greg with three runs short of what would have been a magnificent double century.

As one was walking back the field to pad up, Greg was heard lambasting Lillee for not being able to play one ball and really and truly giving him his piece of mind. At that stage it was felt that Greg was overreacting on his missing a double century. And only later on he explained why he was doing that. It was only to get Lillee sufficiently riled up for him to bowl quickly at us. Well, the aim was certainly achieved because Lillee gave us a very uncomfortable time and it was all due to Greg needling him for getting out. This also showed a keen sense of appreciation of the psychology of cricket and fast bowlers. Not surprising, because his grandfather, Victor Richardson, was considered to be a very good captain and Ian Chappell, who was captaining Australia at that time, was also considered a good captain.

Greg scored 85 in the next match on his home ground, Adelaide, and looked set for his third hundred when Intikhab managed to turn a ball sharply to get an edge off his forward defensive stroke which carried and so he ended that series in a blaze of glory and the man who had been reading a book sitting on a deck chair, getting himself a tan, was the first man to be selected in the Australian team to tour England later that year.

There also he had a magnificent tour, scoring a hundred at Lord's and smacking another hundred at the Oval when both he and his brother shared a giant partnership and both of them scored their hundreds. It would have been a gratifying moment for their parents who had come from Australia to watch that Test. Then Trevor Chappell was playing in the Lancashire League and he was also present and it must have made the entire family happy.

The next stage was the series against the West Indies. Again Australia won this series through the batting of the brothers and fast bowling of Lillee, Thomson and Max Walker. Greg scored two centuries in that series and often came to the rescue of Australia when they needed his batting most.

Then followed the Ashes series and once again Greg batted magnificently and it was he who the opposition wanted to dismiss. Before that he had set a unique record scoring a century and a double century and making most runs in a Test when Australia played New Zealand. The aggregate in the two innings is the highest scored by a batsman in a single Test. He simply massacred the New Zealand bowling which at that stage was pretty thin and with Richard Hadlee still a comparative newcomer and not quite the bowler he is today.

The Ashes series was completely dominated in Australia by Lillee and Thomson. That was a very good Australian team. Besides Lillee and Thomson, there was Max Walker to support them. Then there were Ian Redpath, Rodney Marsh and others and people for a moment forgot the deeds of Greg Chappell, though he scored over 600 runs in that series.

In the inaugural World Cup, Australia came to the final, but it was generally believed that they were not cut out for one-day competitions because there was practically none of this type of cricket in their calendar. But they surprised everyone by their versatility. The Australians then played four Tests in England and here Greg suffered the worst patch of his career. He totalled just 108 runs in Test matches with 70-odd in the second Test being his highest score. But Ian Chappell scored a brilliant 192 in the last Test and decided to step down from the captaincy of the Australian cricket team and that made the way clear for Greg to take over the leadership. There was also talk about his indifferent form in England due to which Ian Redpath was expected to take over the captaincy and it was believed that Greg would recover his form and then take over captaincy in another series. But, the Australian selectors had great faith in Greg's ability and they appointed him as captain. And he proved that faith by hammering a century in each innings in the first Test he was captain and winning that Test. This was a great feat on debut as captain. He suffered very few setbacks as captain of Australia thereafter.

The West Indies in 1975-76 were a great team and their clash with Australia was billed as the World Championship clash between the two teams. Both the sides had a battery of fast bowlers, free-stroking batsmen and possessed fielding of the highest order and that was enough to fill the grounds to capacity. Greg had an excellent series aggregating over 700 runs with 182 as his highest score in the deciding fourth Test. He led the side very well judiciously using his bowlers, Lillee, Thomson, Walker and spinner Ashley Mallet when the West Indies threatened to recover. That was a disappointing series from the West Indies point of view and they lost 1-5 in a series which should have been more closely fought.

The Pakistanis came the next season and they surprised

Australia in the third Test to level the series. It was mainly due to the inspired bowling performance of Imran Khan who only then had discovered the real potential of his bowling. He had begun to believe in himself and his ability to bowl fast. Greg did not have a very successful series though Pakistan seemed to be his favourite team against whom he had scored plenty of runs.

Before the Australian team went to England for the Ashes series, they played the Centenary Test against England in Melbourne to celebrate the 100 years of Test cricket. Though the two teams did not score many runs in the first innings and Greg also did not score runs, his medium-pace bowling brought him some wickets and his slip catching was of the highest order. The Australians won that Test by an identical margin of 45 runs, the same margin by which their predecessors had won a hundred years ago.

It was immediately after this match that the Packer bombshell burst on the unsuspecting cricketing world and turned the official international cricket topsy-turvy for the next couple of seasons. Greg had signed up with the majority of the Australians on that tour and so there seemed to be an atmosphere of distrust between those who had signed and those who had not. There were accusations that those who had not signed were not being given their due and this was due to lack of team spirit and it was, therefore, no wonder that they lost that series 1-3 and surrendered the Ashes which were with them for quite some time. Greg's performances in this series were not in keeping with his high standards, with just one hundred in the Manchester Test, which Australia lost as well. And that was his last notable innings for some time because the Australian Cricket Board had decided that the W.S.C. players would not be selected as they were not available to play in the Sheffield Shield matches the performance in which was the criteria for selection to the Australian team.

He was therefore lost to official Test cricket for the next

couple of seasons and he had to play the W.S.C. cricket before crowds which were sometimes hostile not being the regular cricket appreciating crowd. The W.S.C. cricket was very tough. High standards were expected from every player with emphasis on physical fitness as the players were professionals and were getting good fees for their efforts. Greg had an outstanding season. He played well against the Rest of the World as well as against the West Indies and he had to play under Ian Chappell who had staged a comeback for the W.S.C. cricket.

It was a couple of years before a compromise was reached between the W.S.C. cricket and the Australian cricket officials and Test cricket could be resumed. During this period Greg had fine performances in the W.S.C. and in 1977-78 when we visited Australia we had seen four of his centuries on TV. Greg scored 246 which is considered to be his best against an attack which was really sharp and hostile and the fielding which was of the highest class. And this innings came after fielding for over 600 runs and it was an amazing performance and set to rest any doubts anybody had about Greg's batting.

He scored tons of runs on his favourite West Indies wickets when the Australian team visited the Caribbeans and again proved to the world that he was still the best batsman. Meanwhile, he had some health problems. Just before the W.S.C. Australians went to West Indies, he had trouble with his left eye and fears were expressed at one stage that he would lose the sight in his left eye. Fortunately, for the cricketing world and for Greg himself, nothing untoward happened and he was back to normal in a short time. He has these health problems often and though he is a very healthy man, he is prone to catch viruses which are around. But this does not for a moment mean that Greg is not a fit person and that there is no power in his strokes. He can play a long six-to-eight-hour innings as well as anybody can, as well as Boycott can but probably he would score double the runs accumulated by Boycott in that period.

In 1980, the Australians went on a short tour of Pakistan and there Greg scored a marvellous 235 at Faisalabad to once again show that he loves the Pakistan attack more than anything in the world.

Thereafter, it was India's turn to visit Australia in the new set-up decided by the compromise between the W.S.C. and the Australian Board so that two teams would simultaneously tour Australia in a season. In the first season after the settlement, West Indies and England toured Australia and in the next, we were there along with New Zealand. Each played three Test matches along with a number of one-day internationals for the Benson and Hedges Cup.

The first match was the one-day international against Australia in Melbourne and India won it surprising the Australians and the Indians themselves. After the game, Greg came over to the dressing room along with his Australian colleagues as is the practice and had a word with me about the Melbourne wicket. He had been writing a lot about the deterioration in the quality of the Melbourne wicket and he wondered if I would support him in that. He also wanted to know my opinion about the Melbourne wicket. I told him that though I supported him that a better wicket should have been provided for this game, I could not pass on any judgment having played only one game. This was possibly due to the fact that I did not want the other games to be shifted from this venue to other grounds. Because a wicket where the ball did not bounce much would have been in the interest of the Indian team, with three or four fast bowlers at the Aussies' command. While I made a comment about the wicket for that game, I was not too enthusiastic about making a protest that Greg wanted me to make.

When we played the Australians we found that Greg Chappell was the lynchpin around which the Australian side was built although they had Kim Hughes, Allan Border and Graham Wood as their main players and they had brought back Doug Walters. So if Greg got a big score, the

E.A.S. Prasanna — The smiling "assassin"

Geoff Boycott — Technician par excellence

Glenn Turner — Perfection combined with run-hunger.

Greg Chappell — Mr. Elegance on and off the field.

G.R. Vishwanath — The supreme stylist, little man with a big heart

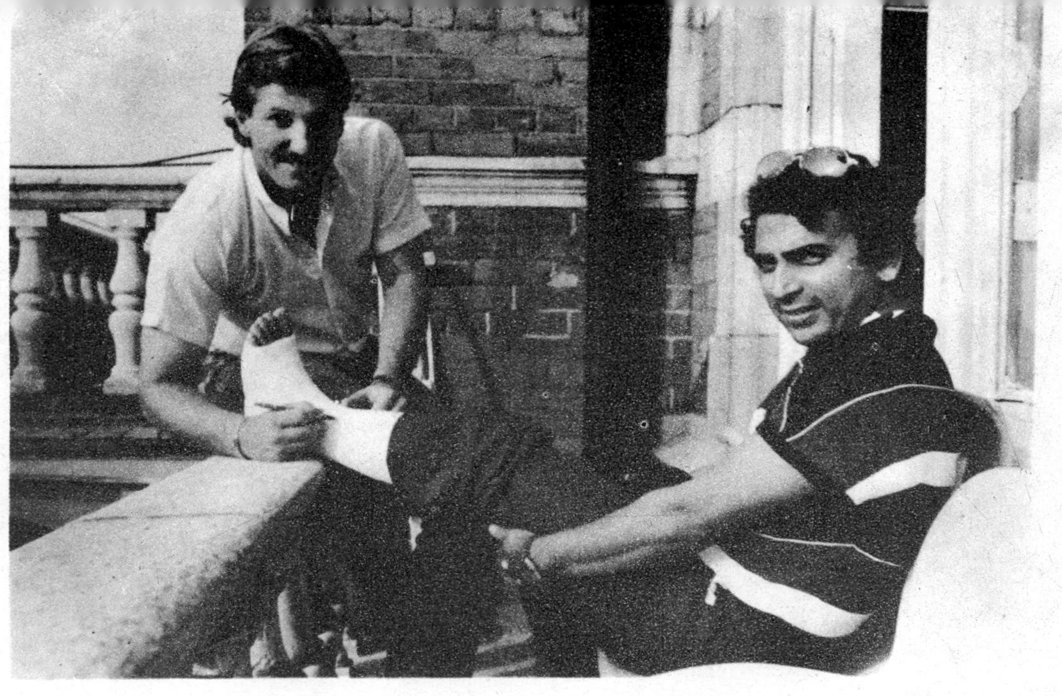

Ian Botham — Big, beefy and the best all-rounder in the world.

Ian Chappell — Growling, fighting Aussie who led from the front.

Imran Khan — Super athlete and the heartthrob of millions of girls all over the world

Australians piled up a big score as a team. This was, of course, proved subsequently when Greg failed in the Melbourne Test for a 'duck' in the second innings and the side collapsed for barely 83 runs. During the first Test, while we went out to toss, we had a very interesting discussion on the dressing rooms being as far off as they are in Sydney. And Greg spoke about the dressing rooms at Lord's where one has to walk long to get to the other dressing room. And as we walked back after the toss and reached our dressing rooms, I realised that both of us had failed to exchange the teams. I think the thought must have simultaneously occurred in Greg's mind because he came running from his dressing room and we met midway in the Long Room, where the members normally sit, and we told each other who the twelfth men were. Greg had a marvellous Test. He scored a double hundred, despite being not fit. He was having a virus infection. Halfway through that innings, he asked me if he could have some water and I told him only if he had some Scotch in it. He was hammering our attack and the only way to get him out was if he would be intoxicated enough to try an over-ambitious shot.

There were stories in some of the tabloids during this Test that the reason for Greg's sickness was a drinking spree the previous evening and not anything else. It was not correct because Greg is hardly a hard drinking man. This showed the kind of pressure he was having at that time and why he prefers to take a break at times from cricket. While the papers went to town pinpointing the reason for his sickness no one gave him credit for that double hundred. In that condition, how many players would have had the energy and the determination the next day to go out and score a double hundred and that also when he had only a slice of toast to eat the whole day. But then that is what happens to famous personalities and it's tougher if he happens to be the Australian captain. Now I understand why Ian Chappell gave it away, why Greg wants to take a break now and then. The pressure on him, his family, his children is tremendous and Greg therefore wisely takes time off cricket and goes to his family to forget the pressures of being a captain and the leading batsman of his team.

The next year he did not have a good series when the West Indies and Pakistan were around although he got a double hundred against the Pakistanis but did not do well in other matches. And by far his worst patch after the 1975 series against England was in that season of 1981-82. He came back with a brilliant hundred against the New Zealanders just when Richard Hadlee threatened to make life difficult for the Australians and one hopes that Greg comes back to his normal run-getting form because there are few finer sights in cricket than Greg Chappell in full flow.

Along with his cricket contacts, he has developed business interests. He is a very successful man in this sphere too. He has got a hotel, he is a director in some insurance companies and generally he is doing very well out of these ventures. For an Australian, he is a rare phenomenon in that he has continued to play at an age when most of the Australians look to their own career than their cricketing ones. Having established himself in the business career, he wants to go on playing cricket and only the pull of the family will make him quit cricket. And that will be a tremendous loss for the entire cricketing world. His batting has thrilled the cricket lovers all over the world, and although he may be surprised to know this—he hasn't played in India as yet—that he has the most number of fans in India than any other part of the world. To youngsters his batting is a terrific example, of how to play correctly also without losing one's ability to play shots and that is what is important to youngsters. He is a superb batting model. As a sportsman he has carried himself through all controversies and tough and tense situations with dignity and he has shown that he is very much in control of his emotions. That I think is his greatest example to budding cricketers.

13

G R Vishwanath

The year was 1968, the venue Hyderabad for the Moin-ud-Dowla Gold Cup Cricket Tournament. A young slim boy was in the nets, facing everything that was bowled at him. The nets weren't very good because it had rained earlier and the wicket was damp. The ball was climbing up, but at no stage did this youngster look in any sort of trouble. The ball that came up to his chin was played down firmly. He held the bat high above his head to let the ball pass safely above stumps. Watching that performance in the nets were some of the then Test stars—Jaisimha, Pataudi, Abbas Ali Baig and Abid Ali. That little performance was an indication that here was a talent above the ordinary and very soon this talent would delight cricket lovers all over the world. The young lad was none other than Gundappa Vishwanath and that exhibition is still fresh in my memory.

The youngster had already attracted attention scoring 230 runs in the Ranji Trophy cricket the previous year on his debut and was included in the powerful State Bank of India side to play in the Moin-ud-Dowla tournament. In those days, the State Bank side included Ajit Wadekar,

Hanumant Singh, Sharad Diwadkar, Ambar Roy and others and so for a youngster like Vishwanath to find a place in the side was signal enough of the tremendous natural talent that he possessed. The selection committee of the State Bank side had confidence in him. That confidence has not been belied and Vishwanath has proved himself to be the best batsman India has ever produced in the 1970s.

Soon after, Vishwanath was selected to represent South Zone in the Duleep Trophy and he scored a fifty on a turning track which had found stalwarts like Jaisimha, Pataudi, Baig groping and his performances brought him very quickly in the Indian fourteen. When the New Zealanders came in 1969, he was selected for the Board President's XI and he scored a neat 68 and in the company of Chandu Borde rescued the side just when the New Zealanders were threatening to do some more damage. Vishwanath had started hesitantly, but Borde gave him confidence, gave him encouragement and Vishwanath flowered and began to play his shots off his own. That season, the selection committee, chaired by no less a person than Vijay Merchant, plumped for young talent which brought to the fore players like Solkar, Vishwanath, to name just a couple, and both of them were included in the side to play New Zealand.

While Solkar made his debut in the last Test against New Zealand, Vishy, as he is affectionately called all over the cricketing world, had to wait till the second Test against Australia who visited India later that season, which was the fifth Test of the season. It is now history that he failed in the first innings being caught off Allan Connolly off bat and pad for a 'duck' and then coming back and scoring a glorious 137, including no less than 25 boundaries, to join a select band of Indian cricketers, scoring a century on debut. With that Vishwanath's place in the Indian side for the next decade or so was almost certain. One hundred was not enough. There were two other innings of 50s, on wickets which were not ideal for batting, that proved Vishy's class and at the end of the series, he was the find and toast of Indian cricket.

The spinners dominated the series against Australia, but among the batsmen, it was Vishwanath and Pataudi who carried the battle to the enemy camp. Vishwanath, with his adventurous play, had won the hearts of the crowd.

There was a little setback for Vishy in the Duleep Trophy match in Bombay, on the eve of the West Indies tour when he twisted his knee and there was a bit of a problem. This resulted in his missing two Test matches on the 1971 tour to the West Indies and he was back in the side only in the third Test. His replacement, Dilip Sardesai, grabbed the opportunity with both hands and scored a double hundred in the first Test itself and thus it was Jaisimha who had to make way for Vishy to play his first Test against the West Indies. A fifty in that innings was not the kind of an innings Vishy was known to play, but considering that it was his first big match of the tour, it was understandable. He took his own time to gauge the West Indies attack and then prepared himself for bigger innings. However, in that series, the big innings did not come. He scored 20s and 30s and when he looked set to be on the top of the bowling, he lost his wicket either to a good delivery or to a brilliant catch. This affliction of getting out early seemed to dog him for quite some time and when the England team came here in 1972-73, he was almost dropped, till he scored a brilliant 75 not out at Kanpur, which is his lucky ground, and thus kept his place in the side.

Earlier on the tour of England in 1971, he had become the first Indian to score a century on the tour and it was his calm, methodical type of batting that got us out of a tight situation that Illingworth had created and brought about on us at the time of our first ever victory over England in England. A score of 180 was all that India were asked to make, thanks to Chandra's marvellous bowling effort, but this target looked distant when we lost a couple of quick wickets and then on the final morning, we lost skipper Wadekar, run out. But Sardesai was a fine player of spin bowling and Vishwanath steadied his bat and slowly and steadily took us to the victory target. With only four runs required for victory, Vishy played an uncharacteristic swish off irregular bowler Brian Luckhurst and ended in giving a catch to Alan Knott. Later, when he was asked why he went for that swish, he said that he wanted to score the winning hit over the fielder's head. Unfortunately, he did not succeed and it was left to Abid Ali to score the winning run.

The 1972-73 series was a period of downs for Vishwanath. He was not getting runs although he seemed to be in no trouble at all. During the time, he was at the crease, but never got a fifty till the Kanpur Test. He was dropped from the side by the selection committee which had met before the Test was over but far from being discouraged, Vishy went on to score 75 not out and thus was reinstated in the side and he went on to score a century in the last Test at Bombay and became the first Indian to score a century on debut and then score another. That hundred was the last by an Indian at the Brabourne Stadium because, thereafter, the venue for Test matches was shifted to the Wankhede Stadium which was constructed in a record time.

The next engagement for the Indian team was the tour of England in 1974. It was a disastrous tour, but Vishy came out of it with credit because he batted in all the matches very well. His performance, particularly in the first Test on a green top at Manchester, was superb and the way he negotiated the quick bowling was an example to the budding cricketers and great morale-booster to the batsmen to follow.

When the West Indies team came down in 1974-75, they threatened to sweep us 5-0, having won the first two Tests fairly easily and were looking like winning the third Test and the series at Calcutta when Vishwanath had different ideas. He scored a scorching 139 and, in partnership with Karsan Ghavri, added runs which put pressure on the West Indies batsmen, batting last. Chandra and Bishan then spun them out and India came fighting back in that series.

In the next Test at Madras, India, at 91 for seven, looked like crashing to another defeat. Andy Roberts was bowling with such speed that he had to put on the brakes to stop in his follow-through. Such was his rhythm, such was his pace, that wickets came his way rather easily. He was stopped by our man Vishwanath. His 97 not out is finest Test match innings I was privileged to see. That attack is the best form of defence was amply proved in this innings. From 91 for seven, Vishy helped in carrying the score to 191 and in the end missed his hundred by just three runs when the last man in, Chandrasekhar, who had defended dourly, surrendered his wicket to Roberts. Vishy's strokes in that innings were unbelievable. His square-cutting meant that Clive Lloyd had to keep two fielders on the thirdman boundary and the way Roberts was bowling that day, it is a tribute to the quality of batsmanship. The moment Roberts bowled on the leg side, Vishy flicked him past square-leg and past mid-wicket and the moment there was an overpitched delivery, he drove it through the covers with elegance. When the innings ended, and both the batsmen came in, it was Chandra who looked the most disappointed for having deprived his mate of a well-deserved century. The knock raised the spirits of the Indian team and the spinners bowled us to victory to level the series at 2-all.

The deciding match was to be played at the newly-laid wicket of the Wankhede Stadium. Before a ball was bowled, the West Indian manager, Gerry Alexander complained about the quality of the wicket and the fact that more than 1,000 runs were scored in the first innings proved his apprehension to be wrong. Vishy, though he scored 98 in the first innings, was not at his best as seen in the previous two Tests. Obviously, he was mentally and physically tired. But such was his form that in spite of committing more mistakes, he still managed to score 95, before edging a ball from Lance Gibbs in the hands of short leg. This habbit of getting out in the 90s stopped Vishy from scoring more centuries in Test cricket than he has at the moment.

The 1976 tour of New Zealand and the West Indies was very successful for Vishwanath. At Christchurch on a green-top wicket, Vishwanath scored a superb 83 and 79 on a wicket which was helping seamers so much. It was an exhibition of masterful batting. When the ball pitched in line with the stumps, Vishy just let the ball go so that the ball went above the stumps and when the ball was pitched up, Vishy drove it. When the ball was pitched shorter, Vishy cut it and the judgment of leaving the good length balls alone which then sailed harmlessly past the stumps, or just above the stumps, was an unbelievable sight. Most of the present-day cricketers would have definitely played these balls and surrendered their wickets. But Vishy's judgment was absolutely correct and he didn't make a mistake at all till he got out. With the match drawn, and India having won the previous Test, the New Zealanders decided on another strategy and thus they left even more grass on the wicket at Wellington than they had kept at Christchurch. And with Richard Hadlee fulfilling the promise and potential he had shown earlier, in this Test, New Zealand won it easily.

When the team arrived in Barbados to play the first Test in Bridgetown, it was Vishy who stemmed the rot by scoring 62 runs. However, the West Indies won that Test and again looked as if they would run through the Indian side. But the fortunes of the Indian team changed in the next Test at Port of Spain and when the third Test was switched over to the same venue, the Queen's Park Oval, because of continuous rains in Guyana, it was Vishy, who, after scoring a brilliant 112, brought India the remarkable victory when chasing a target of 406 runs. When the last day's play commenced in this Test, the policy of the team was to hang on and play for a draw. By mid-afternoon, thanks to Vishwanath's strokeplay, visions of a victory were raised. These visions turned into a reality when Brijesh Patel cut the ball to short third man to bring about that historic triumph. Two strokes of Vishwanath in that innings stood out. He stood on tiptoe and square-cut both those balls which were rising deliveries, to the point boundary and thus took the sting out of Holding's bowling. He showed that the new ball held no terrors for the Indian side. These two strokes were really marvellous and brought victory to us for, if Michael Holding would have got a wicket with the new ball, our chances of a victory would have diminished. Those two strokes took away the confidence of Holding.

In the last Test, Holding, however, had his revenge when on a very quick wicket at Kingston he had Vishy fending at a short delivery and the resultant catch was not perhaps as painful as the fracture that Vishwanath sustained while playing that defensive stroke. He fractured his middle finger of the right hand and, at one stage, it was feared that an operation would be necessary to set the bone right. But luckily it was not needed and thus in the second innings Vishy did not bat at all. Luckily, the next Test on our programme was five to six months away against New Zealand and so Vishy did not miss a Test. Vishwanath again dominated this series and on a rain-affected Madras track he demonstrated once again what a technically perfect batsman he was.

There was a bit of slump as far as Vishy's batting was concerned after this series. The series against England did not find him many runs. But Vishy came into his own on the tour of Australia next year and aggregated about 500 runs to head the batting averages. He played Thomson on their fast wickets giving an exhibition of the highest class and it proved to the world, if any proof was needed, that India may not play fast bowling at home regularly but when it comes to counter-attacking the fast bowling, they had as good as the best batsman in the world.

India went to Pakistan in 1978. At Faisalabad, which

was a new Test centre, Vishy became the first Indian to score centuries against all Test playing countries. And although he could not maintain that form later on the tour, he had already become a popular and respected figure in Pakistan on the strength of that innings.

Later on, when the West Indies team came to India he scored then his highest score in Test cricket–179–in 1978-79. And this was achieved at his favourite ground, Kanpur. It is difficult to say what fascination Visny had with Kanpur for most of his electrifying innings have been played there. There isn't a match staged in Kanpur where he has failed. The only match that comes to mind is the Test against the Australians in 1979 when he failed to get a score of at least 50.

It was around this time that the WSC controversy surfaced and Vishy, who had been approached in Pakistan, was non-committal about it. This is Vishy's greatest strength in that he cannot be easily swayed by others' opinion. He takes his own time to think and decide to take a view of all matters. The WSC offer was one such proposal and he was a little cautious because he had a semi-government job and his priorities lay with India and Indian cricket. And though it was made known to him that there would be no clash with his commitments for Indian cricket, it had still generated enough storm in Vishy's mind so as to postpone taking a decision in the matter.

The Indian Cricket Board rewarded him with the vice-captaincy on the tour of England under the captaincy of Venkataraghavan. I have failed to understand why people say that Vishy would not have made a good captain. He was as tough as any other cricketer and his knowledge of the game was second to none. Thirdly, he was the most popular of the Indian cricketers and the other members would have done anything to help Vishy out. These factors were in his favour but the media had somehow given him the image of a man who was reticent and one who did not enjoy captaincy. This was far from truth and in fact, I am sure that if Vishy had gained the captaincy, he could have proved to be a good captain for India.

The two Test matches he captained for India were the matches where the Indian team was mentally and physically tired and, thus, not in a position to give off its best and so people have probably judged him on those performances. But then Vishy should have been made vice-captain under Pataudi and Bedi, before I was made. Not only was he a senior player, but also a much-respected and popular player.

In that series against England, Vishy was very successful although he did not score many runs that he was capable of after that Lord's Test century. That was another rescue effort as far as the Indian team was concerned and he and Vengsarkar both played magnificently to save India from an embarrassing situation. India were bowled out for 96 in the first innings and looked certain to lose this Test match, but the determined efforts of Vishy and Dilip saw to it that not only was the match saved but the team gained in confidence thereafter. Many people believe that India would have won the last Test at the Oval if Vishy had been sent at his usual batting order, instead of promoting Kapil Dev to that position. This, of course, is a matter of conjecture and this proves cricket is a great game of ifs. It is easy to criticise, particularly after the event. Venkat was criticised for not sending Vishy earlier, but if Kapil Dev, who is a reputed stroke-player, had succeeded in winning the match for us, then Venkat would have been hailed as a genius. But all this a captain has to undergo and the final responsibility is his. Very seldom do they get the credit for having taken a good decision and it's always easy to be wiser after the event.

When the Indian team returned to India, in September, the Australians were already in India and the first Test at Madras was played under sultry and humid atmosphere. Facing a total of 400-plus, Vishwanath once again steered India out of trouble. His century in Delhi was a fine innings and right through the first half an hour of that knock it looked as if Vishy would get out any time. The hallmark of Vishy is that he very seldom plays and misses the ball, but in this particular innings he was often rapped on the pads, he played and missed on a number of occasions and it looked as if he was out of touch with himself. But as soon as the half hour was over, Vishy was back to his dazzling best and cornered the Australian bowling to score a scintillating 100.

Against the Pakistanis, he was not at his best and did not score many runs befitting his reputation of India's top batsman.

Vishwanath's next glorious moment was when he scored a hundred against Australia at Melbourne and India won that Test. The amazing part of Vishwanath's career was that every time he has scored a century, India have either won the Test or have come out of it with flying colours. India have yet to lose a Test match in which Vishwanath has scored a hundred.

The 1981-82 season was perhaps his best season. On the verge of being dropped in the third Test against England, he came back to score another delightful hundred at Delhi and followed it up with his highest Test score of 222 in Madras, sacrificing his wicket on the dot of lunch in order to see that quick runs were scored. He could have gone on and on had it not been for the needs of the side. This again has been a popular trend in Vishy's cricket. He has always played for the side. When there was need for attacking cricket he has done that keeping the crowd in good humour giving them their money's worth. It is, therefore, unfair to judge him on the number of centuries he had scored because if one looks back, one will see that he got out very often in the 80s and 90s trying to play the shots which would have got the crowd to its feet. It has been his single aim to entertain, at the same time enjoying himself during a well-played innings and this is the reason why he has been such a popular cricketer.

He was very much missed in the last series against the West Indies and in the Prudential Cup. But he has not given up hopes of a comeback. He is practising hard and I am pretty certain that India would have to bring back this man, a genius with the bat.

He is a man who has a very good sense of humour. He always comes out with a rib-tickler when things are tense in the dressing room and his sense of repartee is well known among the cricketing fraternity. His popularity, just not amongst cricketers, but also with our crowds, particularly at Calcutta, is legendary and I am waiting to see whether he would come back against the West Indies and perform brilliantly in front of that magnificent crowd of Calcutta. Calcutta, with its fanatical love for sports, deserves a cricketer like Vishwanath and with a bit of luck, I am sure that Vishy will be able to come back in the Indian side and delight not just his fans at Calcutta but also all over India with his wristy stroke-play once more.

14

Ian Botham

Ian Botham is the craziest cricketer I have known. Well, when a guy scores a hundred at break-neck speed, hitting a few deliveries in the crowd and out of the ground at times, rushes in and bowls at a quick pace and takes five wickets during which a few deliveries have whistled past the batsman's ears, dives about and comes up with incredible catches, still has got energy in the dressing room to dip his teaspoon in the pot of tea and try to cause burns to the guy sitting next to him, you have got to call him crazy. That crazy guy happens to be England's No 1 all-rounder and the cricketer who really brings in the crowds whenever England play Test matches at home.

It is cricketers like him who really get the crowd's pulses roaring, and excitement runs high while players like Ian Botham are on the scene. If the above sounds like a very flippant statement, let me assure readers that it is not so, because, in spite of all these achievements that Botham has to his credit, he is a singularly modest man, a man who never cares much for figures and who thoroughly enjoys the game and also conveys its enjoyment to the people. That is why he is so hugely popular with the crowds wherever he goes. And I also mean the word crazy in a good sense and not in a derogatory sense.

The story of Botham's meteoric rise to fame is well chronicled in cricket magazines and many books written on him by authors and so I shall not delve into that aspect as to how he started hitting cricket headlines and how he came to be the cricketer he is today. But it would be of interest to know that when Botham started playing cricket, he played just the same way as he is doing now. The responsibility of playing Test cricket or the pressures and tension of Test cricket do not seem to have mattered to him, not even when he was the captain of the side and he played in exactly the same manner as he did when he shot to fame on the national scene in 1976.

It was just a matter of time before he was picked to play for England and his chance came in 1977 against the Australians and he started off with a dream debut taking five wickets in his first Test and scoring a few runs along with it as well. Among his five wickets, there were a few which were not against good deliveries. But he got those wickets and that is what matters most.

Botham has come a long way since and has to his credit over 200 wickets and 3,000 runs as well plus over 50 catches which speaks of his ability in a much more authentic manner than any words written on him ever will. At the end of the day, it is sheer statistics that go to prove a person's ability and not the words which are written about him. When a person plays Test cricket over a period of time, it is really the figures that should speak. For too long people have gone on saying that a cricketer A, B or C was a great player because he did so well in matches which did not matter, county matches or other first class games. Test matches are really what matters and when the form seen in Test matches is seen over a period of years, the ability of a person comes through and Botham has proved that he is the topmost all-rounder in the world today. His ability to change the fortunes of a match with his batting, with his catching and with his bowling is now legendary and while he is on the field no team can take things easy.

I first met Ian in the "Brylcream" double-wicket indoor championship played early in April in the 1978 season. And at first appearance, he looked to me like one of those French detectives of whom one reads about in novels. I do not know why that impression stuck in my mind but that is the impression I carry of him ever since. He was obviously restricted because of the rules which specified that one could be caught off the net on the side of the wicket and one could not bowl from a long run-up because the lighting was not so good. Yet you could se, the enormous talent that was there in that man. He hit some huge sixes during that event and his strokes used to travel like lightning on that surface which was an artificial one. The way he fielded those scorching hits by the West Indians and the other players was amazing. This man showed completely no regard for the hardness of the hits and did not fear injuries while stopping some of those hits. Fear of injury never entered his mind and he stopped everything that came at him. He and Derek Randall won the tournament that year and also, in the following year, when the double-wicket tournament was organised at the same venue at Wembley, London.

That year in 1978 he routed the New Zealanders and the Pakistanis with his bowling and batting and was really the star of the season. There was nobody to touch him but, at the same time, there were also the unkind remarks that he had scored his runs and taken his wickets against second-rate opposition. He was to prove, of course, later on, that he could score runs and take wickets against all kinds of opposition. But the successes of those years were clearly written off because some of the best cricketers were playing for Kerry Packer. What people forgot was that Ian Botham had not picked the opposition sides and he was only playing against those available and to decry those performances was very unfair. Not that it mattered to Botham because he is the type of person who immensely enjoys playing the game and if he is successful, all the better, otherwise he is not the type of person who would brood over his lack of success and let failures overtake him and subdue his bubbling personality.

When it was our turn to play in England in 1979, Ian Bothan was the one man we were worried about because he was one person who was capable of turning a match. In the first Test, he was not required to do much because David Gower scored a double hundred and Boycott ground out a hundred and fifty and there were useful scores from almost everybody in the England batting line-up. But in the bowling, it was Botham who struck at vital times and, as a fielder at silly point, he put a lot of pressure while the spinners were on and he played his part in that victory with crucial wickets.

When the second Test came along, it was a matter hotly debated whether Botham would be able to get his 100th wicket in that match and thus become the player to get the fastest double. Well, he did that having got my wicket to a brilliant diving catch by Brearley, off his bowling, and that was something which annoyed me tremendously. I was determined not to get out to Botham, particularly in view of the fact that he was in line for his 100th wicket. That over during which he captured his 100th wicket still gives me the shivers because I missed a hundred which was there for the asking, if I would have just kept a little control over my eagerness to attack. The first ball, which he bowled, was shortish, more of an attempted bouncer which did not come up and I gloved it off and went on the second bounce to Mike Brearley in the slips. The next ball was a slower one. I smacked it hard but as the ball came rather slower than intended it went uppishly to Randall's left and he stuck out a hand, not expecting to catch it, but to stop it. The ball fell to the ground with Randall wringing his hands and me cursing to myself for having missed four runs.

Botham seemed to be charged with that particular delivery and the next one was a beautifully pitched outswinger which I played and missed and, off the next ball, which was again a shortish ball outside the off stump I thought to myself that here comes four runs again but the ball was a little closer to my body and as I was a little cramped in playing that shot, a back-foot forcing shot, the ball hit the bottom of my bat, just kissed the bottom edge, and went low to Mike Brearley who dived to his left and held on to it — a marvellous effort. To my mind it was a waste of a wicket as far as the Indian team was concerned. I was fuming to myself, though I offered a congratulatory hand to Ian, who in his eagerness to go over to Brearley, completely overlooked that. I was furious with myself for having missed out on a big score as well as letting the team down

Another over which comes to mind when I was batting with 99 in the Bangalore Test and he bowled to me four genuine outswingers when the ball was not even new and the ball just pitched on good length on the off-stump, forcing me to play at it and then luckily missing an edge. This happened for about four times in that over and the fifth and the sixth ball he brought in and hit me on the thigh pad. But that was one over which I was glad was finished because four times I could have been out though that was not to be. That is what the luck of the game is all about, and one can hardly complain about one dismissal and be jubilant about dismissals at other times.

He played, in the Test at Leeds, an incredible innings of 138 when he smashed all our bowlers all over the park. It was hitting which was controlled and, at the same time, savage Every time, Kapil or Ghavri bowled a little short of a length, it was hooked into the car park of the Leeds cricket ground. It looked at one stage as if he was more keen on smashing Geoff Boycott's car parked in the car park but, fortunately, that kind of thing did not happen and he managed only to smash the confidence of our bowlers. Till he came on the scene in that Test our bowling was looking really good. Kapil struck early blows and Mohinder had managed to get an important wicket. Ghavri had also bowled very well. So it looked as if we would be having England on the run but then this man came in and changed the entire complexion of the game. He had managed to hit 99 runs in the session before lunch and he did not know that he had scored that many because the last over before lunch from Kapil he played out a maiden over, which was unthinkable, considering the mayhem that had preceded in the 118 minutes before lunch. That also goes on to prove that Ian Botham is not a man who looks at figures but just plays his game. Any other man would have tried to get that extra run but that was not the case with Botham. When he got out he was four runs short of scoring 1,000 runs in Test cricket, he missed that coveted double. He eventually did that in the next Test — the fastest double in Test — but it would have been one Test earlier. It proves the point that Botham does not care for records.

In the next Test he was run out due to a misunderstanding

with Boycott which was something of a sight and shall remain in my memory for ever — the way Botham walked off, swearing away at Boycott. Boycott, for once, did not look too repentant and almost seemed to have a gleam in his eye! It seems, the story goes, that in New Zealand while the Englishmen were going for quick runs and for a declaration, Botham had gone in and got Boycott run out deliberately so that the scoring rate would be accelerated with Boycott's departure. Well, the table seemed to have turned over at the Oval and it was a fuming Botham who went off the field.

When we were batting and I had got my hundred, he turned around to me and said that he had dreamt the previous night that I would score a double century and that he would see that the dream would be proved wrong. Well, I did get the double hundred and it was very, very thoughtful of him, that at the end of the day after I was out and the Indian batting was going on trying to overhaul the score of 438 set as a target by England, he picked up the stumps and kept them as souvenirs for me. That was a gesture of a person who has always treated the game as a sport and it was a gesture which goes to show how warm-hearted he is and appreciative of others' performances.

He then moved on to Australia to prove to the doubting Thomases that his successes earlier on were not just against second-rate opposition as they seem to have been thinking. He proved to them that he had the ability to get wickets and score runs against the best that Australia had to offer.

Then came his greatest performance when in the Jubilee Test at Bombay he single-handedly won the match for England. He started off taking eight wickets and the non-stop bowling spell in Bombay's sultry heat was a sheer test of stamina. He put in everything in his bowling. The wicket this time was as green as one can ever hope for a fast bowler. It was hard underneath and, therefore, there was a fair amount of bounce in the track and Botham utilised it in a magnificent way, not giving batsmen a chance at all and running through our side. And when it was our turn to field, Kapil Dev and Ghavri bowled excellently and restricted England to 57 for five when Botham along with Bob Taylor staged a grand recovery. Botham scored 114, a super innings because he did not play a single rash shot. He put his head down and was prepared to wait for a loose delivery and played a very responsible innings. It was an innings which showed that he could play with his head down if he wanted to and if it was required by his side. In fact, it was one of the best I have seen because Kapil and Ghavri were really moving the ball and making the ball talk.

Ian was not finished with the game and in the second innings, he took another five wickets to see that we were skittled out, leaving England only 90-odd runs to win which they did duly without losing a wicket. Ian must have gone back a very happy man because England had not had a very successful tour of Australia, having lost the series 3-0 and therefore, did not have a victory under their belt till the one in Bombay.

It was during the Jubilee Test at Bombay that the offer of playing for Somerset was made to me. Not by Ian as many people believe. But I was not very keen at that stage to get involved with a seven-day week programme of English County Cricket and, therefore, had to decline the invitation. But I took it up later on when I realised that I was required to play only for a short while and not for the full season. That gave me an opportunity of studying Ian Botham more closely and I have been friends with him ever since When you play in opposition, one can never really be friends because there is still a certain reserve which is difficult to break down and there are very few friendships between cricketers of opposite teams. But then having played together for Somerset, Ian has been a good friend after that season.

You come to know a person a little better when you spend time in the same dressing room with him. That was the time I came to know Ian Botham as a person. He has not been touched by all the successes he has had and all the glamour he has been sorrounded with and the adulation received from the crowd. I also found out that he did not particularly like the criticism that came his way sometimes and especially from some of the spectators when he had to give them the old Harvey Smith salute which, as a captain of the England team, which he was then, was perhaps not the right thing to do

The captaincy of England really did not change him and he went on the same way as he had gone about before. And that was the right thing to do. Captaincy is something which succeeds by what once has ben doing before and one need not change after being appointed a captain. Perhaps the Harvey Smith signal could have been replaced by a clenched fist which would perhaps convey the same meaning to the offender and you can get the thing off your chest as well.

In the dressing room he was an absolute terror because he never could sit still and he had to keep on doing something and if he did not find anything to do, he would punch you viciously on the arms, dip his tea spoon in a pot of hot, boiling water and while you were sitting unawares, he would try to cause burns on your hand with the spoon or just a lighted match stick. Many other variations of his technique would starte and stun you. I believe if the British Secret Service or the Police wanted somebody to do a bit of torture, and get information out of people who have not been talking, Ian Botham is the right sort of person to contact because he would get the information out of the guy who has been clamming up in no time flat.

Knowing my fear of dogs, he never missed an opportunity to call a stray dog in Taunton into or near the dressing room which meant I would be stuck up in the dressing room for hours on end. Once I remember going just outside the dressing room, as there are no telephone facilities in the dressing room, into a public call booth which is just ten yards away from the dressing room. The moment he saw me inside the booth, he got hold of a big dog and both the dog and Ian were parked outside the booth and inspite of the fact that there was a big queue outside, there was no way I was coming out of the telephone booth. I stuck around there in the telephone booth for about 20 minutes and the people outside were getting very annoyed with that and I had to signal to them and tell them to take away the dog and Ian Botham and only then would I step out. Ian eventually took pity on me and thank God for that and may God bless him for that! He took the dog away and I came out and heaved a sigh of relief.

At other times he would just lounge about in the dressing room and he could really eat, because any sandwich, any piece of cake or any eatable left over would be devoured by him, hungrily and not only that, in-between the lunch and the tea intervals, he would send for his famous steak and kidney pies and keep on eating them. No wonder, his size increased during that season, because that was the season when not much cricket was played during the early summer which meant that with inactivity, Botham kept on putting weight That perhaps hampered his bowling because one could see that he was not able to bend his back, just as he would have liked and as much as he was doing earlier on and so his outswinger was not as dangerous anymore and a batsman could play him with comparative ease.

He did not have a particularly good season against the West Indians and his figures, both batting and bowling, did not do him justice at all but that did not seem to affect him a little bit. He was horsing around as usual and on the last day of the season there was no play due to rain and both the teams, Somerset and Warwickshire, decided to play a game of football. Botham was at his best during the game and he really enjoyed that game. When everybody was in the team bath at the end of the game, Ian suddenly got out and dumped the pad and boots whitener into the bath while the others were still in there and, amidst angry howls of protests, sped away. Then he sneaked into the Warwickshire dressing room where most of the players were dozing off after a hectic night in Taunton. They were woken with a bucketful of water being splashed all over them. Dilip Doshi was lucky because he was in a three-piece suit and Ian threatened to douse him with water. But I do not know what happened and in spite of urging from me he did not do that to Doshi. He is quite fond of Doshi and obviously did not want to spoil the expensive suit he was wearing. On that day he would not have bothered about anybody else and so Doshi must count himself lucky on that score.

His driving, I mean car driving, is as dangerous as his bowling is, because, just like his deliveries seem to dip in and out between a batsman's bat and pads, he also weaves in and out of lanes, and speeds along at breakneck race which is not permissible by the law. He has been lucky that he has not been caught for speeding but, I believe, that he has been booked recently. The police obviously have newer faster cars now to be able to catch up with him.

I was not very sure about my way around Somerset and when we were playing away matches I would follow one of the players' cars. As it happened, once we were playing at Bath and I had to follow Botham's car. I told him frankly that since I was going to stay within the speed limits he should also strictly follow the same. Botham was really an agitated man when we finally reached Bath. He said that he would have driven faster in reverse gear but for the restrictions imposed by me.

Well, that's Ian Botham the man who has been living his life fully. There are no short cuts for him, no brakes for him. It's just one beautiful innings he is playing and I hope, with advancing age and diminishing reflexes, which is the case with every individual, the fun that he is getting out of the game and giving to the people, who come to watch, does not in any way be diminished and the spirit in which he is playing the game keeps on the way he has been doing so far.

15

Ian Chappell

In the year 1969-70, most of the college cricketers in India, particularly in Bombay, started wearing their hair over the collar. Long hair was getting into fashion in those days and it was also due to the fact that one of the most charismatic cricketers of our generation, Ian Chappell also started wearing his hair long—just an inch or so above his shoulder. Unfortunately, with my wavy hair, I could not wear hair above my collar but the rest of the blokes with their straight hair could do that, being true fans of Ian Chappell.

And then as luck would have it, the Australian team came down to India in the latter half of our winter in 1969-70 and all eyes were really on Ian Chappell. Just a season before in Australia he had caned the West Indies attack for over 500 runs, including three hundreds. And with his flamboyant way of going about things, he was the main attraction. There was, of course, Doug Walters, who had also scored an equal number of runs the previous season. He was the first player in the world to score a century and a double century in a Test match. But then Walters has been a very quiet individual, not the same kind of outgoing personality that Ian Chappell was. Walters was a lot more funnier person than Ian ever was. But most people were eager to see only Ian Chappell when the tour party was announced.

Bill Lawry had come to India in 1965 and so also Graham McKenzie, but then they were two players who attracted attention because of their stature. Johnny Gleeson was another player who attracted attention with his ability to turn the ball both ways without any noticeable change in his bowling action.

Before that series, however, India played a three-Test series against New Zealand and just managed to draw it. So when the Australians came with all their might, it was generally believed that India would be lucky to draw the series. As it turned out, India put up a good performance and it was only because of the lack of solidity in the middle-order batting that cost us a couple of Tests.

The first Test was in Bombay at the Brabourne Stadium and as soon as the first wicket fell, it was a sight for anxious eyes as Ian Chappell came out with his collar rolled up. This, to the Indians, is a belief that the man's head is swollen. The reason for turning the collar up is simple and that is to protect the neck from the fierce heat of the sun or to protect it from a stiff wind if it is blowing. But in India, we treat it as a sign of a guy whose head is little big for his shoulders.

His manners were a bit cocky, a little arrogant, and he only gave a glimpse of his ability then. However, he came back in the Delhi Test with a brilliant hundred on a wicket which was turning and which afforded all kind of help to our famed spinners and then followed it up with a superb 99 at Calcutta.

Over there, I am given to understand that it was the excitement of the huge crowd that dismissed him one short of his century, though I can't believe that a player as experienced and as crafty and professional as Ian Chappell could be dismissed for that reason. In fact, the crowd wanted him to get his hundred and were disappointed when he was out. These were his major contributions in that series along with the ease with which he took some brilliant slip catches. His style was a little peculiar in that he did not really bend down from shoulders as most slip fielders do.

Most slip fielders are used to almost squatting down on the field, but Ian Chappell had a different way of standing. A habit which was picked up in Australia where the ball comes up, the wickets being bouncier. The ball comes over the waist or near the shoulders rather than near the boots as it happens in England and India.

When the Australian team went to South Africa after the Indian tour, their captain Bill Lawry made a statement that Ian Chappell was the best batsman in the world. Of course, Lawry made that statement in all honesty. Ian had scored runs on the England tour of 1968, then in Australia against the West Indies and on the spinning tracks in India also he was successful, where the ball turned from the word go. He had scored about 400 runs on the Indian tour and naturally Bill Lawry was entitled to his views about Ian. A host of other followers of the game all over the world also held the same view that Ian was the best batsman in the world at that time. But this riled the South Africans. They put in more efforts to get Ian Chappell out. Though a lot of people gave excuses that the South African leg of the tour came after the tiring Indian tour, they forgot that the Australians are a tough and resilient lot and if they could not cope up with the South Africans, in 1969-70, the South Africans must have been a really good side.

Australia were really whitewashed in that series in South Africa and Lawry's captaincy was in jeopardy. But the Australian selectors gave him another chance when the England side, captained by Ray Illingworth, came Down Under for the Ashes series. Lawry's performances as captain in this series did not meet the approval of the selectors who thought that he was not able to get as much from his teammates as they would have liked him to do.

So for the seventh Test—this was added later on as one of the Tests was completely washed out by rain—Ian Chappell was appointed captain. Chappell lost that Test but under his captaincy, the side somehow seemed to be a revitalised side and a side with new determination and purpose. Poor Bill Lawry was not even picked for that Test, although he had good performances as a batsman at that stage.

Then it was the turn of the South African team to come down to Australia in 1971-72, but the Australian Government did not give them permission to come over and a Rest of the World XI team was assembled to replace the South Africans. The idea of having a Rest of the World side was the brainchild of Sir Donald Bradman. Gary Sobers, at that time, was staying in South Australia and these two got around in Adelaide for the formation of the Rest of the World XI. Sobers was the captain of the World XI and Ian Chappell that of Australia and thus the void created by the cancellation of the South African tour was filled in for the Australian season.

It was not a truly representative World XI because some big names were missing from it. Boycott and Barry Richards, who were considered to be the best two opening batsmen in the world, were not there and so also Alan Knott, but they had previous commitments and could not join the party. Still, it was a good side, although the side lacked a genuinely quick bowler which would have been a plus point on the hard, bouncy Australian wickets.

In the first 'Test' itself Ian Chappell gave Australia a tremendous start on a slightly rain-affected wicket by scoring a hundred. His hundred was laced with brilliant drives, cuts and pulls. He was particularly superb in playing the spinners of Bedi and Intikhab Alam. Whenever Bedi flighted the ball he was down the track, reaching the pitch of it for driving and every time Bishan pitched it short, he was very savage with his pull. He, therefore, neutralised any advantage the spinners got from the rain-affected wicket. The Australians helped by another decent score from Keith Stackpole piled up a good score and the Rest of the World also did not do badly with Hilton Ackerman and Rohan Kanhai adding over 150 runs for the second wicket and both scoring hundreds.

Ian Chappell believed that the Australians were a better side and so in the second innings he decided to take the attack by the scruff of the neck and carved out another hundred, even more brilliantly than the first innings' hundred. With a century in each innings, he set the tone of the series. Unfortunately, the rains came and the match was abandoned as a dull draw, contrary to Ian's expectations. In the second 'Test' Lillee tore the heart out of us by taking eight wickets for 29 runs, and, although Rohan Kanhai scored another brilliant century in the second innings, it did not stop the Australians from running away with a victory

The third 'Test' in Melbourne, of course, was well fought where Gary Sobers scored that unforgettable 254 not out. It completely dwarfed the efforts of Greg Chappell, who was playing in his first 'Test' of that series and a century before lunch by Doug Walters. The World XI won that 'Test' to tie the score at 1-all and with the Sydney match washed out, the last one was a crucial match for both sides.

The World XI was a better balanced side and their batting was strengthened at that stage by the arrival of the Pollock brothers. We won the last 'Test' in Adelaide to take the series. But one could see that Ian Chappell had inculcated a fierce determination to win and the Australians, as always, were a difficult side to beat. They never seemed to give up and everytime Ian called out in the field for greater efforts, his teammates responded. His leadership was flamboyant. Everytime a wicket fell or a catch effected, he would rush to the bowler or the fielder, embrace him, congratulate him which meant plenty of encouragement to them. The rest of the team members also rushed in to congratulate the bowler or the fielder which amounted to a kind of assault on the bowler or the fielder. But, this kind of feeling brought, also along with it, a sense of participation and team effort and a feeling of one-for-all and all-for-one, and Ian was the vital cog around which the Australian team was moving. The players used to look at him in the field for inspiration and instruction and he became gradually a revered figure as a batsman but also a tremendously respected captain.

So competitive the Australian team became that they also practised the art of 'sledging' to perfection. 'Sledging' is a short term for sledge-hammer and it was a term which was invented because the Australians never felt shy to tell the opposition what they thought of them, whether it was the opposition batsman or the opposite fielder, the Australians were very vocal. The Australians have this habit of giving nicknames for persons or things meaning exactly the opposite of what the nicknames are, for example, somebody, who is a very quiet person, will be called 'Rowdy' meaning making a lot of noise. Similarly, 'sledging' meant the views the Australians had of the opposition on the field would be conveyed to the opposition in as subtle a manner as a sledge-hammer if ever a sledge-hammer can be subtle.

That's how the word 'sledging' came into being and the 'credit' for it should go to Ian Chappell for bringing it into the team effectively. Former players touring Australia have admitted that the practice was there but then in those days, it was not practised by all the team members but by a few cricketers. This is not by way of casting any aspersions on Ian Chappell but just to show how competitive the Aussies were in gamesmanship which in their view was to unsettle the opposition and score over them.

Thus, the team under Ian Chappell came to be known as the "Ugly Australians" because if an opposition player came into arguments with them, almost the entire team together told him what they thought of him. This was unprecedented in a way and, therefore, the Australians wherever they went did not make too many friends. They thought that winning was everything and, therefore, cared a hoot for the norms and traditions of this gentlemen's game called cricket.

Along with Ian Chappell there were Dennis Lillee, another fiercely competitive cricketer, and Rodney Marsh, Ashley Mallett and Greg Chappell lent him able support in his campaign. These were the players who formed the nucleus of the Australian sides of those years.

When the Australian side went to New Zealand in 1973-74, Ian Chappell had a public altercation with Glenn Turner after which Turner declared that he would never share the same dressing room with Ian Chappell. Of course professional cricketers should never make statements like this because somewhere along the line there comes a time when you have to share a room with the same player. Glenn may not agree but then he went to South Africa with International Cavaliers, a team assembled by former Australian captain Richie Benaud and Ian Chappell was also included in the side. Eventually he had to share the dressing room with Ian Chappell.

Anyway Ian Chappell did not come out of it creditably and he was very unpopular with the Australian administrators and his relationship with them was stormy, to say the least. There was a public uproar also when he dropped his trousers to tie a loose thigh pad, though for the life of me, I cannot understand how a player could ever tie a thigh pad without dropping his trousers. What is normally done when a thigh pad comes undone is to request the wicketkeeper and close-in fielders to form a kind of circle around the batsman while he adjusts the thigh pad. Probably, Ian would not dream of asking that favour from the opposition and, therefore, he thought it was right and just changed the thigh pad on the ground. Of course, the media in Australia, which is always looking for something sensational, projected him as someone who did not care for traditions.

Then, of course, there was the incident where Ian Chappell had to appear before Sir Don Bradman for having incited South Australian players not to play in a Sheffield Shield match. He went to the meeting smoking a cigar and with a pint of beer in his hand which certainly did not look the most respectable thing to do.

But then he did what he really thought was right and damned everybody else. This did not make him very popular with the officials and they were always waiting for a chance to get back at him. Chappell also made it clear that he would not give the Australian officials a chance to sack him as captain and, therefore, after a very successful tour of England in 1975, he stepped down from the captaincy though he was available to play for Australia in Australia.

The following year, in 1977, a great coup was staged and Kerry Packer signed all the leading players from Australia and the rest of the world. Ian was the main brain behind this movement and did everything possible to make the World Series Cricket very popular. He went to the extent of ridiculing the India vs. Australia series in 1977-78 and thought that these were not real Test matches.

That was Ian Chappell and, once he stuck by a person, he could be assured that he would give his life for him. He came to Delhi for the Abbas Ali Baig Benefit Match and took this opportunity to try and sound me about joining the Packer series. His approach to me was typically direct and forthright. He came to me near the dressing room and said, "Sunny, I want to have a yarn with you." We then sat around and discussed the pros and cons of joining the W.S.C. and he made a fine impression because he only placed before me the best aspects ahead of me and did not mention the disadvantages, though he made it very clear that it was I who had to make the final decision and that I should make proper inquiries from different people as to the kind of cricket and the kind of security that was involved in the W.S.C. cricket.

Talking to him then, I realised that how much of a morale-booster he must have been to the players. Every time the team was down in the dumps, he had the knack of talking to the players which would boost their morale and make them rally round him. He pointed out that if I did not join the W.S.C. cricket, there would be something missing from my life. It was such type of talk during their team meetings at the intervals that must have made the Australian cricketers do their damnest best for the team. That's what made him one of the great captains of Australia.

He retired as captain and then came again as a player to play against the Englishmen in 1979-80. In this series, the Australians simply overwhelmed the Englishmen 3-0. He would have loved to score runs, particularly against Ian Botham whom he did not rate very highly when he burst on the international cricket scene. The story of his clash with Ian Botham in a Melbourne pub is very well-known. It is one of the few occasions when Ian Chappell came second best in an argument or brawl.

He then became one of the commentators on TV Channel Nine after his cricket was finished and his comments were very, very knowledgeable. In fact, his comments were precise up to the point and he gave a very good insight into the cricketing psychology that takes place when a Test match is on. Later on, so impressed were the Channel Nine people that they gave him a sports programme to compere. It became very popular and here again he did a marvellous job.

One day, not realising that the mike was live, he uttered an abuse which was heard by millions of viewers. He had to apologise and he was suspended for some time. He came back again and he hasn't so far made a mistake, using a wrong word here and there. One can be assured that the defiant spirit of Ian Chappell is still alive and it won't be too far in future to hear that Ian Chappell in the news again.

There is an interesting story about Ian Chappell and it

tells how he became a fiercely competitive cricketer. On his first tour with the Australian team to South Africa in 1967 he was playing in a Test match when a ball came up, off a length, and as he hurriedly fended it off and lost sight of the ball as it went off his bat. The next thing he knew was the chorus of appeal and so he turned round to the fielder who had the ball in his hand and asked him: "Did you catch it?" The fielder said: "Yes, I did." Then Ian Chappell walked back to the pavilion and when he went to the dressing room, the rest of the team members were furious at him and told him what a sucker he had been made and then told him that the ball had lobbed before the fielder had taken it. Ian Chappell was also furious about it and at the end of the day cornered the fielder and checked with him why he said he had caught the ball when he hadn't. The fielder replied: "You asked me whether I caught it but you did not ask me whether it bounced first. Did you?" And it was from then on that Ian Chappell stopped walking and also became a competitive cricketer. He would do everything within his powers and within the rules for his team and he came out of it successfully.

Most Australian cricketers of that era believed that Ian Chappell was a better player than his brother Greg. But that is so difficult to believe because Greg is so correct a player than what Ian looked. They believed that on difficult wickets and under difficult conditions Ian, with his fighting attitude and never-say-die spirit, would come out on top and would play a much more better innings than Greg, who according to them was not as good a player as Ian was on difficult wickets. So the Australians think that if there was one player whom they would choose if it came to saving their lives, it was and would be unhesitantly Ian Michael Chappell.

His attitude on the cricket field for not caring for reputations, not giving a damn to the authorities, is reflected in life. He dressed very casually, hated suits, and only now that he has become a compere for TV programmes that he has taken to wearing ties. But he preferred to be in jeans and open neck shirts and moved around in shorts.

He offended people by running on the field to dispute an umpire's decision in shorts in one of the World Series Cricket matches. And during his time, the Australian cricketers also dressed casually and were often called the most sloppily-dressed cricketers in the world. For then they were just being themselves, dressed in whatever was comfortable and in jeans because these garments were in fashion then.

His attitude towards the discipline of the team was also similar. He believed that each player selected to play for Australia was capable of understanding his responsibilities and, therefore, did not believe in curfews or things of that sort. He is reported to have said that a little beer did not give anybody any hangover and, in any case, it passed off in a few moments in the morning. With such a person at the helm, it was but natural that the Australian cricketers responded to him and gave everything that was possible for him. To ask an Australian not to drink beer is nothing short of sacrilege and so it was too much to ask Ian not to have a beer can in his hand. It was like dictating to a school kid.

Maybe the officials didn't like him, maybe the media, who castigated him at every possible opportunity didn't like him for his abrasiveness and his attitude of not giving a damn. But it was he who brought in the crowds more than anybody else, maybe with the exception of Lillee and Thomson, and it was Ian Chappell, the cricketer, that every cricket lover admired for his style, for his attitude towards the game and for the way he took Australian cricket by the scruff of its neck and brought it right on the top of the world and made it once again the pride of all the Australian sporting public.

16

Imran Khan

When we played Worcestershire in 1971, a skinny boy with an unruly mop of hair came up to bowl. He kept on pitching short his medium-paced stuff. Ajit Wadekar and myself who were concerned in a big partnership kept on helping ourselves to some useful runs, mainly through cuts. Three years later, when we saw this bloke again, he was a little bit quicker but just didn't seem to have filled in physically at all. He still had little freckled face and unruly mop of hair was still there. Years later when we saw this young man he had grown into a wide-shouldered, narrow-hipped man and had all the requisites for a bowler of genuine speed. This man was Imran Khan.

When one saw him first in 1971, one could not have believed that this man in a matter of three or four years would be troubling the best of the batsmen in the world, and make them dance to his tune with his ferocious bowling. In 1974, he dismissed one of our batsmen in the very first over with a bouncer. The batsman tried to duck and held the bat hanging up like a periscope lobbing an easy catch. But then Imran had worked very hard at building up his physique and the result is one of the most magnificent physiques one can hope to see. In 1971 he was still growing. My impression of Imran of 1971 is that the man was a little shorter than what he is today.

One then heard of him when he skittled out Australia at Sydney in 1976-77 and caused Australia's downfall, thus leaving Pakistan with a small target to clinch victory, their first on the Australian soil. At the end of the match, Greg Chappell wrote in his comments that Imran, at times, bowled as fast as Dennis Lillee did. And that we thought was a little bit exaggerated. But then Greg Chappell knew what he was talking and Imran himself has expressed in many of his interviews since then that he himself did not believe till then that he could bowl quick. He went to West Indies from there and though he was not the kind of success as he promised in Australia, he was still fiery and West Indians could not afford to treat him lightly. As Sarfraz was also in the side, there was obviously no bumper war. Because the Pakistani bowlers could have easily retaliated, if not in the same measure as the menacing West Indies fast bowlers. Pakistan had enough guns to cause a little bit of discomfort.

After that brilliant beginning, Imran joined World Series Cricket which saw him away from Test cricket for some time. The 17-year-old lad, who had come down to England in 1971, had now come to stay as Pakistan's main bowler. His success in the World Series Cricket on the harder, faster and bouncier wickets of Australia saw him establish himself as a bowler of world class. People now started talking about Imran in the same breath as some of the West Indian quick bowlers. In 1978, the World Series Cricket episode was forgotten by the Pakistan Cricket Board and all the players were recalled to play in the India vs Pakistan series which was resumed after a long lapse of 20 years. Imran was the one man on whom the Pakistanis pinned their hopes for attack. But at Faisalabad, he bowled far too short. That gave our batsmen enough time to either avoid the delivery or play it down safely. It was at Lahore on a greenish wicket that Imran came into his own and really ran down our batting along with Sarfraz and Salim Altaf for less than 200 runs. Imran bowled really fast and some of his deliveries were being taken by Wasim Bari in front of his face as they were still climbing. Bari was standing quite a few paces behind the wicket. Till then we could not believe that Imran had genuine speed. That performance proved that he had become one of the genuine quick bowlers in the game. He did not move the ball much because he pitched it too short. His main target seemed to be between the rib-cage hoping that the batsman would fend off the ball but that kind of approach does not always pay in Test cricket and he got most of his wickets by bringing the ball up and let the ball do the rest. Even in Karachi, he bowled quick but he was not so successful, as much as one would have hoped, but his furious hitting, when Pakistan were chasing a target, won the game. And it was those 19 runs that changed the complexion of the game. It was altogether an unexpected victory.

He then went on to Australia and New Zealand and bowled superbly and had all the batsmen in trouble. When the Pakistan team came to India, he suffered from fitness problems, having a side injury at first, then a back injury and so he was not able to take part in the full tour. He made a mistake in playing the Bombay Test and then missing out a real green-top in Kanpur which was the Test following the Bombay Test. I think it was Imran's dream to play in the Bombay Test as he had a large following in Bombay. And he did not want to disappoint his fans in Bombay and therefore he played. This was a mistake as far as Pakistan were concerned because that aggravated his injury which had occurred in the previous Test in Delhi and this meant that he had to miss bowling on a real green-top wicket in Kanpur. In Delhi, he bowled three overs of real scorching pace before he broke down. If he would have bowled another over to me, perhaps I would have had to bat with no feeling in knuckles, so badly were they smashed in those fiery three overs. He broke down then and did not bowl again in that Test in which Sikander Bakht went on to take eight wickets and then the marathon knock of Dilip Vengsarkar almost clinched victory for us when we just missed the target by 26 runs.

Came the Madras Test and Imran was fit. The Madras wicket is known to be a hard one which gives enough bounce to a fast bowler. Imran was a dangerous proposition on that track. But fortunately everybody in the Indian team seems to have applied himself to the task and the threat of Imran was nullified to a great extent. In the Calcutta Test Imran exploited a patch which was on the centre of the track and as the ball reared up it made life miserable for the Indian batsmen. The ball really flew at unexpected heights and caught the batsmen unawares.

On this tour Imran seems to have concentrated more on his bowling and his batting is something which has not got the recognition which it deserved. If you see his county record, it is excellent. He is a useful batsman but somehow he has not scored for Pakistan consistently as he should have. Perhaps, when he found a place in the Pakistan side, it had a very good batting line-up. The only time when his turn came to bat, he was required to do some slogging to get some quick runs. This obviously is not the best way to build up one's batting. Imran suffered because of that. But now that

Pakistan require his batting resources and it was so in the last tour of Australia, as his batting in one-day international as well as in Test match was extraordinary, he should bat in higher order. He now realises that Pakistan needs his batting and also that he himself is capable of batting well at Test level and therefore the results are there to see. He is still youngish and that means that there are many years ahead of him as a quick bowler and a brilliant all-rounder.

Off the field, of course, Imran is a lady's man. He has the personality which sweeps the ladies off their feet. During the Abbas Ali Baig Benefit match which was played in Delhi, the players were not put up in hotels but billeted with families. Imran and myself were with one family and one should have seen the rush of girls at this family's house. How they came to know about it and how they contacted him was something beyond comprehension. Still the hordes of girls never stopped visiting him and he always welcomed them and he had time for most of them. Something he is free to do being one of the most eligible bachelors in the cricketing world. I believe, in Pakistan his telephone number has to be constantly changed so that girls cannot disturb him and his family members.

The Abbas Ali Baig match was played in April 1978 and when I went to Pakistan in September 1978, I was a little disappointed to see the change in Imran Khan. He had certainly become less communicative and this was perhaps because I was the opening batsman and perhaps he being the opposition opening bowler he thought he should not be over-friendly with me. But thankfully, when he came down to India in 1979, this attitude of his had changed. He was his normal friendly self and someone who could talk about cricket for hours on end.

The girls continued to surround him on the 1979-80 tour also and the cry "Hi Imran" was something which was heard throughout the length and breadth of the country wherever the Pakistanis went. He is still a popular figure in India, still the heart-throb of thousands of girls, not only in India but all over the world. And I am sure these girls await with bated breath till the "Prince Charming" makes his final choice. He still has a long way to go as far as setting up some more bowling record is concerned.

The recently concluded series against India was a phenomenal personal success for him. He is now not only the leading all-rounder in the world but also a popular and successful captain. It would be a pity if his skin stress fracture were to deprive him of bowling because Imran running in to bowl is a sight for gods.

17

Javed Miandad

Two cricketers in 1977-78 captured the imagination of the cricket-loving public in our sub-continent. One was Javed Miandad of Pakistan and the other was Kapil Dev of India. These two cricketers have taken the cricket world by storm and, within a short span, have won over countless admirers from both the countries.

Javed Miandad made his debut much before Kapil Dev did and he is the one who had been more in the forefront because of his glorious performances in his country and also in the County Cricket which Kapil Dev has only recently started playing.

I remember Javed Miandad as a little kid, just barely out of his teens. He did not even shave then. He had come to play in the Prudential World Cup in 1975. Mushtaq Mohammed was the captain of Pakistan, though not for the World Cup. He had said that Javed Miandad was the most promising youngster he had seen. "This boy should go places," Mushtaq had said in 1974, a year before Javed was picked to play for

Pakistan in the World Cup.

Javed was a very shy and a different character then and not the brash and self-confident and cocky person he is today. I remember sitting down in the lobby of a London hotel when Javed shyly asked for directions to go to a Chinese restaurant round the corner. He was not speaking much of English then and I was not very fluent in Hindi and so there was a bit of a problem making him understand where the restaurant was. But later on, one found him in the same restaurant, eating shyly, sitting by himself. The other thing I remember about him is how he was trying to warn another of his players from trying to flirt with one of the wives of cricketers as Javed knew that the lady in question was the wife of a cricketer,a fact which his colleague in the team did not know and thought that she was just one of the fans who had come to meet the players. That expression on his face trying to warn his colleague, who was still seen flirting, is still vivid in my mind. Of course, Javed would not be averse to flirting a bit on his own now since he has come a long way since he was a little kid in 1975.

In the World Cup in 1975, he did show glimpses of his ability in playing the quick West Indian bowlers and scoring some runs and then chipping in with the valuable wicket of Clive Lloyd. Pakistan had as good as won the game when they had nine wickets of the West Indians down, still needing 62 runs to win. But then Deryck Murray and Andy Roberts played some sensible cricket and took West Indies to a sensational victory. And thus prevented Pakistan from qualifying for the knock-out stage of the tournament.

Javed stayed back after the World Cup and played with a club and then came again the following year to play league cricket. Then he was asked to register with Sussex in order to qualify to play county cricket. In 1976 he took the cricket world by storm by scoring a hundred on his Test debut against New Zealand and with a double hundred in the last Test. He narrowly missed the distinction of scoring a double hundred and a hundred in the same Test when he was stumped out at 85. So, a brilliant Test career was launched. He has not looked back since then and he has been a most consistent scorer in our sub-continent. In fact, if there is one person, who is likely to score the maximum number of runs in the sub-continent, it is going to be Javed Miandad because youth is on his side and he has the confidence and ability to score all those runs.

The tour of Australia following that was a bit of disaster for him because he did not get many runs there as also on the tour of the West Indies that followed. When he came back in 1977 to play against the visiting England, he looked in good shape and though he did not make as many runs as was expected of him, it was obvious that his performances were improving and the trips to Australia and the West Indies had done him a world of good.

The following year it was India's turn to return the visit to Pakistan after almost 20 years. It was resumption of Test cricket between the two countries after a very long time. The last series played between the two countries was in India in 1960 and this was followed by a period of uncertainties between the two countries and the atmosphere was not healthy for any tour, for any sporting contacts and it was only towards the early part of 1978 when the Pakistani hockey team came to India that the climate improved and the conditions were normal for a cricket tour to take place. Before that, however, the Pakistan team had gone through a drastic change due to the Packer saga and which put a lot of pressure on Javed Miandad at the tender age of 21. To be the team's main batsman as well was no easy thing and, obviously, it told on his form and he had a miserable tour of England. Against India, all the Packer players were recalled and Asif Iqbal came back from retirement to play in the series and all the leading players were back in the fold. Thus a load was off Javed's shoulders and as he was just one of the players in a team which boasted of a tremendous batting talent, Javed could play his natural attacking game.

In the first Test he scored 153, reaching his fifty, hundred and 150 with enormous sixers which showed that he still had that cheeky spirit and also showed that he was not afraid of lofting the ball whenever the occasion demanded it. But for the greater part of that innings, he was watchful, waiting for the right delivery to come about and very seldom did he jump out to drive. He batted as if he had made up his mind to score a hundred runs, only in singles, and he took a long time over his innings. But in that match, it was Zaheer Abbas's 176 that overshadowed Javed's innings. Zaheer stroked the ball beautifully from the word go and so Javed was content to play second fiddle to him.

I do not think Javed got too many runs in the second Test, again dominated by Zaheer Abbas with a career-best (for the India -Pakistan series) 235 not out and there was really no need for Javed to exert himself. In the third Test he scored a hundred, very good runs on a wicket on which Kapil had found his rhythm and was beginning to cause a threat to most of the Pakistani batsmen. It was Miandad's running between the wickets in the second innings and his dare-devil batting that won for Pakistan the Test when it looked, at one stage, as heading for a draw.

Credit should also be given to Asif Iqbal and Miandad for the way they ran their singles, for the way they hit good balls for runs and the way they kept on moving the score. I do not think they even thought for a moment that they would not be able to score the runs. And the way they played, they even won the match with three overs to spare, which was a considerable achievement considering the target they had been set.

Then, of course, came one of the many incidents in which Javed was involved. There was running out of Rodney Hogg in the Perth Test in Australia when "Hoggy" went gardening. Miandad picked up the ball and threw down the wicket and appealed for run out which was upheld. Mushtaq asked the umpire to reverse the decision, the umpire refused and "Hoggy" knocked down the bails and created an ugly scene. So that was one of the first incidents in which he was involved. It seems he had picked up a lot of these tricks while playing professional cricket with Sussex and under the captaincy of Tony Greig. There is nothing wrong with these things because they form part of gamesmanship in cricket and, Javed standing in the same position as Greig used to, was not afraid to give a bit of talk to the batsman who would lose his concentration. Javed, who had till then scored runs only in Pakistan, showed that he could score runs outside Pakistan as well, cracking a brilliant 140 on the Perth track against Rodney Hogg bowling at his fastest. Earlier on, Hogg had unsettled the Englishmen who toured Australia but Pakistan was a different story, although Australia won that Test with a brilliant effort of 300 runs scored in the last innings.

Meanwhile because of the registration rules in county cricket he had to change counties and he opted to play for Glamorgan because Imran Khan and Kepler Wessex were playing for Sussex.

The 1979-80 tour of India by the Pakistan team was one of the important events of the year as far as Indian cricket is concerned. Nowhere was a side looked forward to as much as the Pakistan side was. Even the West Indians when they arrived in India in 1966 and again in 1974 with best of the cricketing talents were not looked forward to as much as the Pakistan side. Only the previous year they had thrashed us soundly 2-0. So the cricketing public of India expected that they would thrash us again. Even I had serious misgivings and even months before, in fact in May when we were due to proceed to England, I had written when we saw the itinerary that the Pakistanis would smash us to pulp. That statement was made considering the fact that we had just finished a season in which we played three Tests against Pakistan, six Tests at home against the West Indies and with just a six-week rest, we were leaving for England to play in the World Cup, after which we were due to play four Test matches in England. A week after returning from England we were due to play a six-Test series against the Australians and then the Pakistanis, which meant that we were playing 25 Tests in a matter of 16 to 17 months. On the contrary, the Pakistan team had a long lay-off after that 1978-79 tour of Australia and New Zealand. And even those who played county cricket in England had a sufficient break in between before they came to India. The Indian players would be tired with the continuous playing and perhaps would not be in a proper physical and mental condition before taking on the might of the Pakistanis.

As it turned out, my fears were unfounded. What really happened was that the six-Test series against Australia which we won convincingly 2-0 gave us new hope. We were charged with more enthusiasm to tackle the Pakistanis. Before the Pakistanis started their first Test, there were a number of team meetings where strategy was evolved. Among these was the strategy whereby we tried to limit the scoring abilities of Zaheer Abbas. We succeeded with Zaheer and in case of Javed Miandad, it was difficult to devise a strategy. He was so versatile in his range of shots. It was

Javed Miandad — Great improviser, a provocater of bowlers, fielders, batsmen and umpires.

Jeff Thomson — Pace like lightning.

John Snow — England's hit man of the early 70's.

Kapil Dev — The most natural cricketer in the world.

Mohinder Amarnath — Courage, thy name is 'Jimmy'.

P.K. Shivalkar — Honest trier who missed out.

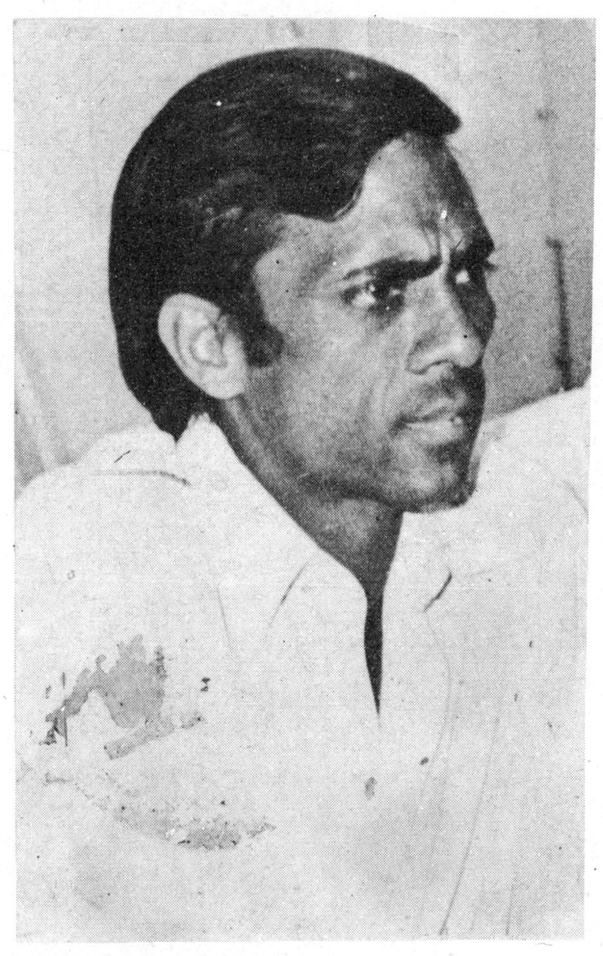

Rajinder Goel — Simply unlucky.

Richard Hadlee — New Zealand's man of steel, super all-rounder.

Javed who we were really afraid of because of his totally unorthodox batting and his dare-devil strokeplay. He was capable of changing the fortunes of the match with his quick running between the wickets and thus unsettling the bowlers. This is what he did although he failed to score a hundred in the series. He played extremely well at all times. Perhaps his best innings was the sixty he scored on a vicious turning track when Dilip Doshi and Shivlal Yadav were really making the ball hop. He batted extremely well, was sweeping Doshi on that turning track with all the control in the world and he was generally making the batting look a simple task. Even in the Madras Test which the Pakistan team lost to lose the series, it was Javed Miandad who delayed our victory with a defiant knock of fifty.

He was always dangerous and in the field he was always brilliant. I once jokingly told him that electric heels should not be allowed on the field because so quickly did he move and chase the ball and stopped it yards within the boundary.

His batting was not exactly from the purist's point of view a delight but from his side's point of view his improvisation was an object lesson to those who were watching. Javed on the field was a tough customer. He had a ready answer to everything. He was not averse to exchanging words with you. But this man Javed is one of the friendliest guys and I particularly think that he leaves all his animosity on the field behind him and he is really a friendly soul off the field.

There was no doubt that he had a sharp cricketing brain. He was always on Asif's side explaining to him and cajoling him to bring a particular bowler on or to shift a particular fielder this way or that way. Javed for all his inadequacies as far as education, etc., is a great cricketing brain which throws up weaknesses in the opponents and plans ahead.

It is a pity that because of internal problems, Javed Miandad has lost the captaincy. But one thing is sure, whether he is the captain or not, his brain will keep on ticking providing the captain with ideas so that the team will do well. I personally feel that he is the one man who is likely to break most of the batting records in this sub-continent. He has time on his side, he has talent in plenty and, more importantly, the determination to do it.

18

Jeff Thomson

When the England team led by Mike Denness arrived in Australia in 1974, they were greeted with Lillee's comeback stories in newspapers. Remember Lillee had been out of action for more than a year due to back trouble which, at one stage, had looked like finishing his career? But Lillee came back strongly, thanks to the hard work put in by him and due to the fitness programme charted out by his doctor to get him back into top physical condition.

Along with the report about Lillee's comeback, there was this news about Australia having discovered another demon bowler in Jeff Thomson. The Englishmen dismissed this story as just another one created by the Australian Press to cause worry to them. The Englishmen were not worried in the least about tackling Thomson because in his only Test two years previously, against Pakistan, he was hit all over for 100 runs and claimed only one wicket. They forgot, for a moment, that Thomson had bowled in that Test with a fractured toe and so they concentrated on how to tackle the fury and pace of Lillee. They went to see Lillee bowling in a Sheffield Shield match and were relieved when they saw him bowling only medium pace in his comeback match.

Then came the first Test at Brisbane in Queensland and the Englishmen were awakened out of their complacency by Lillee and Thomson. Lillee, of course, had very intelligently conserved his energies and saved himself for the big occasion, building his speed, his confidence and his accuracy for the Test matches and did it very gradually and the climax was reached when he went flat out in the Test. So did Thomson. His run-up was not very long. But he had powerful shoulders, he was an immensely strong man and had a whipping action. He concealed the ball behind his right thigh and at the point of delivery, he was just about impossible to be picked and so quick was he that he did not have to move the ball at all.

On a wicket full of grass these two simply ran through the English batting and put back the careers of a lot of established English batsmen. Thommo bowled into the wind because Lillee, being the senior partner, more experienced and craftier, was given the choice of ends to bowl with the breeze behind him to get that additional pace. Yet, Rodney Marsh thought that Thomson, bowling into the steep breeze, was even quicker than Dennis Lillee was and which is saying something.

At the end of the first session, Rodney Marsh turned to slip fielders, Ian and Greg Chappell, and told them that his fingers are hurting from the battering they were taking from Lillee and Thomson's thunderbolts. But he added that despite the hurting feeling, "I still love it."

Australia, thus, found a combination which would match with the legendary combinations of Hall and Griffith, Lindwall and Millar, Statham and Truman of the bygone days. And these two between them put the fright into the England batsmen and gave Australia such a psychological advantage that England never recovered from it at all.

Thomson, prior to the series, had got himself into trouble. He had said in a magazine interview that he liked to see the batsmen on the field with blood flowing because that's the way he could get them out. If he could not get them out bowled, he would like to see them knocked out and sent back to the pavilion. Either way was fine by him. This interview, of course, was great stuff, a nice way of sensationalism to attract attention and invite people through the turn-stiles, but exactly liked by Cricket Boards all over the world. Though the Boards would like people to come for matches in large numbers, this statement of Thomson was not in keeping with the traditions of the gentlemen's game. But the Australians always want to speak their minds and do not worry about the consequences. Thomson later on denied having given that interview, but for a moment it created enough impact and enough reputation for Jeff Thomson.

When the Englishmen met Thomson, though they were confident of tackling him due to his poor performance in the only Test played against Pakistan, they were shaken out of their stupor by scorching, electrifying pace that Thomson achieved. His most dangerous deliveries were those which rose from fractionally short of a length and which gave the batsmen no time to play any kind of strokes. Batsmen in turn had bruised knuckles and blows all over the chest to show for their efforts to get behind the line of the ball. In this Test, everytime he tried to bowl a bouncer, the ball went sailing above Rodney Marsh's head and struck the boundary fence for four byes. And one ball went so high above Marsh's head that it struck the boundary fence on the first bounce, which tells how quick Thomson was and how hard and green and bouncy the track was.

On such a track, Lillee's craftiness and Thomson's pace was enough to destroy the confidence of the best of batsmen, not just the Englishmen, who always shout about other batsmen's weaknesses against pace, without showing any kind of technique or attitude towards pace themselves, considering that in English county cricket, there is at least one, if not two, quick bowler in every county side.

From that Test, Lillee and Thomson became household

names in Australia, but the connoisseurs of fast bowling loved Lillee for his rhythmic approach, delivery action, his strides, his follow-through and also his craft with the ball. The kids, the normal Australian kids, went wild for Thomson, his unruly mop of hair bouncing as he ran in to bowl with his unusual action and moreover his hatred towards the batsmen seemed to stir the children crazy. Suddenly, Thomson found himself the idol of millions of Australian kids and he did not understand how to react to that. His attitude was to be his normal initial self and as he is a calm composed man off the field he took it all, after initial amazement, in his stride. He never refused an autograph to any kid and duly obliged all kids. He used to say, "Never refuse an autograph to any kid, he might have an elder sister."

In those days Thommo became the darling of the Press. What Thomson did was reported with gusto and with a lot of spice added to it as well. But his image of a man, who would like to see the batsmen in pain, suffering under his glare, was one thing and then there was his image of a man who liked to see the sun come up in the morning, spend his time with beautiful girls and basically he was a law unto himself. This image is, however, highly exaggerated, but at that time it suited Thommo and it suited the Australian Press and the Australian team led by the mercurial but outstanding captain, Ian Chappell. It suited them best because it gave them a certain toughness and also brought the crowds flocking to the Tests.

By the end of the fifth Test, Thomson had picked 33 wickets and looked as though he was going to overtake the series record set by Bill—way back in 1930s. This, however, did not come off because on the rest day of this Test, Thommo had an injury. On the rest day, both the teams traditionally go to Borossa Valley which is a vineyard with facilities for playing tennis and swimming. They relax under the shade of a vineyard and enjoy the Australian hospitality and, of course, the wine. Here while playing tennis, Thommo damaged the ligaments in his shoulder and was unfit to play not only in this Test but also in the next. That ruled him out from setting the series bowling record for most wickets taken. Lillee too damaged a foot and went off the field under this handicap. Without the Australian fast bowling twins, the Englishmen had a hey day and amassed a big total with Fletcher scoring a hundred and Mike Denness 188. The mastery that Lillee and Thomson had established on the Englishmen had gone away. The England side went on to win this Test to erase a little bit of the ignominy that they had suffered at the hands of the Australians right through. This victory also helped in regaining their confidence and they left for New Zealand in a much better frame of mind.

At the end of that series, the English Press, which always has excuses, sometimes ridiculous and funny, for the performances of their side, accused the Australians for having resorted to a bouncer war. However, they forgot that the bouncers were, in fact, started by Peter Lever and Bob Willis who bowled short at the Australian batsmen in the first Test and it were Englishmen themselves who started it since they had not reckoned with Lillee's comeback to peak physical fitness and Thomson's arrival, which they thought were figments of imagination of the Australian Press. So to a certain extent the tables were turned on the Englishmen and they lost very badly. That series had caught the imagination of people back in England and so when the inaugural World Cup was due to be played that summer, in England, Lillee and Thomson were ones who were star attractions, even more than the West Indinas who were the favourites to win the World Cup. During the series in Australia, the reports mentioning 'Lillee and Thomson' made headlines in the English Press and that led old ladies in England to wonder why and how a woman "Lillian Thomson" should rip through the England team.

When the team assembled for the World Cup once again all attention was focussed on Lillee and Thomson. After the World Cup, there was a series between England

and Australia in England and that meant that the two bowlers were again to meet the Englishmen, this time on their soil. The English Press had faithfully picked up from the Australian Press what they had been writing about the exploits of Jeff Thomson off the field and painted him with different colours and hues and somehow made him some sort of a villain.

In their first World Cup match played against Pakistan, they all went to see Jeff Thomson bowl and saw him misbehave a little. It was like going to see John McEnroe in action and his tanturms and only being able to see this great player's array of shots without seeing his tantrums. They went to see the bowling of Thomson but along with that they were expecting some other action, just like a gesture here and there at the batsman and Thomson did not disappoint them. Having some trouble with his run-up and having been called for 'no balling' often, he found to his dismay the crowd cheering his discomfiture and cheering every no ball he bowled. Not being used to being booed and not being used to this kind of reception, his immediate reaction was to show two fingers to the crowd. And this gesture, though more out of frustration than anything else, made the headlines the next day. The more perceptive of the writers knew of Thomson's predicament, but the others cashed in on in the hope of producing a good copy, hinted that the Australian umpires were reluctant to find this fault in Thomson's delivery. But the height of Thomson's unpopularity came when he was playing against Sri Lanka. Earlier on, the Sri Lankan batsmen had batted very confidently on a flat Oval track. Then Thomson decided to go flat out and knocked Duleep Mendis on the head. Duleep was lying flat on the ground and Thomson, instead of going up to him and inquiring about his injury, just turned his back away. This gesture of his did not meet with approval from anybody and he was condemned for this behaviour.

Hardly had this incident been forgotten, when Thomson was involved in another. He bowled a yorker to

Sunil Wettimuny which hit him on his foot. Thomson refers to his yorkers as—"sandshoe crushers." As the batsman was out of the crease, writhing in pain, Thomson ran down the pitch and broke the wicket, appealing for a run-out. This again did not meet with anybody's approval and though he was technically right, the ball seemed to be dead and that was what the umpires ruled. Again Thomson had made the headlines the next day. This was all very frustrating for Jeff Thomson and it was not certainly helping him in any way. However, Jeff showed great imagination and determination when in the final of the World Cup, he and Lillee batted sensibly and took the Australians within 17 runs of victory against the West Indians. That was a great final, thrilling all the way and there was some great fielding, particularly by Vivian Richards, great batting by Clive Lloyd and Rohan Kanhai and this last partnership between Lillee and Thomson that almost snatched away the victory from the West Indians' hands.

At the end of the World Cup the Australians applied themselves to the task of facing England in the four-Test series that followed. The bigger problem was to get over the habit of Jeff Thomson to overstep the crease which had by now reached alarming proportions. And this was causing his team management a lot of worries. However, during the Test matches, Thomson came good and although he had the occasional trouble of overstepping, he took care not to annoy the umpires as well as his captain in this respect. The wickets in England that season were more like what you see in Pakistan or India, devoid of any grass and were more whitish in appearance than green. Obviously, the Englishmen were not prepared to take risks with Lillee and Thomson in the attack, supported by Max Walker and Garry Gilmour, who had done very well in the World Cup and was also a force to reckon with.

The Australians won the first Test very comfortably after Mike Denness had opted to field and then suddenly found that the weather had upset his calculations. Thomson, though bowling not at his fastest, got vital wickets and proved that his performance in Australia was not a mere flash in the pan. Lillee, of course, was there taking his usual quota of wickets and on his way to become the greatest fast bowler of the decade. The two completely mesmerised the English batsmen in that Test and this forced Mike Denness to step down from captaincy and Tony Greig took over. He did a thorough job of revitalising the English team and he brought in players who were not outstanding or crowd-pulling but thorough professionals who would do their best for England. One of them was David Steele and he fitted firmly in Tony Greig's plans, batting with care and caution against the twin menace of Lillee and Thomson. Thomson after his first Test success was not quite the bowler he was and the wickets hardly afforded him any help and he was not particularly happy with the cold damp conditions in England, though it was an extraordinarily good summer. Yes, it was a good summer where wickets were drier and there was hardly any scope for seam bowlers to do anything extraordinary once the ball had lost its initial shine.

Thomson returned from that tour without damaging his reputation but also without enhancing it any further. He waited for the West Indians to come "Down Under" later that season for what was labelled as the 'World Championship series.' The Australians completely annihilated the West Indians and it was the pace bowling of Thomson and Lillee that did the damage. We were touring West Indies in 1976 and it was interesting to hear stories about how quick Jeff Thomson was from some of the demoralised West Indians. They admitted they had never played pace bowling of the type Lillee and Thomson hurled at them on that tour.

Throughout that series, Lillee and Thomson bowled short-pitched deliveries at them and completely mastered them, the only exception being when Roy Fredericks scored 169, racing to his century in 71 deliveries. This was one of the most memorable Test hundreds in cricket history.

Apart from that battering, Thomson was his usual devastating self. He was back in familiar surroundings, on hard, bouncier tracks from which he could extract life and bounce. This together with their natural fondness to hook was the downfall of the West Indian batsmen. The Australian grounds being larger than most of the West Indian grounds, their hooked shots were turned into catches. They were not hooking badly, but the shots which would have been certain sixes on other grounds fell short and were made into catches. That was a bit of disappointing series for both sides with such an array of fast bowlers on both sides. It was predicted that it would be an evenly-contested series, but the West Indians at that stage were a talented lot but still were not in that professional, ruthless streak of winning, which they were to fall in in the following year.

For Jeff Thomson that was a satisfying way to make a comeback into big wicket-taking league and he now waited patiently for the new Australian season to start when the Pakistanis were going to visit Australia. He had memories of his first Test against Pakistan when he had a broken toe but did not inform the selection committee. Because of that broken toe, he could not get more than a wicket and was hit for over 100 runs by the Pakistani batsmen. He, thus, had a score to settle with them and he was eagerly looking for that series.

Unfortunately, everything went wrong for him in the first Test itself. Having captured two quick wickets, Thomson bowled a steep rising bouncer to Zaheer Abbas, one of the best batsmen in the side. Zaheer went for the hook and hit it high with the splice of the bat and Thomson, following through, collided with Alan Turner, who was running in from mid-wicket to make the catch and both fell in a heap on the ground. Thomson was then seen getting up holding his shoulder. The collision created a terrific sound like the crack of a pistol and that meant that there was something seriously wrong with Thomson's shoulder. It was later discovered that the shoulder had not only dislocated and fractured but that the injury would heal only after inserting a metal pin in his shoulder. At that stage it looked as if Thomson's career was at a very sad end. However, he made a very good recovery and after having satisfied the Australian selectors went on the tour of England in 1977. That was the year when Kerry Packer had signed up cricketers all over the world. Some of the Australian players were not signed and the result was that there was "clear division" in the Australian team's ranks. Thomson had Pascoe as his partner to share the new ball as Lillee had opted out of the team because of the old problem—back trouble. The Australians could never get going. Then good leadership by Mike Brearley and the emergence of Ian Botham as a world class player and all-rounder combined to cause their defeat by a 1-3 margin.

By the middle of this series, Thomson was involved in a controversy. The WSC people claimed that he had signed up with Kerry Packer, while his agent, David Lord, claimed that in no way Thomson could have signed and, even if he had signed the contract with WSC, it would not be valid for the simple reason that Thomson had a previous contract with a radio station in Queensland.

As a result Thomson had to withdraw from the WSC Australian side and he was brought back in the official Australian side and was the only leading player in the side. Bobby Simpson was appointed captain of the Australian team after a lapse of ten years because there was no one experienced enough to lead the side which was depleted due to signing of the leading players for the WSC. Simpson insisted on discipline at all cost not only on the field but off the field. He wanted the players to stop coming to the ground in 'T' shirts and jeans and insisted on the players wearing the Australian tie and blazer. He insisted that the Australian players must feel proud about wearing their colours being the representatives of the country. This policy brought in a new look to the Australian team. They were a determined lot and with Thomson in their ranks they were raring to go against India.

It was a well-contested series because both the sides were equally balanced. They won the first two Tests mainly because of Thomson's bowling and the second Test because of Thomson's batting at the crucial stage. The Indians won the next two Tests and the fifth Test was the deciding Test. Australia coasted to a 500-plus total and Thomson captured first two wickets and then strained a ligament in his leg and did not take further part in the match. That was a severe blow to the Australians. The Indians almost won that Test falling short by just 45 runs.

Thomson had a very good series and was rewarded with the vice-captaincy of the Australian team that toured the West Indies immediately thereafter. Here, somehow, the old views of Simpson and modern views of Thomson did not agree and created quite a few problems. The relationship between the two was apparently not what should be between a captain and a vice-captain. The result was that Thomson could produce only one electrifying spell in Barbados when he had the West Indian batsmen on the hop and the knowledgeables said that it was the fastest spell of bowling they had ever seen in the West Indies.

After that it has been a series of ups and downs for Thomson and he has been in and out of the Australian team, sometimes due to injuries and sometimes due to the fact that the Australians produced some fine fast bowlers to partner Lillee and Thomson was not always able to keep his place in the team.

He was dropped from the side that went to England in 1981 and he instead signed for Middlesex in the county championship, something he was not in favour of earlier on because it involved playing cricket seven days a week. Over there, he had to return midway through the season as he was required to undergo an operation and Middlesex could utilise his services for only part of the season.

Thomson is not cut out for the seven days a week hard grind. He would love to play for shorter duration and then go fishing in between which he admits is his favourite pastime. He did not have a very successful season in 1982-83 when New Zealand and England toured Australia, nor could he do anything extraordinary in the World Cup in England earlier this year. In fact, he was dropped from some matches because of his indifferent form.

Married to a beautiful wife, who was a model once, Thomson still has a lot of fire in him though the fire seems to come to the surface occasionally, still he is an attractive fast bowler who still draws the crowds. Thomson will go down in the cricketing history as one of the fearsome fast bowlers of the 1970s.

19

John Snow

When the Indian team was playing in the West Indies in 1971, we got regular reports about the series in Australia where John Snow was running through the Australian batsmen and making them hop about. Geoff Boycott was scoring all the runs and John Snow was getting all the wickets. As luck would have it, both of them were not there for the vital sixth Test which was being played. Boycott had broken his arm and Snow broke his finger in this Test itself and was not able to take part in the second innings at all. Their impact on the series was tremendous.

When we came to England, the talk was mainly about these two English players; both had been picked because of their performances earlier on in the winter, but were also in for some criticism for their behaviour on the tour. Boycott had thrown down his bat when he was given run out and Snow had altercations with the umpires about the bouncers. Both were controversial characters, with Snow not half as controversial as Boycott was. But that summer Snow was very much more in the news. Snow had not played against the Pakistanis earlier on in the summer due to some injury and he was due to make his comeback against us in the Lord's Test. Till he actually played, one had no idea as to his bowling action or the kind of deliveries that he specialised in. Of course, it was believed that the bouncer was his lethal ball. But nobody could give us an indication whether he moved the ball off the wicket and either way. That was something which we had to find out ourselves when the Test started.

The Nursery end at Lord's is a place where teams practise before and during the match as nets are out of the ground behind the stands at the northern end from the pavilion. So on the morning of the match, most of the Indian players were trying to get an idea of how John Snow bowls. He bowled off a short run-up to the English batsmen. The balls used at the English nets are seldom new ones and we could not get an idea about his bowling ability but at least we got to see his bowling action.

It wasn't long before that opportunity came and we could see why Snow had been rated as the top fast bowler in the world. But before that, Snow contributed with the bat and led an England recovery with Raymond Illingworth. England were not in a happy position when Snow walked in to bat and he just stuck around there by sheer dint of application and plenty of determination. He wasn't able to read Chandra, wasn't comfortable against Bishan, but carried on gamely for 71, before Chandra had him caught. These runs were indeed invaluable and helped England put up a reasonable total. That batting effort seemed to have warmed him up for the bowling that was to follow. He bowled fast and furiously and soon a short one had Ashok Mankad lobbing a catch to Norman Gifford at forward short-leg. He didn't have too much success after that because he bowled too short and perhaps his line and length was still adjusted to Australian wickets and not the English wickets.

Therefore, he did not get too many wickets in that game and frustration was telling on him. The Indian batsmen have gained a reputation of not liking real fast bowling, though I don't think this reputation is correct when it is hinted that others in the world are more adept at playing fast bowling. No team in the world is good at playing fast bowling and at various times, one has seen that how the best of the teams have fallen. In defence of the Indian batting, it must be said that they rarely get anything above medium-pace in domestic cricket and, therefore, have failed to have enough practice against the bouncing ball. And so their vulnerability to fast bowling is understandable because they just do not have the opportunity to play the kind of fast bowling the rest of the world have. Look at the present performances of India in international cricket and it can be seen that they are sometimes better than those of other countries who regularly get practice against this type of bowling yet do not give good performances.

Well, with this kind of reputation, Snow thought that he would be able to run through the side and when he found resistance coming and at times defiance in the wake of Ajit Wadekar's brilliant innings and another good knock from Vishy and the stubborn defence of Eknath Solkar, the frustration was very evident. When we began the second innings, he tried bouncers, and when he found that they had no desired effect, he was getting a little difficult.

Then came the famous incident which almost everybody knows but I want to recount it for the benefit of those who missed it. Snow was bowling and a ball hit Engineer on the thigh pad and just went down to where short square-leg would have been, in front of the wicket. We were chasing runs at that stage and we were taking quick singles to keep the scoreboard moving. As soon as I dashed off to take that single as the non-striker, I suddenly found Snow coming in my path. As I swerved away, I found Snow following around with me and the next thing I realised was that a hefty shoulder was dug into me and I went sprawling. I reached the crease with my hands and on my knees as the bat was knocked out of my hands. I was furious at this incident and turned round to see Snow standing there with my bat in his hands which he tossed it to me and he was off and away. The umpires had a word with him but it was a very annoying thing and it did upset me a great deal It took me a long while to recover.

Snow was asked to apologise for that incident by the chairman of the England selection committee, when play started after lunch. But he was also disciplined and not picked in the side for the second Test. Peter Lever took his chance, scored 81 and that meant Snow was not in the side for the third Test. But an injury to Lever ruled him out and Snow was recalled for the third Test at the Oval.

When our turn came to bat, Snow's first ball, as expected, was a bouncer to me and he gave me a stare as if to say that because of you I have been suspended for one Test. In any case, that ball was a waste but later he produced a beauty that went through my defence, through my bat and pad to knock my middle stump. I still remember how quickly it nipped back and ripped in through the gate. Snow really bowled well but was not very successful and it is now history how India went on to register their first Test victory in England at the Oval

Snow got me out in the second innings when I offered no stroke, the ball coming outside the leg-stump and I was surprised that I was given out leg before. Be that as it may, the experience of watching John Snow was tremendous because here was a great fast bowler. His run-up was short, not long as you see today in case of most fast bowlers. It was rhythmic, smooth and his final delivery stride, though not really sideways on, ended with a lovely action and he had the whipping method of delivering the ball. He predominantly bowled inswingers or made the ball cut in off the wicket. He could also bowl outswingers but they were not as lethal as his inswingers.

For a fast bowler, he had the usual good bouncer, but he did not have an effective yorker to follow the bouncer. But his bouncer was really very good and he made you play it all the time and did not waste it at all and the ball seemed to be coming at your throat which meant that you had to throw the bat up to protect yourself and then if you were unlucky you would lob up a catch.

It was this bouncer that got him into trouble in Australia because he bowled one to Terry Jenner which did not come up and Jenner turned his back and received a sickening blow on the back of his head. Jenner had to retire hurt. At this stage, the umpires cautioned him for bowling too many bouncers. Snow and an agitated Illingworth argued with the umpires about the ball being called a bouncer In their opinion the ball wasn't a bouncer. As if to prove his point, Snow bowled a bouncer the next ball and turned round to the umpire and said, "that was a bouncer and not the previous one" The umpires warned him promptly and told him that if he did that again, he would be taken off the attack. Fortunately, Snow kept his cool thereafter because of his importance to the England attack and went on with his judicious mixture of bouncers to win the match for England.

In the last Test, just before he broke his finger, he was fielding at the fence and a drunken spectator came up to him and caught hold of his shirt. Snow did not do anything to retaliate. But that was enough for Ray Illingworth to take his side off the field because he thought the safety of his team was in danger. It was then at this very spot when play resumed later that Snow broke his finger while going for a catch off Stackpole and crashing into the wooden fence, dislocating his little finger of the right hand — his bowling hand. He was out of action in that vital innings when the Aussies required 180-odd runs to win and Ray Illingworth and Basil D'Oliveira spun England to a victory.

Snow played in 1972 when the Australians were around and again in 1973, though he was surprisingly not picked to tour with the team to the West Indies in 1973-74. I am sure the England team must have missed him because on the previous tour there in 1968, Snow was very successful as he got quite a few wickets in that series. In fact, in that series, he became the only bowler in the world to get Gary Sobers out twice off the first ball he had bowled to him. He got him out in 1968 and again in 1970 series when he bowled him with a shooter.

We met again in 1975 when the World Cup was staged in England for the first time. Snow was brought back in the England team though he was not included when we were there in 1974. He was going back to his bowling mark when we played England in the World Cup and he turned around and told me "Don't try those singles", remembering the 1971 incident that had taken place at the same venue, four years earlier.

Snowy has always been, apart from that incident, a good friend, off the field. Like all fast bowlers he had got that streak in him when he is bowling to opening batsmen. Even after that 1971 incident, we sat together and had long discussion on South Africa. I remember, myself, Solkar and Illingworth sitting together and it was only when Col Adhikari, our manager, insisted that we got to bed that we decided to part. Not very often does one come across people with Illingworth's experience as a cricketer and at that stage of our career, Solkar and myself were newcomers to cricket and whatever Illingworth was discussing we were swallowing. Snowy was also involved in the discussion and one could see that there was a great deal of affinity between the two.

Cricket lovers in India wanted to see Snow in the England side that toured India in 1976 when Tony Greig captained the side. But Snow was not picked. He had gone more or less off the Test scene, though he made sporadic Test appearances for England.

Later we kept on meeting often and in 1979 when the Indian team was in England, I bumped into Snow. He talked a great deal about Sandeep Patil who had played for his club Edmonton and he thought Sandeep had good prospects. His words have come good. Patil has established himself. At that stage Patil had not played in Tests and John Snow helped him a great deal in playing the moving ball.

Snowy has now set up a travel agency and he hopes that when the new business is settled and it is on sound footing, he will avail himself of a free ticket and come to India, the country he had not visited as a player. Maybe, as a former player he can come on a holiday and perhaps play a couple of matches and show the cricket lovers of India what John Snow the cricketer is.

20

Kapil Dev

In 1978 Raj Singh Dungarpur called me over to discuss the team to go to East Africa. While discussing that team, I remembered an over bowled to me earlier in the season in the Wills Trophy. A young lad called Kapil Dev had not only shown enormous potential but also shown a willingness to learn. I remember telling him in that match he should come closer to the stumps because his outswinger then would be more effective. Mind you, all that happened when we were playing against each other in the same match.

A couple of players from his team rushed to him thinking that I was using a bit of gamesmanship to try and make him bowl the wrong line. But that was farthest from my mind because after a long, long time, there was a bowler in Indian cricket who was promising and fast in the competition and it is always good fun to play against good bowlers, rather than try your ability against lesser fast bowlers. Kapil was a quick learner and in the next over, one could see him making an effort to come closer to the stumps and bowl and as soon as he got that right, it was apparent that he was going to be a force in cricket.

He bowled extremely well in that match in Madras and, with his bowling, set us back a great deal and helped his side to win. His side was strong anyway and could have won in normal circumstances but that was a particularly memorable spell and gave him a lot of prominence and brought him under national focus. This match was at the back of my mind when we sat to pick the team to go to East Africa. This was going to be a friendly tour and the team comprised experienced Test players and those who were highly promising. We had included Pataudi, Vishwanath, Yajuvinder Singh and Eknath Solkar among Test stalwarts and among the youngsters were Kapil Dev and Suru Nayak. The two were picked to get some experience of foreign conditions which could have helped them considerably. Playing abroad against opposition which is different, under different conditions with different bowlers and different players comes in handy at all times and goes a long way in making one a better cricketer.

Kapil did well on this trip. He was not only the bowler who got us vital breakthroughs, but he also batted magnificently, hitting many a towering six and won the hearts of East African cricket followers. One noticed on this trip how Kapil improved match after match and towards the end of the tour in a three-day game against the strongest East African side, he was well nigh unplayable. After the team returned to India, Kapil was selected to play for the Rest of India in the Irani Trophy match at Bangalore. It was a trial game before the team to tour Pakistan was selected. Kapil scored a hurricane 61 and bowled most impressively and thus found a berth for himself in the side to go to Pakistan. Even at that stage, it was thought that he would not really find a place for himself in the Test side. It was thought that the tour would give him a lot of experience and so when the West Indies team came to India later that season, Kapil could be useful then.

However, his performances in Pakistan in the beginning were such that he could not be ignored and he was picked in the first Test at Faisalabad. It was a good strip which afforded a fair amount of bounce to the new ball bowlers and in the first few overs Kapil forced Sadiq to discard his green Pakistan cap for a helmet. As it turned out, it was a wise move and, in the next over, a bouncer from Kapil hit Sadiq flush on the helmet and went away for four byes. With that one delivery Kapil had proved that he could not be taken lightly in Test cricket and India, after a long, long time, had not only a bowler who could use the new ball, but also bowl with fire.

Thereafter, there was no stopping Kapil. He scored 59 as a nightwatchman and thus earned a tag of an all-rounder. He confirmed being an all-rounder later in the season when he scored a century against the West Indians. The only time the tag of an all-rounder did not befit him was on the 1979 tour of England when this dynamic cricketer failed with the bat. He bowled with his customary fire and efficiency in the Test matches and also in other matches but somehow failed to get the runs. He used to be out in his eagerness to hit the ball in the air, rather than take his time and play his shots. This, of course, was solely due to inexperience and which was amply proved on the 1982 tour of England, when he almost scored 300 runs in three Test matches.

After that 1978 tour, it has been a case of a rising career graph. He is now reckoned to be one of the top all-rounders in the world, if not the topmost all-rounder today Today people talk about Imran Khan, Ian Botham, Kapil Dev and Richard Hadlee as the leading all-rounders in the world. It is indeed difficult to pick the best all-rounder among them all.

But one thing is sure that any captain would love to have all four of them in his side and win a match. Because all of them are attacking cricketers; all of them have turned in sterling performances; all of them have performed under pressure and have proved that all of them have the flamboyance and ability to take on any opponents at any given time. Picking the best player out of them is basically a subject of extensive exercise and there would always be people who would agree with you and also disagree with you on merits and demerits of the four.

In Kapil's case he has the disadvantage of not having a strike bowler along with him which means that the entire pressure of taking wickets is entirely on him. The opponents also know that since he is the only player capable of running through the side, and are extra careful while playing him and thus he does not always capture the kind of wickets that is expected of him. Also during Kapil's time, the Indian batting has not been consistent, with the result that he has hardly time to take off his bowling boots and put on his batting shoes before he is called upon to go in for the rescue act. This has undoubtedly put on a lot of pressure on Kapil and it has, at times, made him play some loose shots which have brought about his early dismissal.

But with greater experience and added responsibility after becoming the captain, such shots have become rarer and will definitely contribute to a consistent performance in future. And I am convinced in my mind that if Kapil had more experience, the 1979 Oval Test which we drew and did not win, falling short by nine runs, could easily have been won. Kapil went there, promoted in batting order, and the first delivery itself he tried to whack out of the ground and ended up being caught at long on.

Today, the same Kapil would have nudged a few runs in

singles and twos and got his legs moving, then had a good look at the bowling, and played his shots. He could have certainly taken India to that incredible victory. There is no place for ifs and buts in cricket and one can only live in a dream world if one tries to think what would have happened, if it was this way or that way.

His greatest triumph, however, has been India winning the Prudential World Cup, earlier in June this year, under his captaincy. Nobody could have dreamt that India, so often the underdogs in one-day cricket, could have ended up as winners. But Kapil led by example in the game against Zimbabwe when five wickets had gone for 17 runs to a mixture of good bowling and poor strokes. Kapil went out and played an innings that is truly unforgettable. His first 70 to 80 runs were really calculated in the sense that he pushed and nudged the ball and only hit those which he was convinced should be hit.

After that, he had enough confidence and when he saw that he had partners who would stay with him, he launched a counter-attack the like of which one had never seen before. It was absolutely unbelievable stuff. He was hitting the bowlers as if at will and we were applauding each and every shot. Our hands become weary but each shot was absolutely thrilling. When he was around 160, we all had our hearts in our mouths. We knew that the record score of 171 was so near and perhaps Kapil was not aware of it, and in his anxiety to get as many runs as possible, he would perhaps play an ambitious shot and get out.

It was obvious at this stage that he was a tired man and may hit a tired looking shot and get out. But fortunately, he didn't do that and went on to make 175 not out which is a record in the Prudential World Cup. Then he came on to bowl four overs of tight medium-pace bowling and did not give Zimbabwe players any respite at all.

That was the turning point of the tournament and thereafter, the Indian team really went from strength to strength and took in their stride, Australia, England and the West Indies. With this win, Kapil has become a household name in India, which, of course, he was, but he became a household name all over the world where cricket is played. His grinning face holding the Prudential Trophy with sheer joy stamped on it has become as memorable as the win itself.

His brothers have started a hotel and named it after Kapil. 'Hotel Kapil' is a tribute to him from his brothers for all the glory he has brought to India and the family name has been placed on the top of the cricketing world. His success has given encouragement and impetus to thousands of youngsters all over the country and not only in metropolitan cities. This will act as a spur to many youngsters to give off their best in international cricket.

Kapil's advent to international cricket is the best thing that could have happened to Indian cricket because we had spinners who earned a name for themselves and the country but there never was a fast bowler to lift the country's prestige so high in the past. With Kapil's example before them, boys in the street are walking to their marks purposefully, coming in from a distance and hurling the ball quickly at the opposing batsman. Today's cricket is jet age cricket where speed is more important than subtleties of spin and speed, and speed follows the batsman wherever he goes and with the likes of Kapil Dev to inspire the youngsters, more and more of the younger lots will take to fast bowling and it will be for the good of Indian cricket. And even if all of them cannot make the Test grade, at least they will be able to provide adequate practice to our batsmen so that they are not found wanting when facing the fast bowlers of other countries.

Kapil's brand of cricket is also the attacking brand of cricket which makes him a crowd pleaser everywhere he goes. It will certainly go a long way in seeing that the cricket India plays is the kind of cricket which will bring in the crowds. No longer Indian cricket and Indian cricketers will be called 'dull dogs' as was the case in the early fifties and people will believe that the Indian cricket team plays attractive type of cricket.

It has been a rapid rise for a lad who batted at No. 11 in East Africa to come to the fore as one of the leading all-rounders in the world. Kapil, to this date, remains the same simple guy that he was in 1978, with, of course, a lot more confidence with the way he deals with people, than he had in 1978. This confidence came as he gained more successes in international cricket. But along with this confidence, and along with these successes, his attitude towards people has not changed. He is still polite, and courteous to the senior cricketers and is prepared to listen to everyone. These characteristics are difficult to find in recent years and Kapil is richly endowed with these along with his many-splendoured cricketing abilities, cricketing talents that God Almighty has showered on him. He is still 24 and has years and years of Test cricket ahead of him and, I am confident, that these years will be the years when Indian cricket will keep rising and will reach its zenith and standards unheard of before.

21

Mohinder Amarnath

When I started writing this book, sometime last year, Mohinder Amarnath did not figure in the list of "The Idols" I have seen. Until then he had always been a very fine player who had not somehow produced a performance up to his potential at Test level. The transition from a very fine player into a great player came only last season when, with the consistency which is the hallmark of great players, he started producing 100s and big scores in all the matches that he played.

The dividing line between the great players and good players is that the great players score runs when the team really needs them, while the good players score runs when everybody else is also scoring runs. Mohinder Amarnath's performance in the last season was outstanding. His batting displays in the West Indies ought to have been preserved on films because he showed that the West Indies bowling could be attacked and attacked successfully and consistently. Apart from that his ability to judge which balls to leave alone clearly separated him from other players in the team. No wonder, therefore, that he got 300 runs more than the next best batsman in that series for India.

One first heard of Mohinder Amarnath in 1965 when the Cooch-Behar Trophy matches were in progress in Bombay. The newspapers in those days used to cover the university and Cooch-Behar Schools Tournament in greater detail and gave them plenty of prominence. Amarnath bowling with a short run-up attracted attention because of his similarity of bowling action, though not the delivery stride, with his illustrious father, Lala Amarnath. Scribes, who have also seen his father in action, went on to describe how Mohinder resembled his father in his run-up and also his ability to make the ball swing late both ways. It was thus as a bowler that Mohinder first came to the notice of the cricketing world.

His elder brother Surinder was a batsman and though Mohinder was also a useful batsman at that stage, nobody paid much attention to his batting ability. During the visit of the London schoolboys later that year, both Mohinder and Surinder were in the Indian schoolboys team. Although they didn't have outstanding successes their ability was never in doubt and it was only a matter of time that they would follow in their father's footsteps and become Test players. Both are quiet and it was very difficult to get from either of them anything. However, if a leg-pulling session is on, both join in to pull someone's leg or also get their leg pulled. But as it has happened, at schools level, when sons of former Test players are involved, no one fools around with them too much for the simple reason that schoolboys being schoolboys and being anxious about their future, they do not want to jeopardise their chances. The father may get annoyed with them and so the Amarnaths were left with themselves.

Both of them immediately played for the Punjab in the Ranji Trophy and as one who had played with them in the schools tournament, and who was not even in the reckoning for the Ranji Trophy Cup, I used to follow their progress in the tournament with great interest.

The All India schools side that year was a very strong

side with Eknath Solkar as captain, Ashok Gandotra, another talented player, who went out of firstclass cricket too soon to concentrate on his career, Ramesh Nagdev, who, but for his migration to the USA, would have made the higher grade, and the world would probably not have heard about Sunil Gavaskar; the Amarnaths, Milind Rege, Arun Kumar, Asif, Ajit Naik and Dhiraj Parsana. All these cricketers were a lot of fun. This side was full of cricketers of promise and most of them went on to play for India or their State with distinction.

Mohinder was soon making progress, mainly as a bowler, and though his pace was of a friendly variety he was a shrewd mover of the ball, keeping the ball just outside the off-stump and getting the wickets as the batsmen played rash strokes, underestimating his ability. It was, therefore, not much of a surprise to find his name in the Test 12 at Madras when the Australians came here in 1969. He stood up courageously to the Australian fast bowlers and made his name by clean-bowling Stackpole and Ian Chappell. That, however, was the last Test of the series and there was no way Mohinder could find a place in the team next year when the Indian team went to the West Indies because Tiger Pataudi was no longer the captain and he was instrumental in picking Mohinder for the Madras Test.

After that successful tour of the West Indies, the Indian team was to go to England and for the last place in the team Mohinder and Kirmani were selected, but only one was to go depending upon whether Engineer was available for the tour matches other than Tests. Subsequently, Engineer's county, Lancahsire C.C., decided that he could not be released for other matches and so Kirmani had to go as second wicketkeeper and Mohinder was out of the team. There was this unusual inclusion of three wicketkeepers in the side. At this stage, Mohinder developed the phlegmatic attitude that has remained with him all these years. Disappointed for missing the tour, he kept quiet and he never tried to make an issue out of it. He went on training and practising in his own way trying to prove the selectors wrong.

It was not until 1976 that Mohinder came back into the Indian team for the tour of New Zealand and Australia. On that tour he impressed everyone with his ability to take a few knocks on the body. He was not at all worried by the pace or spin. In fact, in the first Test against New Zealand, which India won, we were indebted to Madan Lal and Mohinder for their invaluable partnership which gave us a big lead and thus enabled 'Pras' to strike his form and bowl us to victory. In the second Test at Christchurch in the cold and windy conditions, he and Madan Lal kept on bowling for hours and captured five wickets each. In the last Test at Wellington when New Zealand routed India, Mohinder stood bravely against the battery of their fast bowlers with a courageous display of batting.

With his elder brother Surinder showing indifferent form, Mohinder was promoted to No. 3 in the series against the West Indies and he rose to the occasion manfully. In one of the Tests, I was at the non-striker's end and I remember a ball from Holding, who was twice as quick in 1976 than he is today, rose awkwardly and Mohinder was caught unawares but he was unperturbed and he shouldered arms and took it on his chest and did not even try to rub the part where the ball had hit him. When I walked down the track to ask him if he was alright, he said, with a shy smile on his face, that it was okay. He obviously must have been in pain. That must have been his way of saying that it was indeed a painful blow. Then in the last Test he was the only player to offer some resistance, scoring a fine 58, with three sixes when Holding was at his ferocious best.

At the end of the series I was convinced that Mohinder, if he showed the same kind of application and a little more discretion in the choice of balls he picked up to hook and score runs off, would not only be more consistent but would also become a great player. But, unfortunately, that wasn't the case because immediately thereafter, in that winter, New Zealand and England toured India. He did not score as many runs as were expected of him. That was the series when Tony Greig used his famous tactics and thus a lot of established players found themselves out of the Indian side. Mohinder was no exception. He found himself out of the side, for Madan Lal then was the only genuine new ball bowler in the side and with Chandra, Prasanna and Bedi in the side, the Indian team could not afford the luxury of another seam bowler. The spinners used to come on the scene within a couple of overs as the ball started turning almost from the word go. The exercise of opening the bowling from the other end used to be entrusted to a batsman who had to turn his arm over for an over or two at the most.

However, Mohinder was the first to be selected when the side to tour Australia was announced for the tour in 1977-78. Here too his liking for pace bowling was evident for he handled Jeff Thomson at his best and fastest. His hooking was thrilling to watch and his running between wickets was a greater joy for me. We batted together on many occasions and he responded to my calls for singles. I am a great believer in taking singles because not only it keeps the scoreboard moving but it keeps the strike rotating also and as a result no bowler gets to bowl too many balls continuously at you.

Mohinder's courage was again to the fore in the second Test. He was batting with 80-odd runs when a ball from Sam Gannon smashed into his right temple as he went to hook it just before lunch. Mohinder was carried off the field and a big lump was formed just above the eyebrow. It was hideous, black and blue and really looked bad but Mohinder just got it attended to during the 40-minute lunch interval. And contrary to all advice he went on to bat again, scored 90, before falling to another short ball. However, the century he missed came in the next innings when he played all bowlers with ease. At the end of the series he had established himself as No. 3 batsman for India. But cricket can be a very funny game and also a cruel one.

When the Indian team went to Pakistan in 1978, Mohinder, in spite of these excellent performances, found himself down the batting order with brother Surinder taking his No. 3 spot. Mohinder batted lower down in the first two Tests. It was in the Lahore Test that Mohinder took another painful blow when he turned his eyes away from a short ball from Imran and was hit a sickening blow on the back of his head and fell down unconscious. We all feared his well-being. His wife—they had married only six months ago—was most upset at that. However, 'Jimmy' came out of that crisis without any scars and was subjected to a bumper barrage as soon as he came out to bat. He fell to one such bumper while trying to hook and fell on his wicket. Soon a whispering campaign was started that he would always get out to short-pitched balls.

Surinder Amarnath was indisposed during the second innings of the last Test and Mohinder was promoted to No. 3. With Chetan Chauhan falling early and the new ball still fresh, it was expected that the Pakistani bowlers would see that no ball is pitched in his half of the wicket in view of what had happened previously in the series. Sarfraz and Imran banged more deliveries at him which were short-pitched and thought that Mohinder would back away and get out. But instead, Sarfraz and Imran saw the courageous side of Mohinder who hooked and timed his strokes perfectly. However, his innings of 58 was the only knock of note in that series and there was intense pressure on him to keep his place in the side. Therefore, when he failed in the first innings of the Bombay Test against the West Indies which followed on the heels of the Karachi Test, Mohinder had to go. Anshuman Gaekwad was picked to bat in his place. Chetan Chauhan and I opened the innings. But when Chetan was injured, Gaekwad opened and Dilip Vengsarkar was promoted from No. 5 to No. 3 position. There was a thrilling partnership between Gaekwad and Vengsarkar and the latter thus clinched the No. 3 position for some time to come.

But players of the class of Mohinder cannot be kept away for long and he came back in the last Test at Kanpur where everyone scored as India amassed 644 and Mohinder scored his second Test hundred and made sure of his place in the team to England in 1979. It was here in England that he again got hit on the head and sustained a hairline crack which meant that now there was a big question mark against his ability to play the short ball. People forgot that he would hit most of them and it would be the odd ball which caused injuries. But since injuries had come fairly frequently, it was, therefore, a tough decision for the selection committee to make. Mohinder produced a fitness certificate and because of his known ability, the selection committee was forced to include him for the last Test at Bombay against the Australians in 1979. It was anticipated then that he would be bounced at and that's what happened. Rondey Hogg bounced one and Mohinder in an attempt to play that ball slipped and fell on the wicket. He was batting in the old sola hat which the players used to wear in 1930s and 1940s and this came in for much ridicule.

The sola hat is tough but not quite a helmet. Mohinder, who is a professional cricketer in his attitude, did not wear a helmet for so long apparently because his father would not allow his sons to wear one. With this dismissal, which was unfortunate, Mohinder missed out and was not selected against the Pakistan team which came to India. It was in this series that Sandeep Patil made his mark and with Yashpal Sharma showing dogged qualities, the Indian middle-order looked settled with Vengsarkar at No. 3, Vishwanath at No. 4, Patil at No. 5 and Yashpal at No. 6 and with Kapil and Kirmani to follow. It was, therefore, a tough job for 'Jimmy' to break into the side unless some of these players failed consistently.

Mohinder seemed resigned to his fate and knowing fully well that he had no chance to stage a comeback then accepted a contract to play in Western Australia in the 1980-81 season. He went to Australia even before the Irani

Trophy match, which is considered to be a selection trial and, in fact, the team to tour Australia was to be selected on the basis of performances in this match. He did not take his chance and play in this match otherwise he would have been considered for selection.

In the 1981-82 season, Indian cricket saw another young player come up in Ashok Malhotra. And Ashok Malhotra was in addition to the players mentioned earlier who have been consistent in our middle-order batting. And it was only when Sandeep Patil failed in four consecutive Tests, Malhotra took his place and did a good job during the first Test innings he played. And he was considered to be a promising cricketer. Consequently, it was difficult for Mohinder to stage a comeback for two consecutive seasons. However, his name did come up for selection when the team was being picked to go to England in 1982, mainly because of his phenomenal innings of 170-plus in that incredible final of the Ranji Trophy when Delhi scored over 700 runs to beat Karnataka who had already totalled 700.

The selection committee, however, decided to bring back Patil. Mohinder was also considered mainly as a batsman and with Patil, Malhotra, Vishwanath, Yashpal and Vengsarkar in the side, forming a solid middle-order batting, Mohinder lost out to these players. It was a pity that people made a big noise about his omission. They forgot that Mohinder was now coming into consideration only as a batsman and he had to miss out because of superior performances of the others.

Undaunted, Mohinder came back at the beginning of the 1982-83 season, scoring a hundred and a double hundred. He was selected to go to Pakistan and the axe now fell on Malhotra. What happened afterwards is now history and you all know what a magnificent comeback he has made in Test cricket. People say that the use of helmet has changed his fortunes and helped him. They also believe that his two-eyed stance has also helped him. I would not like to argue with them. All I would like to say is that Mohinder had the courage, ability and the vital element in cricket that every successful cricketer needs and that is luck. It was with him. He grabbed this opportunity with both hands and not only consolidated his position in the Indian side but has become, in my opinion, for whatever it's worth, the best batsman in the world. Nobody plays fast bowling better than him. Nobody plays fast bowling with such an assurance than him and this is more praiseworthy because the Indians do not get fast bowling to play in their own country.

Off the field, Mohinder, called 'Jimmy', is always smiling and likes to joke of others and at his expense too. He is basically the quiet type and does not venture to express his opinion, unless he is asked. He never meddles in other people's affairs and in recent instances has shown that if there is a controversy, he can take care of it by dismissing it off in a very mature manner. He has done himself justice even though he is only 33. He is a fitness fanatic and a very dedicated cricketer. There are yet plenty of years ahead of Mohinder and with two series in India this winter, Mohinder, I am sure, will utilise these Tests to consolidate his position.

The best years of Mohinder, which are ahead of him, will be savoured by Indian cricket followers, because India is playing mainly at home and thus it will be the Indian cricket followers who will have the opportunity to see Mohinder at his very best.

22

Padmakar Shivalkar

One of my favourite cricketers has been Padmakar Shivalkar. 'Paddy', as he is affectionately called by fellow cricketers and cricket lovers, has played cricket with nothing but complete enjoyment. And perhaps the only sad thing is that he has not been picked to play for India in an official Test. I always admire this man's uncomplicated approach to life just as his approach to the wicket was so simple and rhythmic.

It is an irony of fate that players like Shivalkar and Goel were born at the same time as Bishan Bedi was. And so were deprived of playing for India in Tests. Any other country would have gladly picked them up and included them in the side for Tests.

Paddy's ill-luck was that when he came on the scene, Bapu Nadkarni was already an established left-arm spinner for Bombay. And Nadkarni used to get plenty of wickets in addition to a number of centuries which 'Bapuji' used to get with monotonous regularity in local as well as Ranji Trophy cricket. And when Bapu Nadkarni was about to bow out, in came Eknath Solkar and with his extraordinary fielding and ability to bowl, a bit of seamers as well, blocked Shivalkar's entry to big cricket for some more time. And so Shivalkar had to wait for a very long time before he got picked for Bombay

He had gone to Australia with the Cricket Club of India team in 1962 and impressed everybody not only with his figures but also with a bagful of wickets. On those hard Australian wickets, he bowled brilliantly, teasing the batsmen with his flight and forcing them to play shots which normally they would not have played.

So it was finally in the 1967-68 season that Shivalkar was selected to play for Bombay in the Ranji Trophy Championship matches. I was then in the reserves for the Bombay team and I can recall the excitement with which he came on the eve of the match to our room and talked about how he just needed a little luck now that he had his break so that he could become a permanent fixture in the Bombay team. It took him a couple of seasons to do this but since then he hardly looked back and only in the last couple of seasons has the selection committee decided to do away with his services and bring in some young aspirants.

Padmakar Shivalkar's has been a real, tremendous success story. He started off like everybody else in those days at Shivaji Park Gymkhana and in early sixties this Gymkhana produced cricketers of highest quality, much the same way as Dadar Union used to do in sixties and seventies.

Shivalkar started his career there and attracted attention of the cricket followers in the city. Cricket followers in Bombay are most discerning and because a lot of cricket is played in Bombay, it becomes easy for them to spot talent. Then the name Shivalkar started buzzing around the Bombay club circuit, and he soon became the highest wicket-taker in a Ranji Trophy season. Like all bowlers, he was very proud of his batting ability and he saved Bombay on a couple of occasions by staying there stubbornly till the regular batsman had got the winning run. In those days only one team used to qualify for the knock-out rounds from West Zone and the matches used to be very close in the league stage and on a number of occasions, Shivalkar has come to the rescue of Bombay with his batting ability. There used to be, invariably, a mix-up when he and Abdul Ismail were batting and there were occasions when both batsmen were at the same end and one was run out. These mix-ups were a great source of all-round hilarity in the dressing rooms and we all used to enjoy it to the full.

In the dressing room, Paddy used to be, to start with, very very quiet. But then as he became an established member of the Bombay team, he opened out, and showed that he too had a dry noughty sense of humour. In fact, he was the player who was very helpful in the thick of tension. His remarks would help break tension all around. You need players of this character in moments like this.

Paddy was very good as a thinker on the field. He would spot the batsman's weaknesses right away and start attacking him accordingly On a turner, he was absolutely unplayable and even now, when he is in his forties, it is impossible to score runs off him on a turning track. Today, the old nip, of course, is not there as before but it is very difficult to take any liberties off him. This goes on to show how bowling has become such a mechanical exercise for him. This perhaps gives one the impression that his heart is not in his bowling but so much has been his body used to running up and bowling that the dainty three-step run-up that even if you want to, cannot score too many runs.

When we were on tours with the Bombay team, Paddy would always buy a memento for his family members which showed how dedicated he was to his family On tours we would try and guess as to what Paddy would buy for his family as a memento.

Today he is a very accomplished singer. A few years ago, he approached me to cut a disc with him and I was very happy to do that and he sung his version of the disc in a very professional and lilting manner and a particular song composed by Shantaram Nandgaonkar is about how one misses an opportunity if the luck is not on one's side. Paddy put his heart and soul in rendering that song. It was almost the story of his cricket career, how he came so close to getting an India cap but could not do so. The lyrics of that song were very touching, so also the rendering of the song by Paddy. Now he sings at a lot of programmes and shows and is very popular because he sings without any fuss and he has good control over his voice.

Shivalkar's behaviour on stage has been impeccable, just as his behaviour on and off the cricket field. He has carved out a niche for himself as a popular singer. He is totally engrossed with his singing and spends a lot of time practising the same. When he is running in to bowl, one gets the impression that he is humming a tune under his breath. Most certainly, he does that while fielding on the boundary fence and it goes to show that he is practising for the evening's function or show.

A simple man, a modest man, he likes to wear sports clothes, sports shirts particularly when he is not playing cricket. He has always given off his best for his team, and this too knowing fully well that he is not going to get an India cap — he gave nothing but the best. It speaks volumes for the man's contribution to the game. He was the one who always wore a smile. Keep on smiling, Paddy There are very, very few cricketers like you in the world Your contribution to the game has been just as immense as all the top Test players.

23

Rajinder Goel

There are two cricketers who were desperately unlucky not to have played for India. They are Rajinder Goel and Padmakar Shivalkar, both left-arm spinners of the highest order. But because of the presence of Bishan Singh Bedi, these two have not been able to play in Tests. Before Bishan came on the scene, they had to contend with Bapu Nadkarni and Rusi Surti who were more of all-rounders than specialist bowlers and, of course, that genius of all-rounders, Salim Durrani. So they could not come into the India side.

Once Bishan came on the scene, he was certainly miles ahead of them as far as bowling was concerned because of his variation and, therefore, Bishan could not be displaced at all. But still given the choice of facing Bedi and Goel at their peak, I would prefer to play Bishan because with his flight, Bishan gave you a bit of a chance of coming down the track and converting those deliveries into drivable balls, while Goel, with a flatter trajectory, was almost impossible to hit.

Not that he could not flight the ball, the flighting was minimal and because he could obtain turn on any track, the flighting was just not necessary.

Rajinder Goel has got over 500 wickets in the Ranji Trophy, not to mention the wickets he has captured in the Duleep and Irani Trophy matches. This is a record in the Ranji Trophy and looks as if it will stay for some more time. There are not too many people with 400-plus wickets in the Ranji Trophy playing today and the only person in this category is Venkataraghavan and he will also take some time before he can catch up with Rajinder Goel. Meanwhile, Goel plans to play for another year and thereby complete over 25 years playing in the Ranji Trophy which will be another record for him.

I do not know if any other player has played for 25 years in the Ranji Trophy though there are some careers which have been going on for quite some time. Notable among them being Ashok Mankad's which started in 1962 and he is still there on the scene after 20 years, though he missed out one season because of differences with the Bombay Cricket Association selection committee. His stamina is unbelievable for a man who is over 40 and once given the ball he can bowl right till the end of the day's play without seeming to ose any of the nip that he possesses. Of course, the turn today is not as sharp as it used to be a few years ago, nor is the nip of the faster one, of which he claimed many of his victims, bowled or leg before, as quick as it used to be some years ago. The accuracy is still there and the willingness to bowl long spells is also still there.

The advent of Kapil Dev on the Haryana scene certainly has taken off the load off Goel's shoulders and now he does not have to work as hard as he used to before. He is a simple man and a totally unassuming person and a person who is an ideal to follow because of his behaviour on and off the field.

He is an absolute professional, who takes pride in his craft and who for ever is trying to think the batsman out. His batting is strictly No 11 stuff though he has got a few runs by throwing his bat about, the best shot of his being the sweep shot which he plays even against the quicker bowlers. But it is really a pity that somebody like him could never get a chance to represent the country and one fails to understand why, when we picked two right hand off spinners in the side, he was not picked. In partnership with Bedi he could have worked wonders where victories were missed by just a few wickets, or by a few runs.

When he was unexpectedly picked for the Test side in 1974, because Bishan was disciplined, he was a surprised man and he had to buy a new pair of boots, a new bat and the entire kit to make it to the Test. It is a pity then that he was dropped and two off spinners were picked but then against the mighty West Indians, there was no place for anybody to make a Test debut. I have a feeling that the selection committee was not prepared to play him because if he had taken a few wickets, Bishan's return to the team would have been delayed for some more time and it would have been quite embarrassing for the selectors concerned.

He had been on the fringe of Test cricket for a long time and played in the unofficial Test against Sri Lanka and did very well but he was considered not good enough to be picked even on a tour with the Indian team which would have meant that he would have at least worn Indian colours, although he would not have technically won India cap because he had not played in a Test match. But the man has still gone on playing Ranji Trophy cricket, knowing fully well that he had no hopes of playing for India and done it with great pride, with great honour, and done his job faithfully as he knows how to do. I wish there are more cricketers like Rajinder Goel in this country. I wish there are younger cricketers who follow the example of Goel and keep on serving their state associations for a longer time even if somehow due to fate, they cannot play for their country

When we played North Zone in the Duleep Trophy, it was him whom we were afraid of than Bishan Bedi because he was the one who pegged us down, it was he who would take the wickets on a turning track and it was he who was the most likely to run through the side and he has done that on a few occasions and caused enough problems, chipping in to take a lot of wickets, just the vital wickets, and then waiting being withdrawn from the attack till he was called again and then again delivered the goods.

He is the one bowler whom I have really dreaded facing in my life because I have never been able to feel comfortable against his left-hand spinners and Goel has been the one who, because of his flatter trajectory, has not given the opportunity to step down the track and drive. Our bowlers, who bowl with a flatter trajectory, often commit the mistake of either bowling short or overpitched and so can be driven, cut and pulled, but Goel did that very, very seldom in his career and that too perhaps when he had started bowling his 25th or 26th over. All the overs before that were deadly accurate. We were lucky to scratch a single or two off those and lucky if we survived.

He was an ordinary fielder. He took most of the catches that came his way and even now he throws without any trouble. His throw is perhaps not as powerful as it used to be, but it is as accurate as his bowling has been and that is very important.

He is a simple man, modest, almost self-effacing about his tremendous achievements in the Ranji Trophy. He is a person who is a pleasure to talk to and an ideal for the younger cricketers to follow. Although he is not a Test cricketer, to me he is one of the greatest I have played with and it's been a privilege playing against him.

24

Richard Hadlee

No other cricketer has stirred the imagination of the sports loving public of New Zealand more than Richard Hadlee has done in recent years. New Zealand has produced its great players over the years, and Bert Sutcliffe, John Reid, Glenn Turner are names that come easily to one's mind. But Richard Hadlee towers above them all.

In sheer performance, charisma and crowd-pulling ability there's no one who has done as much for New Zealand as Richard Hadlee has done. I remember my former office colleague and friend, Tony Fernandes, who had gone to Tasmania to play a season of club cricket, came back and was raving about Richard Hadlee. At that stage the New Zealand team had gone to Australia to play a three-Test series. The year was 1973 and Richard Hadlee, though not very successful, impressed Tony Fernandes who came back and said: "Here is a bowler of whom much will be heard."

Tony hasn't been proved wrong and Richard Hadlee has simply improved with time and now after almost ten years in

Test cricket, Richard can claim to be one of the finest new ball bowlers that have played a Test match.

Unfortunately, Richard's batting ability has not been given the kind of importance that one would have liked and because perhaps of his inconsistency with the bat he's not being talked about as an all-rounder in the same breath as Ian Botham, Kapil Dev and Imran Khan.

He's got a beautiful run-up, he generates genuine pace and has one of the best outswingers in the business. Having played county cricket he has added the inswinger to his repertoire and he is certainly a most difficult and awkward customer on a green and lively wicket.

His run-up starts off in somewhat an old fashion because his body seems to move forward and he leans forward and then instead of taking off his right foot comes back as though he's going in the reverse and then suddenly he starts off again with that run up of his accelerating into a beautiful action and a fine side on delivery, as classical as one would hope to see.

He is an intensely competitive player as the Australians have found out and no wonder the Australians who are very competitive players themselves liked to do battle with someone like Richard Hadlee. The Australian crowds also find him a customer that they cannot ignore, for blokes like Tony Greig, Richard Hadlee who are great competitors are people who cannot be ignored. Either you love them or you hate them. There's no in between as far as these cricketers are concerned.

Richard Hadlee was almost a one-man unit for the New Zealand team for the last few years, until Geoff Howarth came on to the scene and established himself with his quiet firmness, dignity and took over the New Zealand captaincy With Geoff doing such a good job of leading New Zealand

Richard found the pressure on him taken off to a great extent and one found Richard's performances improving by leaps and bounds. Till then because Richard was the only world class player in the New Zealand side the pressure was so much on him that one got the impression that he tried too hard. Because he is such an outstanding great fast bowler although he got wickets, when it came to batting he wasn't able to contribute as much as New Zealand would have liked him to or he himself would have liked because the bowling had taken such a heavy toll of his energies.

But with Geoff Howarth coming on to the scene and scoring runs fluently for New Zealand this pressure seemed to have gone off and New Zealand seemed to have become a better side because with Geoff there to score his runs and Richard bowling his heart out and New Zealand fielding being top class as always, it became a side which, though not having too many outstanding or world class players, always fought for every run in the field. So even if the New Zealand team did not score too many runs, the fielding of its side gave the impression that there were much more runs at hand than the ones on the board. Because you had to really get through the cordon — people used to dive about, throw themselves at the ball and generally be very mingy about giving away runs on the field.

When the Indian side landed in New Zealand in 1976, Richard Colliage and D.L. Hadlee were the main bowlers for New Zealand. Richard Hadlee was in the New Zealand fourteen but not in the playing eleven. In the second Test at Christchurch he was picked to play in the side and though he did not get too many wickets he bowled at a good speed and gave enough trouble for the Indian batsmen to think about.

At this stage India was one up in the series and the last Test was to be played at Wellington. Normally a very windy place

— probably the most windy place in my cricket playing memory and where, with a green wicket the ball would certainly help the seamers. What was predicted before the match was that Richard Hadlee would be made the twelfth man. But the New Zealand selectors decided to pick him in the eleven and he became an instant hero by capturing four wickets in the first innings and by following it up with seven in the second innings to destroy India and level the series for New Zealand.

That was the beginning of Richard's exploits and thereafter, barring injury, he has been a permanent fixture in the New Zealand side.

The following year when the Australians were in New Zealand, Richard Hadlee captured the imagination of the crowd. First, he smote the great Dennis Lillee back over his head for a six. He played a very defiant innings that had the crowd on its feet. And when he went in to bowl the crowd started chanting "Hadlee, Hadlee" as they used to shout "Lillee, Lillee" when Lillee used to bowl in Melbourne. That was the first time that the New Zealand crowd got so involved in a cricket match and in backing their own particular player. The Australians and the New Zealanders, being neighbours, have always had an extra bit of competitiveness in their matches. The New Zealanders feel that they have not been treated in quite the manner that they should be by the Australians, and the Australians have always treated the New Zealanders as kid brothers and beginners in Test cricket. And therefore, they have not always sent the best possible side to New Zealand.

All that, of course, is changed now and the full Australian side goes to New Zealand to play in its games. Richard Hadlee was, perhaps, one of the persons responsible for bringing about this change because he showed with his performance that there was a backbone to the New Zealand side and the Australians could ill afford to send a second side to New Zealand anymore.

Since the time the Auckland crowd got up and gave him the kind of support he wanted, Richard Hadlee has become the darling of the New Zealand cricket-loving public. Ever since then, Richard, whenever he comes on to bowl, at all the possible N.Z. centres, evokes this chant of "Hadlee, Hadlee" and it is quite menacing for the batsman who is facing the ball. But perhaps not as menacing as the Calcutta crowds' chant of 'B-o-w-l-e-d" everytime Chandra used to come in to bowl. That was something else altogether and that perhaps will never be matched because of the sheer numbers of the Calcutta crowd.

Richard, after that performance, was one who was eagerly watched. In the series when the New Zealand team came down to India after the Indian team had been there earlier on in the year, he and Glenn Turner, who was captaining the side, were the two people who were most eagerly awaited. Both of them did not disappoint, because Glenn with his impeccable technique and Richard with his aggressive attitude ensured the attention of all the people who had come to watch the New Zealand series.

India won the series rather easily, winning 2-0, and it was mainly due to first class bowling by our spinners — Bishan, Chandra, Venkat and Prasanna — who really bowled well. Our batting also stood up to the test in impressive fashion and that made the task of the New Zealand cricketers a little more difficult.

Richard bowled excellently in the first Test as well as in the second Test though with not much luck. He had quite a few chances "grassed" and he used to beat the bat very often without getting the edge. At this stage of his career the inswinger was not a very prominent part of his bowling armoury and in fact he rarely bowled the inswinger, he just concentrated on the outswinger and the ball that went straight through.

He had, also, a surprisingly good bouncer which came up of a short length and invariably you had to play it. Either you played it in front of your face or you tried to hook it. Mohinder Amarnath got a fair share of Richard's bouncers and although he scored quite a few runs off them he was never able to hook it as well as he has hooked other bowlers.

In the third Test there was a bit of an ugly incident when Richard got upset with a decision when the umpire decided not to give Anshuman Gaekwad out hit wicket when all the New Zealand fielders thought that Anshuman had hit the wicket though Anshuman himself believes he did not touch the wicket at all. However, with the bail having fallen the New Zealanders were a very upset lot and there were ugly scenes around. Richard, for once, could not control himself and he flung the bail at the umpire, hitting him in the stomach and said a few things which made the air around a little blue.

But then that is competitiveness and at that stage the frustration of the New Zealand players was reaching boiling point, having gone through a rough and tough tour and this is one of the reasons why they could not 'stomach' a decision which did not go in their favour.

However, Richard was not to be on the field for a long time after that because the heat got to him and he suddenly collapsed while he was fielding on the deep fine leg fence. Madras, at most times, can be pretty hot, and stuffy, and Richard had just bowled a spell of two or three overs and suddenly found the heat too much and just collapsed and had to be carried off the field and did not take any further part for that day at all.

The New Zealanders lost that series fairly easily by the margin of 2-0. But the performances of Glenn Turner and

Richard Hadlee were memorable ones in that series. By the time the Indian side played Richard Hadlee again in '79 in the World Cup he had already become a famous name. He had played for Nottingham in the county championships with distinction and along with Clive Rice he had formed one of the most dangerous new ball attacks in county cricket.

The experience of having played county cricket added a lot more guile to his bowling. He now just did not come in and bowl as quickly as possible but he kept himself in reserve and only rarely did you come across him bowl a genuinely quick delivery. He concentrated more on using the new ball well, swinging it both ways, testing the batsman outside the off stump and also coming in with a surprise bouncer. These are the varieties he added to his bowling after he had played county cricket.

In '79 he bowled very well in the World Cup match at Headingley. The wicket was just ideal for him, just slightly green, and with enough bounce in it for him to exploit it. He never gave us much of a chance and although we mustered up a fair total he saw to it that we did not pose an imposing total.

Later on, just before we played the last match at the Oval, the penultimate match of the tour was against Nottinghamshire and Richard along with Clive Rice bowled on a real green top and defeated our team. It was only the second defeat for our team in the county games. The first one was the unexpected one at Gloucester where Mike Procter had run through us.

The Holts Trophy and prize money was at stake which would have run into quite a few thousand pounds for Gloucestershire but Nottingnam prepared a real green wicket and saw to it that they too got a part of the share by defeating our team.

It was in this game that Hadlee hit Mohinder Amarnath on the head with a bouncer and caused a crack in the skull which, though not very serious physically perhaps, was not very good for Mohinder as far as his confidence was concerned. His bowling in that game was an object lesson on how to keep the ball up and never give the batsman any rest. At the other end Clive Rice was faster but certainly did not look as dangerous because Richard was the one who was making the ball move around and do all kinds of things off the wicket.

The 1980-81 season in Australia, in which India shared a tour with New Zealand, found Richard Hadlee one of the main attractions of the tour and he did not belie the expectation, by constantly playing aggressively with the bat and bowling with real speed at the Australians. His clashes with the crowds, became fairly notorious, and the crowds used to love to bait him when he came on to field at the fence in-between his overs. The Australian crowd being what it is and their attitude towards New Zealanders, it was but natural that one day Richard would lose his cool and do something drastic! That's what he did in one of the finals of the Benson and Hedges matches when he picked up a spectator and threw him over the fence as the spectator had come across and stopped him from fielding a ball which was just going to the boundary. That was Richard Hadlee's competitiveness and not any antagonism against the spectator. He apologised the next day although he made it very clear that he wasn't impressed with the attitude of the Australian crowd towards the New Zealand side.

We went down to New Zealand immediately after that tour of Australia. In the three Test matches, we lost 1-0. In the first Test Richard bowled New Zealand to victory when we had to chase a total of 250 runs on a wicket which wasn't looking as lively as it did on the first day. I had put New

Zealand in after winning the toss because the wicket looked very green and lively and I thought with Binny, Yograj and Kapil Dev in our side it was better to put the other side in and see what Kapil would do.

Kapil and Yograj got quite a genuine amount of pace out of the wicket but unfortunately for us they seldom found the target and that allowed New Zealand to settle down and post quite a good score. Surprisingly, when the Indians batted it was not Richard who got most of the wickets but Lance Cairns who destroyed our batting with his medium paced swing. Richard, perhaps, like Kapil Dev had tried a bit too hard on that wicket and although he beat the batsman he wasn't able to get the wickets.

In the second innings our bowlers found just the ideal length and we dismissed New Zealand for just over a hundred which left us to score 250 runs to win. We thought our chances were fairly good if we got off to a good start but that wasn't to be because Richard got Chetan Chauhan, who had been batting consistently, cheaply and then ran through with four important wickets that really set us back in that game.

After that in the Christchurch Test as well as in the Test at Auckland Richard did not have much to do because the wickets did not enable him to do much. The Christchurch Test was, of course, ruined by rain for the major part and in the Auckland Test the ball was turning a fair bit.

Yet, simply by that first Test in the second innings when he got four wickets he had seen that New Zealand had ended up on the winning side again, just as his own performance had seen New Zealand beat West Indies for the first time in New Zealand the previous year.

He cracked a hundred and also got wickets in every Test though it was a tour that was marred by the West Indians' displeasure at the umpiring decisions of New Zealand's umpires. However one cannot take away the credit from the admirable qualities shown by the New Zealand team in playing together so much as a team that even the mighty West Indians could not get away from the pressure tactics and competitiveness shown by the New Zealand team.

This facet shown by the New Zealand team of intense competitiveness has come only from Richard Hadlee. Geoff Howarth, although competitive, is a fairly mild person compared to Richard who being a quick bowler and having a temperament for a quick bowler brings out the competitive element in the rest of the team. And that makes it an altogether formidable combination.

However, off the field Richard is a very warm and very friendly person who is always willing to have a chat and a drink. He's come to India and has played a couple of benefit matches as well and he has always appealed to the Indians because of his warm, outgoing nature off the field.

There's one story of how a collector of photographs and albums from newspaper clippings over the last so many years — a person called Shashikant Zarapkar — went across to Richard during the benefit match played for G.S. Ramchand and inquired timidly of Richard whether he was Fred Titmus. That was the only time that Richard was found stumped for an answer and also his sense of humour at that stage failed him because he turned around and asked if he was looking as old as Fred Titmus did. However, that was just a mild thing and Richard quickly saw the humour of it and was very happy to go through the album and sign some of the pictures which Shashikant Zarapkar so religiously collects.

His wife also plays cricket. She represents New Zealand in women's cricket. Richard's father also played for New Zealand and was chairman of the New Zealand Cricket Council after he retired from competitive cricket. His brother Dayle played for New Zealand and his other brother,

Barry, was in the 1979 World Cup side though he did not play an official Test for New Zealand. So it must be quite a family as it has produced so many international calibre sportsmen in New Zealand.

Richard always travels with a medicare bag which takes care of his minor injuries. There was a season, 1980, when he was plagued by far too many injuries and hardly played in the county championship. That almost made him want to give it up and he said that he wouldn't be coming back to play for Nottinghamshire. But the supporters of the Nottinghamshire County Cricket Club prevailed upon him to change his mind and come back and told him that even if he was absent for the major part of the matches it did not really matter. And that was a tremendous compliment because for an overseas player to be as popular as Richard, is, a tremendous tribute.

Richard did not disappoint them because when he came back in 1981, he was bowling over a slightly shorter run up and along with Clive Rice he destroyed most of the county attacks and Nottinghamshire won the county championship for the first time in many, many years. Richard's contribution to that was immense with the ball and with the bat and his competitiveness must have rubbed off on his colleagues at Nottingham as well.

He and Glenn Turner, are the only two professionals, in the true sense of the term, that New Zealand has produced. Glenn has had many a row with the New Zealand Cricket Council about this and therefore has not been playing Test cricket, but Richard has somehow managed to get everything together and still be available for New Zealand.

And I just hope for New Zealand cricket and for the cricket-loving public in the world that Richard Hadlee continues to play for many a long time, although I hope that everytime I play against him he gives me a half volley first ball so that I can get off the mark!

25

Rodney Marsh

Today Rodney Marsh has the highest number of victims behind the stumps. And he is considered to be the best in the wicketkeeping department in the world. And to think that when he started playing for Australia, he was nicknamed "Iron Gloves" by the critics in Australia and England. I am not too sure if the same critics have retracted their words. Most critics seldom do that. They just jumped to conclusions after seeing him in action in just one Test. The first Test for any cricketer is bound to make him nervous and tense and that's what happened to Marsh. He might have dropped a couple of catches, his gathering might not have been the cleanest, his collection of throws might not have pleased the purists, but there was no denying the fact that he had the determination to do well and in this respect he was a typical Australian as far as competitiveness was concerned.

Perhaps the critical analysis of Marsh was based on his being compared with his predecessor Brian Taber and it was thought that he was not good enough to replace Taber. But Brian Taber has recently said that Marsh is one of the best wicketkeepers that he has ever seen and that should silence everybody concerned.

If that is not enough, his record speaks for himself and though there are people who would always run down statistics and statisticians, it has to be admitted that over a period of time, it's only statistics that give one an indication of a player's class. Over a short period, it might not be possible to judge the class of a player but over a long period, it's statistics that tell you how good and how bad the player was. There is no point in saying that a player had plenty of class if the record does not prove it. Too many players have this 'class' tag, who are not able to produce it in the Tests and, in spite of this they carry the 'class' tag. Rodney Marsh does not fall in this category and his performance has been superbly consistent right through.

When he first played for Australia in 1970, he was a roly-poly cricketer, overweight and came in for criticism for that as well. In the following year, having played in six Test matches against England, he had made up his mind to lose weight and this he did by hard training and sensible intake of food.

Rodney has not been lucky to keep wickets to top-class spin bowling. It would have been a great sight to see him keep to the bowlers of the calibre of Bedi, Pras and Chandra. Being a giant in his own way, it would have been interesting to see him keep wickets to the unpredictable Chandra, because Chandra himself at times did not always know what he was going to bowl.

People in India have been rather unfortunate to miss Rodney Marsh in action just as they have missed Greg Chappell, Dennis Lillee and Jeff Thomson. With the sort of programme chalked out between the two Boards, it is extremely unlikely that these players would be seen in action in a Test match in India. All of them are well past their prime, they are now above 30, and the Australians are known for their reluctance to continue in the game beyond that limit. The Indian spectators should keep their fingers crossed and if these players are not able to play in India in a Test match, they should hopefully be able to come down for an odd benefit match and share their talents with the Indian cricket fanatics.

Rodney Marsh has the batting ability to add to his excellent wicketkeeping. And that must have tilted the scales in his favour when he first came on the Test scene. He did not let the Australian selection committee down on either count. In the second Test match on his home ground, which was the first ever Test in Perth, Marsh scored 92 not out and Bill Lawry came in for heavy criticism for having declared the Australian innings when Marsh was only eight runs short of his Test hundred. Lawry has always been an uncompromising skipper. He always put his team's interest first before individual glory and therefore, when the team needed a declaration, he applied the closure. It was the same Test in which Greg Chappell made his memorable debut with a Test century

Marsh has not looked back since and has been a regular member of the Australian team, and, in fact, has been the first name to be ticked off when the Australian team is selected in recent years. The only time he missed to play in the Tests was when he opted to play for the WSC. His tally of catching victims would have been even greater because he missed out on a number of matches during that three-year period. Certainly the Australians missed him more than anybody else. It is an acknowledged fact, and Dennis Lillee agrees, that many of his victims were gained only because of Marsh's tips to him as to how to bowl to a particular batsman. Lillee had publicly acknowledged this fact by rushing down the wicket, after taking a wicket, to congratulate Marsh.

Besides Ian Chappell, Rodney Marsh has been one of the shrewdest cricketing brains in Australian cricket. Standing next to Ian Chappell who was in first slip, Marsh learnt many a trick from Ian, not only of the cricketing variety but of gamesmanship too. However, this aspect of Marsh was evident when Ian Chappell was around and now after Ian's retirement, it has disappeared completely. Captains do influence their colleagues as far as behaviour on the field is concerned and with Ian Chappell it was always a no-holds-barred contest between his team and the other teams and he would go to any length to ensure a victory. The Australian team in those days was, therefore, labelled as 'Ugly Australians'. But Rodney Marsh is far, far away from this tag and his image has been of the friendliest variety.

When we first saw him in 1971 during the Rest of the World Series in Australia, Marsh was still a corpulent cricketer. He has since lost a lot of weight and it is unbelievable. He was at least 30 pounds lighter than what he was in 1970. He continued shedding weight and he is now one of the fittest players today.

It is a sight to see him in the dressing room with a towel or shorts around his waist. He has got thick muscular legs, almost like tree trunks. Somebody said that his legs should have been on his arms and his arms on his legs and then he would have been a better and prettier sight. It was one of his Australian colleagues who said that. But the fact remains that Marsh has very strong legs and it is only in the recent years that his knee is giving him problems. If he would have been the same weight as in 1970, you can imagine how he would have carried himself for all these 13 years.

I will not forget the way he bumped into me one night during that Rest of the World Series. A fire had started in a building near which we had gone partying. Tony Greig and myself went down the street to see the fire. The heat generated by the fire was intense and we were continuously shunted by the firemen and police personnel. Suddenly, we saw Rodney Marsh walking in and staring at the fire with a lost expression on his face. We wondered whether he was staying in that building. Thankfully it was not so and so the three of us went down to a cafe for something to eat and that's where he told that he was walking down the streets a bit nervously because he was expecting to be a father and his wife was in the advance stages of pregnancy. It was truly an unforgettable sight.

In the restaurant, one could hardly believe the way Marsh and Greig talked. Both were at loggerheads on the field in the previous two games. Such is the spirit of cricketers that all the harsh words that are exchanged on the field are easily forgotten and many friendships are made which last for years and years.

After that World Series, we again met after nearly ten years in 1980. We played Australia in 1977-78 and again in 1979 but then Marsh was with the WSC. He could not come to India with Kim Hughes's team in 1979 because of the Packer connection. I found him to be a very amiable person, and not the hard competitive cricketer that he had been made out to be by the Press.

To be sure, he was tough on the field and no one expected him to be otherwise. What was refreshing was the way he would come down at the end of the day's play and have a word with us, not necessarily on cricket, but on any other topic. He had a keen interest in India and said that he was regretting that he had been unable to play in India and he was hoping that he would be able to do this. This desire of his looks very doubtful now.

The wicketkeepers of all teams make a beeline for him to know about his experiences and take valuable tips of improving. They were also prepared to have a tip from him to improve their batting. And he has always obliged. He has the ability to spot the weakness of others and he passes on this information to his captains. He advises the captains as to what type of field should be set for a particular batsman. From behind the wickets, he constantly encourages the bowlers when the bowlers are getting a thrashing. This way he ensures that the bowlers' spirits don't droop and in this way Marsh has contributed a great deal more to Australian cricket.

It's a pity that he was never given a chance to lead Australia and I am sure that he would have done a marvellous job if he was given that opportunity. Perhaps, it is Australia's loss and the opponents' gain. But Rodney Marsh would not let such things affect him although there was a period in the late 1979-80 when there was a bit of resentment that Kim Hughes was asked to lead the side in preference to Marsh. There was also a bit of ill feeling in Western Australia when Hughes was appointed skipper after Marsh had successfully led West Australia in the Sheffield Shield competition in the previous year, but the true sportsman that he is, he did not show any resentment, but carried on doing his job as best as he could and that was wicketkeeping. Not for a moment he showed any signs that he was deprived of the captaincy. Whenever Hughes asked for his guidance on the field, he gave him everything in the interest of his side. He is a perfect teamman and therefore he is held in high esteem throughout Australia.

With Ian and Greg Chappell and Dennis Lillee, he has dominated the Australian and world cricket over the last decade. Along with the other three, he has been talked about as the most controversial cricketer in Australia though he has not involved himself in as many controversies as the other three cricketers. He had his fair share of them but now he seems to be mellowed with age. Therefore he is less of a headache to the administrators and officials.

He is very good at golf as well where his brother Graham Marsh has earned a reputation for himself as a professional golfer. At one time it was just touch and go whether Rodney Marsh would take up golf or cricket. There was some sort of understanding between the brothers and one of them opted for apparently golf and is doing fairly well at it. Similarly Marsh has done remarkably well in his chosen profession. Rodney Marsh is an epitome of a hard-working cricketer who has risen above criticism and above his own performances. And he is a fine example for budding cricketers and particularly budding wicketkeepers to follow.

26

Rohan Kanhai

Rohan Kanhai is quite simply the greatest batsman I have ever seen. What does one write about one's hero, one's idol, one for whom there is so much admiration?

To say that he is the greatest batsman I have ever seen so far is to put it mildly. A controversial statement perhaps, considering that there have been so many outstanding batsmen, and some great batsmen that I have played with and against. But, having seen them all there is no doubt in my mind that he was quite simply the best of them all.

Sir Gary Sobers came quite close to being the best batsman but he was the greatest cricketer ever and he could do just about anything. But as a batsman I thought Rohan Kanhai was just a little bit better.

My first impression of Rohan Kanhai, my first view, was in the game in 1958 when the CCI played against touring West Indians. I don't really remember much about that game but in the Test that followed I remember quite clearly how brilliantly Rohan Kanhai batted and made our bowling look

Rodney Marsh — Gutsy player who overcame initial problems to be acknowledged as the best of his kind.

Rohan Kanhai — Friend, philosopher and guide.

S. Venkatraghavan — The patient Indian.

Sir Gary Sobers — The greatest.

Syed Kirmani — Keeper of India's fortunes.

Viv Richards — Does anybody bat better than he does today?

Zaheer Abbas — The big hundred specialist.

Sir Donald Bradman — Idol of Idols

very easy. He drove, he pulled and he cut with time to spare and he looked a cut above everybody. Between periods of studious defence he would come out with an explosive shot which went like a rocket to the boundary When Manohar Hardikar bowling his first over in Test cricket got him out leg before most of the stadium erupted in joy. But I was disappointed because Rohan had missed his hundred. Perhaps it was not a patriotic feeling at that stage but I thought — my hero had failed to score a hundred and that was very disappointing.

He made up for it in the latter part of the series with 256 at Calcutta which is still talked about and a series of other knocks which proved what a great player he was.

The other memorable part about that 1958 Test which, incidentally, was the first Test match I ever saw, was Rohan's fielding. His anticipation, his sprinting to the boundary to chase the ball, stop it a few yards inside and then hurl it back parallel to the ground and into the wicketkeeper's gloves were thrilling. I stood up in my seat everytime he did that to get a better view from the North Stand.

The next time that Kanhai came to India was in 1966 with West Indian side which was then captained by Gary Sobers. Bombay didn't see him at his best and that was the first match which I saw from the pavilion, though, according to the Cricket Club of India rules, I was not really entitled to sit there because I was under 18. Thus I got a closer look at my hero and also there was Jaisimha who was my Indian idol and I saw both of them in "the flesh", so to speak, from close quarters and went home feeling thrilled.

Jaisimha, though he appeared nervous — and who wouldn't be having to face Wesley Hall and Charlie Griffith — still managed to smile a lot and convey the impression that he was thoroughly enjoying himself.

Rohan Kanhai, on the other hand, seemed very temperamental He would sit in his corner of the players' enclosure and would not look too happy with the world. Maybe, he had problems at that stage and I know each Test cricketer goes through a period when he has other problems. There are many Test cricketers who get very worked up during Test matches and are hardly ever their normal selves. They're grumpy, they're grouchy and very irritable and which is not really their normal self at all in fact, away from it all — away from the Test match scene — a lot of them would be jovial and absolutely topclass company, but when the Test match gets to them a lot of them become irritable, grumpy and grouchy.Not good company at all.

Maybe that was what was happening to Rohan Kanhai that day In fact, I was surprised later when the Test started at the shot he played and got out to It was the first time they were playing Chandra and Chandra really had all of them foxed. Chandra bowled a short one and Rohan tried to hit it out of the ground but only managed to hit it high in the air and Abbas Ali Baig from mid-wicket ran back about 25 yards and took a beautiful catch.

That was the end of Rohan in the first innings. In the second innings too he didn't score too many. At least I don't remember anything about the second innings. What is memorable about that match is the batting of Clive Lloyd when he clubbed Bapu Nadkarni savagely. I don't think Bapuji was ever treated as roughly as he was treated in that particular Test.

The next occasion to see Rohan was when we played against them in the West Indies in 1971. Rohan was reticent at first; he wouldn't make much conversation excepting a very, very formal and polite "hello" and for me, a newcomer, it was impossible to get close to him and have a couple of words with him.

One had heard so much about his falling sweep shot and I was looking forward to it and he didn't disappoint when in second innings during his marathon 158 not out he played a few of those shots off Prasanna. That made my day, and also the fact that he had scored a hundred which meant that one could have a longer, closer look at his batting technique.

Our new ball bowlers did not trouble him too much and he seemed to go on the front foot almost immediately even before the ball was delivered. But one could see when he was batting to the spinners, particularly when Bishan was bowling with Prasanna, that he would wait till the ball was in the air before committing himself either forward or back. In this way he found enough time to play his shots and the only time he had a bit of trouble in that innings was when Eknath Solkar came on to bowl and he did not know whether to go forward or back because Eknath was bowling at a much quicker pace than Bishan Bedi or Salim Durrani was bowling at.

At the end of that innings when I went to him and said "Well played" to him he smiled and said "Thank you" and asked me what my name was and what I did. After I replied he just nodded his head and raised his eyebrows when I mentioned the words "opening batsman" He turned round and said, "Well I wouldn't want to be an opening batsman ever. Thank God I'm not an opening batsman. All these crazy fellows trying to knock your head off."

I instantly warmed to him. All my apprehension after I watched his temperamental behaviour in 1966 vanished with that one remark. From then onwards it became easier to get to know him and slowly our friendship developed.

What won me over completely thereafter was the interest he took in my batting even though I was in the opposite side.

If I didn't play a shot which was right and if I turned back and looked in the slips I would see him shaking his head to show his disapproval. And if I played some good shots, at the end of the over while passing from slips to slips he would mutter under his breath "good shot" or "well played" or something like that. That was his way of giving encouragement to an opponent and I instantly appreciated that simply because this was my first series and Test cricket being what it is today none of the opponents go out of their way to be helpful to their opposite numbers. In this way Rohan Kanhai showed himself to be different than most Test cricketers, while I must also add that Gary Sobers was also very much in with his appreciation everytime our boys did well. And these two great cricketers proved that you don't have to be nasty to your opponents at all and still be able to win matches.

The other thing that got us closer was the fact that he was very much interested in seeing Alvin Kallicharran don the West Indian colours. Kali and I and, of course, Vishy, the three shorties hit off almost instantly from the first time we met. In fact, I remember a very funny incident when Kallicharran thought during the West Indies Board President's XI match when he had got out cheaply in the first innings that he had lost his chance of ever playing for the West Indies. We were at a barbecue dinner and Kali was crying about the fact that he had muffed up his chances. There was Vishwanath, probably an inch shorter than Kali; myself, maybe, quarter of an inch shorter than Kali, Vishwanath with four Test matches experience behind him; myself, with no Test experience. We were consoling and advising Kali like veterans not to give up and that he should fight it out. That was also the beginning of our friendship and when Rohan came to know that the three of us were good friends he was amused about that because, he said to Kali later on, "It's quite natural that the three of you, with just an inch separating you, all should get together and become friends." People were talking about Kallicharran as the left handed Rohan Kanhai. Now Kali is a very fine player indeed but he could never be a Kanhai and for that matter nobody could be a Kanhai.

After that first hundred he used to get a few good scores of 30s but never went on to score a hundred in that series. We met again in England playing against the counties. He was, as usual, pretty good though he seemed at that stage a little less warmer than he had been in West Indies. I don't blame him. Probably it's the weather, the English weather, that made him seem a little less friendly than before. During my trip to Bermuda where I was part of a double-wicket tourney I spent some time with Kanhai. We were together during that period and I spent a lot of time in Bermuda talking to him, trying to take out the finer points of batting from him. It was very difficult to get him to talk cricket at the end of the day particularly because Bermuda wasn't as serious as other cricket centres were and so he didn't seem very keen to talk about cricket though he came out with a little bit here and there. But one got the impression that he wasn't very happy talking cricket. In fact, there were traces of annoyance when I pestered him about batting and I thought at that stage that it was better to leave him rather than get him annoyed, upset and perhaps lose his friendship in the bargain.

There was a surprise waiting for me, when I returned from Bermuda when I was informed that I was selected to play for the Rest of the World party which was going to replace the South African team. The invitation to the South African team was withdrawn by the Australian Government and therefore they had hurriedly formed a Rest of the World side and

Rohan was going to be one amongst them.

Well, that was tremendous, because I thought this was just the right opportunity for me to be with two of the greatest players that I have ever seen — Rohan Kanhai and Gary Sobers — and learn from them. It is a fact that when one is touring, the players in the team come to know each other much better because you spend most of your time together. You spend times of joy and there are sad moments; there are tense moments and there are happy moments which are all there on a tour and this is the time when you come to know your teammates a lot better.

So I was very keen on this trip and fortunately for me it was good to have not only Rohan and Gary, there was the very competitive Tony Greig, there was the perfect gentleman Intikhab Alam, there was Graeme Pollock who came down just before the third Test, and there was Bob Taylor apart from our very own Bishan Bedi and Farokh Engineer.

Farokh and I had gone earlier on to Bangkok. The team had come from London and we joined the flight on to Australia. It was good to be with the blokes and one could feel instantly that each one was trying to size up the other. It is a very difficult task to get people in the same country from different regions together. That's the time also when the first few days are very tentative. So you can imagine how tentative and how wary each one must have been when people from different countries came together to play for the Rest of the World.

However, Gary Sobers with his magnificent approach and his total lack of any (to use the Indian word) "nakhras" put everybody instantly at ease. He is and has always been such an unassuming man that it was very easy for the ice to be broken amongst the teammates. This was helped to a great extent by Norman Gilford and Tony Greig and also the dry humour of Richard Hutton.

The first few days, however, Rohan seemed to be in a shell of his own. He didn't want to mix around too much. He'd been to Australia a few times before, in fact, the previous year he'd come down to Tasmania to coach, so he knew a lot of people and had a lot of friends in Australia and obviously wanted to spend some time with them before the major part of the tour began. It was therefore difficult to get to Rohan Kanhai and to speak to him, to talk to him about batting because he was preoccupied with his friends.

He did take me to a couple of parties and it was good fun meeting his friends in Australia. But soon we were back to the serious business of playing cricket and one could see how much dedication Rohan showed to batting. He trained a lot, practised a lot and was very keen to see that he was successful. However, injuries came his way quite often and deprived him of playing many matches.

He missed the first match because he was struck in the indoor nets in Melbourne by a ball from Asif Masood which just shot off a good length and hit him a very painful blow on the left forearm. Our fear at that stage was that it was broken. It was badly bruised, swollen, but luckily for us it was not broken. But he missed that game because of that. He also missed the next one and there's nothing about the first part of the tour which was really outstanding.

Came the first Test against Australia at Brisbane and Rohan was raring to go. Brisbane at that stage was very, very hot and Rohan was wearing his white floppy cap while batting. He batted at No. 3 and along with Ackerman got a hundred in that game.

At that stage we didn't think that Lillee would be a great danger because Ackerman and Rohan had played him so well while scoring their individual hundreds. He seemed to be no danger at all and McKenzie looked just a shadow of his great self. However, the Test at Perth was a different story altogether. Lillee knocked the Rest of the World side out for 59 runs in their first innings. This was a pathetic performance in spite of the fact that the wicket was by far the fastest one had encountered. With the kind of batting line-up that we had there was no excuse for us to get out for 59 and that too within the two hours before lunch. We had time also to come down for 10 minutes' batting in the second innings during which time we lost Farokh Engineer. which meant that we lost 11 wickets in that session.

It was during this Test that the greatness of Rohan Kanhai's batting became evident to me. I had the rare opportunity to stay along with him in a partnership and it was simply amazing the way he played that day.

Earlier on in that innings of his a short ball from Lillee hit him in the chest. It was painful but he shrugged off all help and stood his ground. The next ball expectedly was another short one and Rohan imperiously hooked it wide of midwicket for a four. That was a great shot. An absolutely unbelievable shot because Lillee was bowling genuinely quick and to have the time to get up on one's toes and smash the ball down like a forehand overhead shot in tennis takes some talent.

Our partnership lasted for about two hours and during that time one got an object lesson on how to play quick bowling from Rohan Kanhai. After I had fished outside the off stump to McKenzie he walked down the wicket and said, "What are you trying to do? You just stay down there, don't worry about your own runs but just give me the support I need and I'll get the runs."

That's precisely what he did. He just smashed the ball to all corners of the field and scored 117 I've seen quite a few century innings, but that, to my mind, ranked as the best century I've ever seen. For sheer guts, for sheer technique for the sheer audacity of his shots, that century was worth preserving on film.

However, another hundred — a double hundred in the same series and in the next Test by Sir Gary Sobers completely erased from the people's mind Kanhai's hundred. But I feel Rohan's was the greater hundred. It was a hundred played under more tension... it was the hundred played when the bowling was really fierce. Mind you, I'm not knocking Sir Gary's 254. It was a great innings, all right. But Rohan's 117 in Perth was just that shade better.

After that innings Rohan seemed to have gone into a bit of decline. He didn't play the Melbourne Test nor did he play the Adelaide Test — being laid down with injuries — and that was a blow to our side. He'd been hit so often on his arms or on his chest and had gone for so many X-Rays that after one trip from the radiologist, Richard Hutton refused to sit next to him saying that he would be 'radioactive'

During that tour Rohan and I became good friends. He took a genuine interest in me. He was very disappointed that I wasn't scoring many runs and he tried to explain to me how important it was as an opening batsman to try and see the new ball off. His favourite words used to be: "Give the first hour to the bowler and the rest can be yours."

And this was precisely what I was not able to do because on that tour in my very first match I scored a hurricane 30 and a very impressionable 22-year-old got carried away with all that publicity about fast scoring and tried to repeat it in the rest of the games — at least until the second Test ended, with disastrous results. It was during the Perth innings that Rohan told me the importance of building an innings — of staying there when the other batsman was scoring a lot of runs, so that the other batsman keeps on playing his shots and does not come under any pressure.

These are little things, but one has to learn these things and it was great education to be at the other end while Rohan Kanhai batted.

We met quite often after that. He used to come over for the benefit matches in India or he used to stop over on his way back from some trip. He had a lot of contracts to play cricket in Australia and invariably on his return journey he would stop over in Bombay and stay with his friends and we would spend an evening or two together.

Rohan has plenty of friends in Bombay and I'm sure all over the world as well. With the ladies he's utterly charming and wins them over by his impeccable manners.

He used to tease me a lot in Australia in 1971 when he used to say that in 1961 when the West Indies team was first in Australia, there used to be a line of girls outside his room. He seems to like Australia as a place and he's tried to settle down there but not with success and has returned to Blackpool in England where he now lives.

Even now in league cricket he's scoring runs and passing on tips to younger players. Whenever we're in England we meet — he always phones up and wishes the team luck. He is now very much involved in organising tours to different parts of the world and only couple of years ago he took a Rest of the World team to Pakistan to give their players practice before they went to Australia.

He'd love to bring a team to India and perhaps he might do so very soon. I know people in India have a soft corner for Rohan and would welcome him with open arms if he brought a team over to India. I am also one of the many Indians who are genuinely fond of the man not just as a cricketer but as a human being. I have had the honour of naming my son Rohan after the great man and if only Rohan

Gavaskar becomes half as good a player Rohan Kanhai was (if he becomes a cricketer at all) I shall be a very happy man indeed.

27

S. Venkataraghavan

Ramakant Desai ran up to bowl with that smooth run-up of his, pitched the ball just short, outside the off stump. Barry Sinclair, the New Zealand vice-captain, square-cut powerfully but uppishly and when most heads were turned towards the boundary, a tall and slim figure stood up with a half jump and snatched the ball with complete ease. The entire Brabourne Stadium rose to a man to applaud this magnificent catch by a youngster who was playing his first series. That youngster was Srinivas Venkataraghavan, India's veteran cricketer today.

He has since then become almost a specialist in taking overhead catches, particularly off the slashes off- spin bowlers which come at blinding speed. That catch was of a kind that the Indian cricketing public and the Bombay crowd took notice of and took this pencil-thin youngster to their hearts. Bombay crowds love a brilliant fielder and Venkat had won their hearts even before he had started to weave his magic web over the batsmen of the Test playing countries.

The next Test was in New Delhi and it was here that Venkat gave notice to the cricketing world that another class spinner had arrived on the scene. He captured eight wickets in the first innings and five in the second. Apart from that he was brilliant in the field. With a performance like this behind him, he should have been the automatic choice in the Indian teams thereafter but strangely, with the advent of Prasanna and his comeback, Venkat found it hard to hold a place in the side.

I remember watching Venkat bowl in the Test against the West Indies the following year when he trapped Gary Sobers plumb in front with a quicker delivery. However, the umpire thought otherwise and did not give Sobers out. Sobers then went on to score a brilliant 50, but as soon as the appeal had been negatived, he turned round to Budhi Kunderan who was keeping wickets, and with a grin said, "hard luck old chap". That was one chance the Indian team had in trying to contain the West Indies team to a reasonable total. Venkat bowled well but without success and shall I say without much success in that series and, towards the end of it, he was replaced by Prasanna. Before that, the Indian selectors in a bold move had picked Bishan Bedi to play in the second Test, after having watched the Sikh in the Board's President's XI match at Delhi. So with Chandra in the side, Prasanna making a comeback and Bishan beginning to establish himself, Venkat found himself out of the Indian side.

That season was memorable because the spin trio, and later on the spin quartet, came into being that year. They used to mesmerise the batsmen throughout the seventies. Venkat made the trip to England in 1967 but Tiger Pataudi did not seem to have much confidence in Venkat. He plumped for Prasanna who had more variation and more spin than Venkat and was the better bowler of the two. It was this tour that saw Prasanna come into his own and he was an automatic choice in the side that went to Australia and New Zealand within two months of the England trip.

Venkat was inexplicably dropped from the side and Prasanna consolidated his position capturing 49 wickets in eight Test matches in Australia and New Zealand. It was a superlative performance but it also meant that Venkat had by now realised that he had a competitor and would have to fight hard to get his place back in the Indian side. Venkat has always been a fighter and the word defeat does not seem to be present in his mind at all. He never gives up. This never-say-die spirit must have been strengthened during this period of absence from Test cricket and must have been developed to perfection in the season that followed.

When the New Zealand and Australian teams returned the visit in 1969-70, Venkat was back in the Indian team but merely as a third or fourth spinner and would come on to bowl only when Pras and Bishan were tiring. He never let go the opportunity, though, and saw to it that after the two bowlers had finished their stints, runs were not easy to come by, off his bowling. His job then was to see that he bowled tight so that both the spinners would come back and strike the vital blows. To my mind, this is where Venkat lost out to Pras and that too in the larger interest of the side. Venkat realised that he would have to be more economical than Pras and so he sacrificed his natural loop and beautiful flight which he had when he first came on to the Test scene. So Pras could get wickets at the other end.

Not many people, except those who had seen Venkat in action in the 1965 series, would realise that this change had taken place. I don't think Venkat is the type who would talk about it as well and it is only now in recent years that with

Pras off the scene, Venkat has come back to his original style, giving the ball plenty of air, inviting the batsman to play his shots and thus getting wickets. That, plus his physical fitness, as well as the never-say-die spirit, have kept him in remarkable shape and kept him going as a Test bowler even now.

In 1970, to everybody's surprise, Venkat was appointed captain of the South Zone team. This was a clever move engineered mainly to see that he became the vice-captain of the Indian team to tour the West Indies in 1971. To many, this move also seemed deliberate and done with a view to see that Venkat did not get a raw deal when bowling for South Zone. The South Zone team also included Pras and the previous captain also tended to rely more on Pras and not as much on Venkat. With Pras tending to tire quickly, it was Venkat with his stamina who bowled long spells while Pras came in short, quick bursts, to take quick wickets. Venkat was duly appointed vice-captain of the Indian team and, with Pras also in the side, it was going to be difficult for both bowlers to play in the same Test team. Chandrasekhar was not in the side and thus our spin combination included Salim Durrani being an all-rounder, Eknath Solkar also capable of bowling left-arm spin, Bishan', of course, and Pras and Venkat.

To Venkat's credit it must be mentioned that he never dominated and made use of his position and ,was fair in his treatment of Pras. Pras, however, was injured and did not play in some Tests so Venkat clutched the opportunity with both hands and ended up as the highest wicket-taker on this trip. With India winning this series against the West Indies for the first time ever, Venkat had no problems in being appointed vice-captain again. However, this time instead of Chandra being dropped, it was Salim Durrani's turn to be axed and Chandra went to England. On this tour also India made history by winning the series for the first time ever and the chief architect of our success at the Oval was Chandra when he destroyed England for a mere 101, taking six wickets for 38 runs. But what people tend to forget is that Venkat kept such a tight leash on the batsmen and did not allow them to take any liberties with his bowling. He also dismissed the troublesome Alan Knott to a brilliant catch by Eknath Solkar and thus he also had his share in this success.

When the England team returned the visit in 1972-73, Venkat found himself in the background with Bishan and Chandra among the wickets. Chandra took a record 35 wickets in the series, closely followed by Bishan and with Pras coming on with his flighted guile, Venkat found himself relegated to the rear. This must have been a severe blow to one who was the vice-captain of the country the previous year but again it went to strengthen Venkat's resolve not to give up.

In 1974 India visited England with Ajit Wadekar as captain and Venkat as vice-captain. This tour produced different results altogether, India being whitewashed completely 3-0. It was a trip beset by weather problems and other problems and it never appeared that the Indian team would do anything of significance on this trip and that is how it was.

The West Indies team, which was in the process of building itself as the champions of the world, came to India in the winter of 1974-75 and that was a winter of turmoil which marked the exit of Ajit Wadekar as the captain, followed by Tiger Pataudi as captain. This was a severe blow for Venkat who was vice-captain till just a few months earlier on the trip to England when Pataudi had declined to join the team for reasons that were best known to him. In those days, people did not bother to know if a player withdrew due to personal reasons or business reasons.

To my surprise, I was told on the eve of the first Test that I was appointed vice-captain but was asked not to make it public. That led to an embarrassing situation when Tiger Pataudi was injured during the first Test while taking a catch and had to go off the field. I knew I was the vice-captain but as I was fielding on the deep mid-wicket fence, it took me some time to reach the centre of the field and realise that Pataudi had gone off without informing the seniors as to who was to take charge. Venkat felt that he being the vice-captain on the previous tour, he would automatically be the captain. Traditionally and normally, the seniormost player takes over if the captain goes off. So Farokh Engineer thought that he would be in charge and to all of them it came as a surprise when I rushed and told them that I had been appointed vice-captain and I would be in charge. It really was very embarrassing when seniors like Chandra, Engineer and Venkat were in the side and someone like me who has just started his career was asked to captain them. However, I never had any problem but I really did feel sorry, at that stage, for Venkat.

When Tiger Pataudi got injured, I was appointed captain for the second Test in Delhi but hardly a week before this match, I injured my index finger playing for Bombay against Maharashtra on a matting wicket at Nasik. With the then chairman of the selection committee turning up only on the morning of the Test match, India woke up that morning of the second Test without a captain. It wasn't a situation for anybody to make his captaincy debut. Venkat, who had been asked to lead the side, must have been hardly prepared to do the job. How can one discuss any tactics or strategy when one does not know who is going to be the captain? Thus, it was, that Venkat's debut as captain was a disaster. Added to that was the decision of the umpires to start play in spite of a rain-affected wicket, just half an hour before lunch. For the life of me, I could not understand how the umpires could not wait the extra half an hour before lunch, take lunch and start play after lunch. After all it is five-day game and there is enough time that can be made up.

With the umpires insisting on play starting early, India lost quick wickets, never recovered from that situation and lost the Test. But worse was to follow. Having captained the side in this Test, Venkat found himself relegated to the position of 12th man in the next Text. What a demoralising blow it must have been for him, but never did Venkat show that he was hurt by the treatment meted out to him by the selectors nor did he ever say anything to anybody. He just carried on gamely bowling to the Test players in the nets, giving fielding practice, taking his share of catches and making himself useful in the dressing room. He was back in the side, however, soon and at the end of the series Pataudi announced his retirement from Test cricket. That meant that India had to find another captain.

The selection committee once again showed its whims and fancies by disregarding the claims of the appointed vice-captain for that series and appointing Venkat as captain for the Prudential World Cup. This was probably due to the fact that Venkat at that time was playing county cricket for Derbyshire and was thus experienced enough in the finer points of one-day cricket to be able to lead the side. However, England proved too strong in this game and they rattled up a record score of 334 which only recently has been bettered by Pakistan in the last World Cup, and with my inexplicable innings of 36, India had no chance whatsoever in that tournament.

Back home, Bishan was appointed captain for the tour of New Zealand and West Indies. The reasoning of the selection committee was now beyond anybody's understanding. They had started off by making Venkat the vice-captain in 1974, then recalled Pataudi as Capt. making me vice-captain in 1974-75. Then after Pataudi's retirement, recalling Venkat as captain and making me vice-captain and finally making Bishan captain in 1976. However, this was an enjoyable trip but with Chandra, Pras and Bishan being among the wickets, Venkat found it difficult to get into the side except when Pras was injured. Here again he didn't let the side down and bowled particularly well in the West Indies and it was only due to Kirmani's lack of experience of the West Indies wickets and his poor' keeping in that series that Venkat didn't get the rewards that he deserved. There were many moments when the great Viv Richards was stranded out of the crease, but with Kirmani found wanting, he could get back and make most of his 'lives' to start a tremendous sequence of runs.

When New Zealand and England came to India in 1976, Venkat again found himself in and out of the side. It surely will not do anybody's confidence much good to have such treatment. However, Venkat had a big heart and, as a result, he kept on doing his own things and went on about his own ways.

The Australian tour in 1977-78 wasn't a very successful one for him and when the Indian team went to Pakistan in 1978, Venkat didn't even play a Test. Zaheer and company had literally hounded Chandra, Bishan and Pras and Venkat, not having played in a Test, escaped the wrath. So, he was picked to play against the West Indies team. He bowled very well in that series. The only disappointment was that he was not able to run through the side on the rain-affected track in

Delhi. The Indian team had put up a massive total and the West Indies team collapsed against Ghavri and Kapil Dev. They had to follow on on a rain-affected pitch but Venkat could not do anything extraordinary with three left-handers in their side.

At the end of the season, I was deposed as captain, allegedly because of some statements my wife made to the media and Venkat was once again appointed captain of the Indian team to tour England. That tour started disastrously with England scoring 600 runs in the first Test and beating us comfortably by an innings. Thereafter, rain came to our rescue more often than not and we went into the last Test again facing a defeat. Fortunately, that was not to be and we just missed winning the Test by nine runs with two wickets left. A victory would have been possible but for some fairly tough decisions by the English umpires which left us struggling when we should have been in a position of dominance.

On the flight back home it was announced that Venkat was deposed as captain and again it was a blow that he took very well. However, midway through the Australian series that followed, Venkat found himself out of the side. Shivlal Yadav, the young Hyderabad off-spinner, had come to the fore and was bowling very well and was getting wickets while Venkat was finding it difficult to get them. Thus, Venkat after three Test matches was dropped again. He was out of the side for almost three years when he was picked to go to the West Indies in 1983. On this trip he bowled well without getting any rewards and was very useful to some of the youngsters who would go to him for advice. His comeback after a gap of three years is proof enough of the man's fighting spirit and it is something worth emulating by the youngsters.

As a captain, Venkat was difficult to understand mainly

because he set very, very high standards and if he found anybody falling short of the expected standards, he was not averse to giving the player concerned a firing. In fact, his temper has become something of a joke in the Indian team. Venkat takes it now more sportingly and he also understands that his temper is the cause of a bit of leg-pulling, but he is very sporting about it and often laughs at himself. This temper of his was perhaps the reason why he was not able to get the best out of the players that he had.

I have found him to be good company because right from the beginning, from my first tour, way back in 1971, we got along well. In 1971 in Jamaica, when I was nursing an injured finger, Venkat, who is a bit of a palmist, read my palm and predicted big things for me. From that trip itself, I was more interested in finding out from him whether I would make the trip to England because no cricketer's education is complete without playing in England. He said that not only would I make the trip, but I would also be successful on this current trip and I was amazed when his prediction came true. I did not know whether his predictions were merely a way of giving encouragement to a young player on his first trip or whether he could really read one's palm. I have not asked him about this to this day and I would rather believe that whatever he said, had come true.

On the 1976 trip to the West Indies, where Dilip Vengsarkar was making his first tour, one could see the personal interest that Venkat took in Dilip and impressed upon him that with his height, he could make an excellent close-in fielder. Dilip has a very safe pair of hands but his reluctance to stand in the close-in positions is, to me and to the Indian team, very surprising.

Venkat was good company also because he could talk on a variety of subjects and it is particularly refreshing not to talk cricket at the end of a day's play. If we went out for a meal together, Venkat would talk on any subject but cricket and that was great relief. Venkat has been dropped from the side that won the World Cup in England in 1983. But knowing the man and his determination, one can be certain that he would be raring to go when the Indian season begins and was, in fact, back in the Indian side. He had not played a Test against Pakistan but he achieved that ambition when he played at Bangalore in the first Test. Here is wishing him luck and may he achieve the success that is his just reward but which has been denied to him for a long time.

28

Sir Gary Sobers

The greatest cricketer I ever saw was Sir Garfield Sobers. He was the complete cricketer. He could bowl medium-paced and he could be quick when he wanted to; he could bowl spinners, the orthodox as well as the Chinaman variety. He could bat at any number and he opened the innings once in Tests and, I am sure, he could keep wickets. As far as fielding was concerned, he was one of the safest catchers in the close-in positions and till the later years, when his bowling used to tire him out, a swift-moving fielder in the outfield.

My first trip to West Indies in 1971 saw the West Indies captained by Gary Sobers. Gary had run into a bit of controversy having just toured Rhodesia to play in a double-wicket tournament. The Governments of Jamaica and Guyana were not very happy about it. I also think, though I could be wrong, the West Indian public wasn't happy about the fact that he married a white Australian girl, because, after all, Sobers was a national hero in the West Indies, much like what Vivian Richards and Andy Roberts are in Antigua today.

In the first Test match of the series at Jamaica, Sir Gary scored 40 runs but, even before that, when we batted, he took a blinder of a slip catch off Jayantilal when he had dived sideways and picked that ball up inches from the turf. As he tumbled and came up with the catch, I turned round and said to Eknath Solkar, who was sitting next to me, "Wow! all I want to do now is to see Rohan Kanhai play his falling sweep-shot and it doesn't matter if I play on this trip or not."

I was on the injured list at that time with a whitlow on my middle finger and so was just a spectator as far as that match was concerned. That match also showed how Gary Sobers can tear an attack apart, while Rohan Kanhai, in the second innings, resorted to playing a waiting game. Gary went out with the intention of showing the Indian bowlers where they really belonged. He just smashed everything. Neither Bishan nor Pras could make any difference to him. He had stormed into the 90's, when Ajit gave the ball to Eknath Solkar and, wonder of wonders, Solkar got him caught behind when trying to essay a back-foot drive through the covers. But then that was typical Sobers, no caution for him. He just went out and played as he could naturally. Thanks to that effort, as well as Rohan Kanhai's marathon effort, the West Indies saved the game.

That game also showed that a great cricketer like Gary Sobers can also make a mistake unaware of some of the laws of the game. With the first day's play having been washed out completely, the match became a four-day contest and, therefore, the follow-on margin became 150 runs and, since we had a lead of more than 150 and less than 200 runs, Ajit very rightly enforced the follow-on. This completely stunned Gary Sobers and he had to be told by the umpires that Ajit was right. But I also believe that this stung Gary Sobers no end, because this was the first time in so many matces that an Indian team had enforced a follow-on on the West Indies team. When he went out to bat the second time, the determination could be seen in the way he handled the bowlers. That was one of his missed centuries and there were not many more occasions when he got out in the 90's.

When the second Test started, I was making my debut and got to see the great man at very close quarters. He was bowled trying to sweep Venkataraghavan and I was in leg-slip. I thought that it was a very unbecoming stroke, particularly of such a master batsman as he was, but obviously, we could not be complaining because once we get somebody like Gary Sobers for less than 50 it's a bonus.

That evening we started our innings and aware that I was making my debut, and with a not very impressive score by his team, Gary had crowded me with fielders. I managed to survive that evening and, the next morning, Vanburn Holder, who was very much quicker than what we saw of him in 1974 or 1978 — in fact, he was genuinely quick in 1971 — bowled me a shortish ball outside the off-stump and I went for a back-foot drive and the ball just moved away and took a thick outside edge and went low to Sobers at second slip. Gary missed that catch and, though he tumbled in trying to take it on the rebound, the chance was grassed. That was the first time, to my mind, Sobers looked human. There was nothing one could do after that excepting try and capitalise on this lapse — a very unusual lapse — by such a great fielder.

When he was bowling he tried everything. He tried bouncing; he tried bowling across; he bowled around the wicket; he bowled seamers and he bowled spinners; he bowled back-of-the-hand stuff and one could not but help admire the versatility of this man. It just seemed that there was nothing in the world which was impossible for him. But then, that was not his day and we managed to get a fairly useful lead.

In the second innings, Salim Durrani bowled him a beautiful delivery, pitching just outside his off-stump and as Gary went out to push, the ball sneaked in between the gap and bowled him. Here I must say that Gary was never one of those who pushed the pad forward, he always played positively and never used his pads, unless he was beaten, but the first idea, the first aim, was always to meet the ball with the bat unlike what we see today where players push the pad forward hoping that the ball would hit the pad and not the bat. With Gary's wicket, we knew that unless the tail wagged or unless there was an astonishing recovery by the West Indies, we were in with a chance of winning that Test. And so it happened. We won that Test. That was also the time when I took a photograph with Sir Gary Sobers just outside the dressing rooms, my first photograph with the great man and it is something I treasure.

Came the Guyana Test and once again Gary didn't do too well, neither did the West Indies. When our innings started Grayson Shillingford bowled me a similar kind of delivery like the one Holder had bowled in the second Test. Only this one was shorter, and I thought I would square-cut it. The ball bounced a little more than I expected and, off a thick outside edge, went to Sobers at second slip and, wonder of wonders, Gary grassed it again. That was the fifth ball of the over and as he passed by, I could hear him explaining to Rohan Kanhai, who was in first slip, that he did not see the ball at all. And it could be quite true because Guyana is one place where the background makes it very difficult to see and sight the edge. Most people believe that slip catches are easy, they look easy when you are 75, 80 or maybe even a 100 yards away because you have that much more distance in which to see the ball travelling from the bat's edge to the fielder. But when you are out there in the middle and it is like a rocket coming at you from barely ten yards, it is very, very difficult.

I wasn't unhappy because it was the second time in the series that Sobers had given me a 'life'. Then later there was another 'life' from Sobers though not technically a 'life'. It was when Noreiga was bowling and I was 94 on my way to my first Test century of my career. Noreiga bowled and as I moved to play forward, Sobers, who was at short square-leg, trying to anticipate, rushed to his left and tried to pick the ball up almost off the bat but, unfortunately for him, the ball jumped up a bit, took my glove and went to where Sobers was originally in position before he left for the ball. Sobers's flailing right hand was worthless and instead I got myself one more run. Therefore, when the next day's play started, Sobers said to me jokingly, "Man, let me touch you because I need some of the luck which you seem to be having"

Remember, he was having a fairly lean trot by his standards and after his score of 93 in the first Test at Jamaica he had not scored very many runs in his last three innings and people were talking that he should be dropped but then this is what happens when you are such a great player as Gary Sobers and nothing short of the best at all times is expected of you. Well, Gary went out in the second innings and hit us for a 100, though many from our side believed that he was caught for a zero by Dilip Sardesai of Salim Durrani at silly mid-on. The very fact that we could have two short legs, Dilip Sardesai and Eknath Solkar, just goes to show how uncertain Gary was till that innings. After he got his bearings and the pitch started easing, Gary hit Bishan and Salim Durrani for enormous sixes; the one of Salim Durrani, which was a gift-wrapped full toss, was hit out of the ground, clean over the pavilion, into the car park. This one was a drawn Test and that meant that we were still one up, but what was more ominous was the fact that Gary Sobers had scored a 100.

In the next match against Barbados, Sobers scored another 100 and one could see that the great man was just coming in form. There was no letting up after that and, true enough, in the first innings of the fourth Test at Barbados, he smashed us for 178 glorious runs and the 'Bajans', as the Barbadians are called, went wild. Here was their home-grown product, their national hero, doing everything that they wanted and wished him to do. The strokes were all there, the delicate late-cuts off the off-spinners, the flicks through mid-wicket off the front-foot and off the back-foot off the left-hand spinners and he was virtually standing, without moving his feet, and crushing Abid Ali on either side of the wicket as if to say, "I don't need foot-work against your pace"

For a 21-year-old like me it was a great education and Gary didn't let up even after his 100. In fact, he just accelerated to put his batting in one more gear and was away. What the West Indies lacked in that Test was a good off-spinner because the foot marks made by Eknath Solkar's bowling follow-through were just right for an off-spinner to exploit. I think, at that stage, Gary did not bowl his Chinamen because he was having some trouble with his shoulders — his Chinamen would have been perhaps equally dangerous to the right-handers.

With only one Test left and India still one-up, the West Indians were obviously looking for the kill and no one was more determined than Sir Gary Sobers. The Test started in a bit of controversy about the toss. Both Sobers and Ajit thought that he had won the toss. For the great sportsman that he is, Gary did not make waves and gallantly allowed Ajit to have the right of winning the toss. This kind of thing can happen quite often if different coins are used. It happened to Venkat and Mike Brearley in 1979. It happened once to me with Kallicharran.

When they batted, the West Indians were obviously in a big rush because they had to force the pace and dismiss us quickly in the second innings to get in with a chance and Sobers scored another 100. That made it four tons in a row for him, before a ball from Prasanna that kept low, bowled him as he went in for a cut. Before that, when our innings started, Gary was in the second slip, as usual, and there he dived to his left to catch Ajit, off John Shepherd and as he fell clutching the ball to his chest, the impact drove the ball into his chest and left him feeling dazed. He went off the field at lunch, didn't take the field again and Joey Carew led the side for two days. The second day we did not hear a word from Sobers though he was in pavilion, otherwise, the dressing rooms being adjoining, one could always hear his hearty laughter coming through.

On the third day, as soon as we arrived at the ground, we heard that inevitable laughter and we groaned because we knew that Sobers was fit and he showed how fit he was by knocking off another century. He still continued to come up to me every morning saying "Let me touch you for luck" I do not know whether he really believed in that or he was just pulling my leg. But if a great man like Sobers pulls my leg, it does not matter at all. Remember the first time he came and touched me and said, "I want to touch you for luck', he got his first 100 that day and maybe like most cricketers who believe in superstition, and are a bit superstitious, Sobers thought that this was bringing him luck? Whether it was or not, he did not have to rely on luck at all. All the natural talent was there and it was just a question of him getting into his batting rhythm. At the end of the series, he paid me a great compliment privately, when he said that I should get a lot of runs in England and his words of advice were: "try and avoid cutting in June but do that only in July and August". He also said that I should go on with my hook shots, though there were times when I hooked in the air and he said that "such a shot you play well and you have not got out so far in a Test match. It has got you many runs, just keep playing it". The very words that he used, "Your team should do well in England", were a great source of encouragement to me because coming from a man of great skill these were words that were highly cherished.

We met him again in England when we were playing the Nottingham county game and Sir Gary didn't play in that game. County cricket being such a tough game, he had to take a break from cricket, and he could take a break only in a non-championship game against the tourists. He was there with his son Mathew and watched us very keenly and had a word for almost every member of our side.

When the proposed South African tour of Australia, later that year, was called off, Gary Sobers persuaded the Australian Cricket Board to include me in the Rest of the World's side to play Australia that season. My opening partner was to be Hylton Ackerman and Farooq Engineer was going to be the third opening bat. Geoff Boycott and Barry Richards were at that stage the acknowledged best opening batsmen in the world but Barry Richards was contracted to play for a club in South Australia and so was not picked. I don't know why Geoff Boycott was not picked.

When we landed in Melbourne, Sir Gary Sobers was there to welcome us and tell us about the incident involving Tony Greig, Hylton Ackerman and Don Bradman. Ackerman and Tony Greig had arrived earlier from South Africa and at the Adelaide airport Gary Sobers had gone to receive them along with an elderly looking gentleman. When the introductions were made, Greig and Ackerman, who were feeling sleepy from their long journey, did not quite catch the name of the person Gary introduced and so when Ackerman had to leave to go to the toilet, he handed over his overnight bag to the elderly gentleman and left. After he returned from the toilet he tried to make polite conversation and asked the elderly gentleman, if he had anything to do with Australian cricket, to which the elderly person smiled and nodded and said, "Yes, a little bit" Ackerman then posed the question which has become a well known story now. He asked the elderly man, "I'm sorry, I didn't get the name, what did you say your name was?" and the person replied "Don Bradman" Ackerman looked at that stage as if he could have been swallowed by the earth.

I don't know who actually made the boo-boo. Ackerman said it was Tony Greig and Tony Greig said it was Ackerman who asked that question. Well, whoever it was, both Gary and Don Bradman had a hearty laugh.

During that tour of Australia, Gary was criticised for not being with the team particularly for net practices and instead playing golf. In fact, Gary was there for most of the net practices that the team had. But it was only after we played a three-day game, that he opted out of the next day's practice, particularly because one travelled long distances in Australia, to get to the next centre. That accusation was very unfair because Gary was really concerned about the performances of the team as this was a team which he and Sir Donald had selected and, therefore, he was very keen to see that this team, which he had helped to raise, would give a very good performance of itself.

The first 'Test' was drawn and that was our first sight of a bowler called Dennis Lillee In this 'Test' Ackerman and

Rohan Kanhai got 100s and Sir Gary was hardly under any pressure. It was the second 'Test' which turned the tables and after Australia were all out at the end of the first day we started our innings next morning and the wicket which seemed to have sweated under the covers assumed dangerous proportions. Dennis Lillee made the ball fly from just short of a good length and he had both Clive Lloyd and Gary Sobers off successive deliveries trying to fend off the balls from their chins caught in the slips or caught behind by the 'keeper'. That was great bowling and even in the second innings Lillee bowled extremely well in spite of one of the greatest, if not the greatest, 'Test' centuries I have seen by Rohan Kanhai.

It was at this stage that the Australian press really started to give Gary some stick with regard to his absence from net practices and his fondness for golf. And so Gary was really a charged man when the third 'Test' began at Melbourne. Ackerman opened the innings and he obviously still hadn't recovered from the previous evening's revelry, the 'Test' having started on New Year's day and one could make out as one walked out to bat with him that he wasn't going to be in any good shape to do any good. He was bowled third ball by Lillee for a 'duck' and Lillee also got Graeme Pollock who had flown in the previous day from South Africa edging a catch to Marsh. Gary was out to the first ball, be played when a short rising delivery from Lillee was nudged straight to second slip Keith Stackpole and the look Gary gave Lillee was one which was full of meaning. It was for the second time in succession that Dennis Lillee had got Gary out playing a shot like that and Gary certainly wasn't pleased about it.

Another remarkable thing is that Gary never wore a thigh guard in his life and the bat which he used was always a light weight one unlike the heavy ones which are in vogue now.

The speed with which the ball went to the boundary showed what superb timing he had and that one does not always need a bat with a lot of meat to hit the ball as powerfully as one wants to. One six off O'Keefe was lifted effortlessly into the stands and that too without advancing down the track. People who have been fortunate to see that film, have raved about it. But remember that those were just the highlights which were shown and what can really be seen or how much be seen in half-an-hour of highlights. Till his 50, the ball met the middle of the bat consistently but with the minimum of foot work, but after 50 the foot started going to the ball and the ball started going more speedily to the boundary. This was really vintage batting and one which completely turned the match upside down as far as the Australians were concerned.

When we fielded Gary contributed with two sharp catches at leg slip to get rid of the Australians and we levelled the series. That was a great way to start the new year on a victorious note, and we were all buoyant with hope that with our skipper in such great form, Ackerman and Kanhai who had already hit big hundreds, we would be able to beat the Australians.

The fourth 'Test' was at Sydney and that's where Bob Massie who had already played in Melbourne but not with much success came into prominence. He took seven wickets, including that of Sobers, and the moment he took Sobers's wicket, he obviously was noticed and not only that he also had Graham Pollock's wicket and so Bob Massie immediately attracted attention of the cricket loving public of Australia. Rain spoilt that game but we were not in a great position at that stage and Gary was bowled in the second innings by Inverarity when he tried to turn a full toss to mid-wicket, missed and the ball went off his pads on to the stumps.

Came the last 'Test' and the series was still 1-all and both the teams were looking for a win, but with the Adelaide wicket noted for its spin, the Australians brought Mallett and it was expected that Intikhab and Bishan would do wonders for us. That is what happened. Both Intikhab and Bishan bowled extremely well although there was a very good partnership between the Chappell brothers. At one stage, Intikhab took two wickets in an over and we had a very close field when Inverarity came in to bat. I was at silly mid-on where very few cricketers are comfortable and as Intikhab bowled that ball and Inverarity played it, I was taking a step back as the ball shot off a thick inside edge and I caught it. Sobers, who was at backward square-leg, came to me laughing and said, "You were retreating when the ball came to you. Any way, well caught", and I said to him," Well, I am not used to standing in that position!" He said, 'Don't worry, you are too small a person to make a target'. If I were standing there, I would be a bigger man and a bigger target because of my size". There was some sense in that kind of talk.

We duly won that 'Test' to win the series 2-1. The Australian side was just shaping up at that stage with the up and coming Gregg Chappell, Dennis Lillee with Ian Chappell making his impact as a captain. The only problem they were facing was a sound opening partner for Keith Stackpole at that stage. There was Massie as well. Rodney Marsh had proved to his knockers that he was a world class wicket-keeper in the making and so the Australian side was really looking good.

It was during this last 'Test' in Adelaide that a farewell dinner was organised and Sir Don Bradman came and spoke at length how the tour came about, how important the tour was and how the tour had gone. This dinner was only for the members of our team and the manager and Sir Don Bradman was a special invitee. Bradman then spoke about each member of the team, what were his impressions about that member and how he contributed to that tour. Before that, welcoming Sir Don to the dinner, Gary also spoke of the role that Sir Don had played about getting the tour going and also giving it every encouragement. While this was going on a very senior cricketer, sitting next to me, said, "Well, these two chaps keep on praising each other, don't they?" That may have been so, but there is no denying the fact that these two cricketers were the greatest ever cricketers the world has ever seen. One, Sir Don, the greatest batsman the world has seen and Sir Gary, the greatest cricketer the world has seen up to now.

Thus ended for me the first tour with so many top class players from the world and my only regret, apart from not getting a century in the unofficial Tests as well as in the first-class matches on the tour, was that I could not get a big partnership with Gary Sobers. There could have been so much to learn from Sobers had I batted along with him just like batting along with Rohan Kanhai in Perth taught me so many things. One thing I noticed about Gary when he was at the other end was that he never gave any kind of advice to his partner. If the partner played a bad shot there was no shaking of the head or no glare, or stare but Gary would simply get back to his crease and stand and stare stoically elsewhere. Similarly, if the partner played a good shot there would just be the hint of a smile and a nod so that the partner would know that while the shot was appreciated, it was not necessary to be carried away by that. This is what I noticed when India played the West Indies and also in our brief partnership. Still it was an experience which I was not fortunate to have and I really cannot go and tell my grandchildren that I had a partnership with the greatest cricketer of them all.

On that tour Gary had grown a beard because his razor got stolen during the first match of the trip. He bought another one. That too got stolen. He bought a third one. That too got stolen, obviously by people not with the intention to steal but to keep something as a memento of the great man. But Gary resolved at that stage not to shave again on the tour. His remark was simply, "I cannot afford to buy razors all the time". So he just grew a beard, but he was lucky because he did not have much of a growth on his cheeks and just the chin and underneath the chin could one find a bit of hair.

Sobers was fond of the night life and we once went to a night club together and I was astonished at the way he could knock a drink. He kept on having a dig at me for having a coca-cola and said that coke was more harmful to the intestines than liquor. I told him at that stage that I wasn't worried about my intestine but I was worried about my brain to which he gave a hearty laugh and said, "that's a good one." But to his credit, he never forced me to try and drink with him unlike some of our senior cricketers who try and force the youngsters in the team to have a drink even when the youngsters don't want to. Fortunately, this trend in Indian cricket is now on the wane but, certainly, was there when I was a beginner and an attempt was made to see that all the youngsters also joined in the drinks. This trend has virtually disappeared since 1977 and I think it is better today that in the Indian team, we find very, very few players who take alcoholic drinks or smoke. In fact, the one addiction of the current Indian team is that of music and that is the thing that they get their kicks from.

I kept on meeting Gary off and on after that and always the greeting was "How are you then, my little fellow" and the greeting was always very warm and affectionate. On the '76 trip some of the Indian cricketers were fortunate to be invited to his house in Barbados for a party which the boys thoroughly enjoyed, but what one did not enjoy afterwards was Gary's driving in his Jaguar car, through the narrow streets of Barbados when he was dropping us back to our hotel. The streets of Barbados are very narrow and also with sharp curves and the way the great Gary was driving we thought we would be lucky if the four of us in his car at that time reached the hotel safe. It was Prasanna who asked him why he drove so fast and how did he know that there was no other car coming from the opposite side when he was taking a sharp curve. Gary replied, "It's my nose, man, I can smell a car if it's coming the other way."

Whatever it was, his nose must have been sharper than ours as we had never smelt a car. All we knew is that we were happy that we reached back safely although those 15 minutes from the time we left his house till the time he dropped us back to our hotel were one of great discomfort and worry. But that is Gary. He lived his life like that, fast. He played his cricket fast and not only did he enjoy life but he also gave enjoyment to those who came to watch him play cricket

29

Syed Kirmani

In 1967, Ajit Naik, who was the captain of the Indian Schools team to England, invited me to meet the vice-captain of the team, but he warned me before that, 'don't be surprised, although we have a schoolboys team, the vice-captain smokes and so don't get upset by it at all'. Actually, I did not understand the reason why that should be surprising because lots of schoolboys get up to more mischief than smoking.

I was eventually introduced to Syed Mujtaba Hussein Kirmani. What struck me was the warmth of that person and his charm, the way he talked in typical Hyderabadi manner, very polite, bending down almost to the ground while being introduced and generally being very respectful. That impression of Kirmani has not changed over the years since he became a Test player and now what must be universally accepted even by the Australians and recognised as the best wicketkeeper in the world.

In the recently-concluded Prudential World Cup, he won

the best wicketkeeper of the tournament award and if proof be needed that he was the best wicketkeeper in the world, it was provided by this award. I say that he is the best wicketkeeper in the world for the simple reason that he has been keeping wickets to the spinners and keeping wickets extremely well, right for the seven-eight years since he has been playing Test cricket. Of course, like any other wicketkeeper, he has had a bad patch. In fact, he had a terrible series in 1976 in the West Indies. But the standard of wicketkeeping that he has displayed has been of the very highest order. The consistency he has shown over that period is enough proof that he is amongst the top wicketkeepers of all times.

Rodney Marsh must be having an edge on him because Marsh stands up to the faster bowlers and thus he is able to see the ball a little more when he brings out those incredible catches. But then Syed Kirmani has also brought off so many incredible catches off the medium-pacers when he is standing back. Where he scores over Rodney Marsh, is in keeping to the spinners.

To get back to Syed Kirmani's rise to Test cricket, that schoolboy tour of England in 1967 was highly successful for him and opened up the doors of the Ranji Trophy cricket for Mysore as soon as he returned. Mysore has been struggling to find at that time a good wicketkeeper, though Budhi Kunderan was keeping wickets. But Budhi, perhaps, found the duties of both wicketkeeper and captain rather strenuous and so he must have been very much relieved when Kirmani came on the scene.

Incredible though it may sound now, when Kirmani went to England with the Indian Schools team in 1967, he went in as a batsman and not as a wicketkeeper. They had two regular wicketkeepers in the side and it was known that

Kirmani could keep wickets. He was not picked as a wicketkeeper. But in the Mysore side they picked him as a wicketkeeper and he has not looked back since.

Kiri himself recalls how he started keeping wickets in the matches that the boys played in streets using a brick as a glove and that 'keeping glove' was harder than what he uses now. His beginning, therefore, has been right from the bottom rung and that's how it should really be since there are no short-cuts, no half-measures to the top.

Kirmani first came into prominence when he played in the Ranji Trophy match against Bombay in Bombay. He scored runs and kept wickets very competently and showed that his temperament was suited for the big time. That match against Bombay brought a lot of young players in the national reckoning, particularly Brijesh Patel and Kirmani, to name only two, while Vishwanath, who was already a Test star, once again proved his progress towards greatness in that particular match by scoring an incredible 95. Thus, with the all-India schools tour behind him and performance at the Ranji Trophy level brought Kirmani into focus and in the limelight to attract attention of the Test selectors.

When the Indian team was going to tour England in 1971, there was some doubt about Farokh Engineer's participation in all the matches of the tour and there was a tussle for the last spot in the team between Mohinder Amarnath and Syed Kirmani. Krishnamurthy had already been chosen as Engineer's deputy and another wicket-keeper was required only if Engineer was not available for the county games. Engineer was at that time only available for Test matches. Eventually, this was resolved when Lancashire C.C., for whom Engineer was playing, intimated that he would not be released for all the matches and that he would be released only for Tests and an odd game before the first Test. Thus, Mohinder Amarnath was dropped and Syed Kirmani came on the trip to England. He didn't have much scope on that tour because Krishnamurthy kept wickets in most of the county matches and Kirmani was there just to get some experience.

I remember a very funny incident. Syed is very fond of taking his afternoon nap and this he does religiously if the team is not on the field. And if the side is batting, you can safely assume that between lunch and tea, provided the situation is alright, and he is not required to bat, or be padded up, Kirmani would be in some corner of the dressing room fast asleep. On this tour, he was just doing that, sleeping in a corner when the late Ram Prakash Mehra, the second official on this tour, woke him up pretty roughly and asked him to watch Allan Knott. We were playing Kent then and he wanted Kirmani to watch Knott and improve. Mehra believed that Kirmani, who was then a youngster, could learn much by watching Knott. Kiri complied and got up, watched the proceedings with an air of boredom written all over his face and as soon as Ram Prakash Mehra got up to get a fresh packet of cigarettes, he slipped away into the physio room, stretched himself once again and was fast asleep. When Mehra got back, he could not find Kirmani and he inquired about his whereabouts. Someone said that Kiri was watching Allan Knott from near the sightscreen. Mehra was impressed by this and remarked that one has to push the youngsters a bit otherwise they will never try to learn.

We did not want to disillusion Mehra at all, but not watching Allan Knott at that stage or any of the other top cricketers, hasn't in any way affected Syed Kirmani. Because one can learn only a bit by watching the great players, but to assimilate that knowledge into your own game is extremely difficult. One has his own style, a set pattern of play and to change it after watching someone else is very difficult. To adopt good points from great players to improve your own game is to get mentally prepared for the same and just keep them in mind while having your own style.

Kirmani had to wait in the wings for a fairly long time, although he made another trip to England in 1974 as Engineer's deputy. The 1976 tour of New Zealand and West Indies found him as the first choice wicketkeeper ahead of Krishnamurthy, though the latter was on that tour and had been consistently the second wicketkeeper to Engineer. Engineer had not been picked as he could not come to India and play in the domestic cricket as stipulated by the Board then.

Kirmani was capped as a wicketkeeper in a Test match for the first time in the Auckland Test. He kept wickets confidently. His batting was also very spectacular and proved on many occasions that, as a batsman, he was difficult to be dislodged. It was, however, in the second Test of that series that he gave a superb display behind the wickets when the conditions were blistery, biting cold. Our spinners could not do well on that grassy wicket. They could not even turn the ball an inch as they could not grip the ball. Thus, we had to rely on our medium pacers who made life difficult for the New Zealanders. Kirmani took some excellent catches and one catch in particular, off Glenn Turner, was outstanding when he dived full length to his left to pick up a leg glance. This has now become a hallmark of Kirmani and his catching of the fine leg glances, with which a batsman normally expects to get him four runs, has now become legendary.

However, after this magnificent debut in the three-Test series in New Zealand, Kirmani's form somehow fell of when the team went to the West Indies. Viv Richards, who was to embark on his run-getting spree in that series, benefited by Kirmani's lapses and the main bowler to suffer was Venkataraghavan. In fact, the situation was such that in the last Test after Rafique Jumadeen skied the ball up in the air, between the wicketkeeper and myself, at leg slip, and when I made the catch, Venkat rushed and thanked me for taking the catch because Venkat had lost confidence in Kirmani's 'keeping in that particular series.

Perhaps, the memory of that series was in Venkat's mind when, as a captain, he was a party with the selection committee to drop Kirmani for the 1979 tour of England.

However, when Kirmani returned to India in 1976, his' keeping was once again at its best and the West Indies tour aberrations were soon forgotten. The cricket lovers at home then got to see with their own eyes that the country had found an adequate, if not better, replacement for Engineer. Kirmani, of course, was not the same kind of batsman as Engineer was. Engineer was flamboyant, dashing, in his approach and his shots were sometimes outrageous, very bold and very daring and he was a crowd pleaser. Kirmani's batting was more careful. His approach was merely push and prod, not that of a hit-for-four-runs approach. That meant that it was more difficult to get Kirmani out than Engineer because the latter's enthusiasm meant that he was prone to make the odd mistake here and there. Kirmani's mistakes were induced by a bowler.

In 1977-78, when the Indian team went to Australia, Kirmani's inclusion as a wicketkeeper batsman was certain. He was more than a useful batsman and many times down the order, he contributed handsomely and saw to it that the Indian team would reach a respectable total. His wicketkeeping on that tour was of the highest class and it was no wonder that when the World Series Cricket were looking for Indians to be part of its cricketing activities, Kirmani's name figured very prominently in that list. Kirmani thinks very carefully and after having weighed the pros and cons, he was prepared to join the WSC. The fact that it did not materialise and everything was sorted out between the WSC and the world cricket officials is another story.

That was used as an excuse, or so it appeared, when Kirmani was dropped from the team which went to England in 1979. If Sunil Gavaskar would have been captain of that Indian team, he would have been accused of regional considerations in dropping Kirmani. But in this particular instance, the captain and the manager came from the same State and the wicketkeeper to be the beneficiary from the dropping of Kirmani was also from the same State as that of the captain and the manager. At that stage, these facts didn't enter into anyone's mind. And why should it? For Sunil Gavaskar is the only captain who is thought capable of such regional considerations being shown and none else in Indian cricket is capable of showing such considerations when he is involved in picking a side!!! I am making these comments because the dropping of Kirmani in 1979 agitated my mind considerably and I felf the same way when Chetan Chauhan was dropped in 1981-82, as many cricket followers all over the country felt then.

There have been other selection omissions which have caused plenty of anguish, notably those of Karsan Ghavri and Dilip Vengsarkar, but these stories will have to wait for another book.

When Kirmani came to know that he had been axed from the tour of England, he was in a daze. He jumped into a taxi and asked the driver to drive anywhere, as long as he pleased. I do not know how much the taxi fare came to, but the damage caused to Kirmani's purse would not have been a fraction of the damage caused to him psychologically.

The Indian team to tour England in 1979 had to undergo a physical conditioning camp at Bangalore and Kirmani had arranged his wedding date during the camp so that he would be able to take his wife to England with him for a sort of cricketing honeymoon. These plans did not materialise and it was a tremendous blow to him mentally. But typically of the man, he came out bravely, fought back and worked hard to regain his place when the Australians came in 1979. Sent as a nightwatchman, he contributed an invaluable 65 and outlined his usefulness as a batsman as well.

He did not look back since then and in the last Test of that series he even scored his maiden Test century. This was when he was sent as a nightwatchman again and he responded in the humid heat of Bombay to score a brilliant hundred. That effort sapped his energies to such an extent that one found Kirmani on his knees in between deliveries when Kapil Dev walked back to his bowling mark to send the next delivery. It appeared at that time that Kirmani was saying his prayers, but in fact, he was so tired and the heat had so drained him off his energies that he was in no frame of mind to stand up. But he kept well and proved what a good 'keeper he has been over the years.

Since then he has been on the upgrade and everytime there is a talk of replacing him with another wicketkeeper, he comes back with a superlative performance to silence his critics.

The latest example being the World Cup which India won and his wicketkeeping was of the highest order and he won the best wicketkeeper award in the World Cup tournament and the presentation was made by no less a personality than Godfrey Evans, one of the greatest wicketkeepers of yester years.

Success in international cricket hasn't spoiled Kirmani. He is the same affable person that he was in 1967, showing the same courtesy, showing the same charm and ability of winning friends. He has plenty of friends spread all over the world and so too are his fans who have become his friends now. He has also made it a point to go wherever his fans are and meet them.

He is a very religious person and never forgets to say his prayers during the day. He has also made a couple of trips to Mecca in recent years. After his first trip to Mecca, he shaved his head and sheared his hair completely. He thus solved a sort of a problem. His receding and thinning hairline required him to comb his hair across the rest of the head when he disembarked from a plane or when he was waiting to be introduced to a guest or a VIP. It has become now easy for him as he need not worry about his hair flying away and exposing his balding pale. One thought that this would enable him to be punctual at functions or to be ready to leave with the team, but Kirmani just loves his sleep and it is not always that he is on time. The team members always laugh when he gives his excuses for being late and the bus or coach rolls away.

Kirmani has many, many years of international cricket ahead of him. He is very conscious of physical fitness and keeps himself in trim. He is not much of an eater and doesn't drink at all and his only vice, if it may be called so, is smoking, but in recent years he has been able to cut it down considerably.

It will be very difficult for any wicketkeeper in India to replace him in view of his recent form. I cannot visualise this barring an injury to him. Of course, little injuries do not bother him as such is his commitment to the Indian team.

When he was the vice-captain in the West Indies, he confessed that his ambition was to go to the top, be at the helm and get out by 1989. That is after six years and I sincerely hope that his ambition of becoming India's captain is fulfilled. His dedication is well-known, his ability is legendary and I am certain that his experience which has been gained over the years will certainly help him in achieving his ambition. I wish him well. I also wish to express now great an admirer I have been of his cricketing abilities and I also pray that he goes on and on as long as he wishes to.

30

Vivian Richards

When the Indian team arrived in England in 1974, one of the first games they played was at Eastbourne against a Robbin's XI. During this game which was captained by Brian Close who was also captaining Somerset, he was asked what kind of a team he had. And Brian Close, normally not a man to waste his breath praising cricketers, went on raving about a young West Indian lad who was making his debut for Somerset and who he thought would be one of the best batsmen the world would ever see.

There were knowing glances exchanged by the other county cricketers who were present as if to convey the impression that, well, this is what Brian thinks — it doesn't have to be necessarily true. But I knew that this was something that had to be taken very seriously because in 1971 Brian Close had given us a tip about a horse which then came through at the unbelievable odds of 14 to 1.

I remember that very vividly simply because I had my wallet picked just the day before which left me penniless and it was only because of the tip Brian Close gave that I requested another teammate to put a pound for me and ended up getting the odds.

That was a bet which came in very handy and I knew then that Brian Close does not waste his words. So when he talked about Viv Richards in such glowing terms even before Viv had played first class cricket for the county, we knew that we would get to see a star when we played in Taunton later on in the summer.

It was bitterly cold in Taunton when we did land up there and Viv was seen loitering about in the covers, very quick on his feet and very eager to get on with the game. When his turn came in to bat, he smashed Abid Ali imperiously through mid on for four and the crowd just sat back expecting some more fireworks. However, Abid had the last laugh when he forced Viv to play another attacking shot off the back foot at a ball which was pitched up for that kind of a shot and the resulting inside edge spread-eagled his stumps.

So we saw Viv Richards for a very short period and one could not form any impressions about his batting though his fielding was outstanding. Later on in the summer one came to know that he had been picked for the West Indies team touring India later on and one looked forward to see how this man had made progress.

He became the first West Indian to get a 100 on that tour in the first match itself and although the West Zone attack wasn't exactly menacing, one could see that the young man had adapted himself very well to the wickets and the shift in the bowling from pace to spin. He looked a predominantly on-side player but he also cut the ball well.

But even in spite of his scoring a 100 one did not expect him to be picked in the side ahead of people like Lawrence Rowe, Alvin Kallicharran, Clive Lloyd, etc. But it was during the same game in Poona that a defect in Lawrence Rowe's eye was detected and Rowe had to fly back to London to get his eye treated which left a batting place vacant for the West Indies, and Viv Richards, with his hundred as well as his brilliant fielding, was a certainty to play.

His Test debut was certainly not as auspicious as a batsman — Chandra got him out quickly in both the innings. But his debut was memorable for his fielding. In the Indian first innings he caught both the openers, Farokh and myself, brilliantly and treated the Bangalorians to as fine a spectacle in fielding as one could see when he was in the outfield. His running, picking up and throwing on the turn and throwing on the run were unbelievable. The power of his throws was to be seen in the way Derek Murray wrung his gloves every time he received a ball from him from the outfield.

The West Indies won that Test largely due to a superlative innings of 163 by Clive Lloyd which turned the scales completely in the West Indies' favour and when the second Test came along, Viv Richards decided to announce himself to the cricketing world and to the bowlers of the Test nations that a new star had arrived.

192 was the number of runs he scored. But more than that it was the manner in which he scored those runs that were memorable. I was injured after having been appointed to lead the side in place of Tiger Pataudi who was also injured but I decided to make the trip in any case — and what a wonderful sight it was to see Viv Richards playing.

Bishan Bedi had been recalled to the Indian side after having been dropped for disciplinary reasons in the first Test at Bangalore and he, Venkat and Chandrasekhar were a formidable attack Yet, Viv treated them in a cavalier fashion particularly after he got his hundred. He was watchful, but never dull till he reached his 100. But once he reached that magic figure he just seemed to go berserk and was smashing everything out of sight. To Venkat, he just stepped out on the track and lofted the ball into the adjoining football ground — a hit which must be at least a 100 yards if not more.

He also lifted Bedi and Chandrasekhar into the crowds for huge sixes. There were four sixes in his 192 and many other attractive shots. The West Indies won that one also with ease.

The Indian team came back in the third Test, thanks to a great century by Viswanath and his fighting partnership with Karsan Ghavri. The West Indies started very confidently and it was Viv Richard's dismissal — two short of his fifty — that turned the tide in India's favour, from which India did not look back for the next couple of Tests.

The third and fourth Tests were also won by India to level the series with one Test to be played. This was the fifth Test at Wankhede Stadium in Bombay, a new venue, and all kinds of doubts were expressed about the quality of the wicket and about the stadium. All these doubts were proved wrong and the West Indies won this rather high-scoring — high scoring in the first innings — game rather comfortably midway through the last day.

Clive Lloyd scored a mammoth 242 not out and with that effort a brilliant 100 by Roy Fredricks was overshadowed as also Viv Richards' two little gems in both the innings. His effort in the second innings when he scored 30-odd runs in half an hour, playing shots which have now become his hallmark — moving away to the leg side and hitting the ball through the offside — were played with such ease and with such a carefree attitude that even in the opposition one could not but admire the man who played such shots.

The West Indies duly won that Test and with that the series. And at the end of the series Viv Richards had justified his inclusion in the West Indian side. He had just one big hundred to his name but plenty of other 30s or 40s.

Somehow he seemed to be getting rushes of blood to his head when he was in his 30s and 40s to try for an ambitious shot and get out when a little more care would have assured another 100 for him.

His impetuosity got the better of him on those occasions and fortunately for India, these periods seemed to come more often when he was in his 30s or 40s.

When we next played against him in 1976 all the old impetuosity was gone. The aggressiveness was still there but it was tempered to the extent that one thought that Viv was a little predetermined in the choice of ball to defend.

During his Test century in Barbados, his first of the series, he seemed to be able to despatch the good balls into the crowd, yet when the half volley was bowled he would block it very meticulously, very religiously, almost copybook fashion. This was perhaps his way of tempering himself and telling himself to play a long innings and not get carried away.

He was the scourge of our attack and he scored runs in every Test match that we played. He had a 100 in the first Test, he had a 100 in the second Test, and he had a 100 in the third Test. And he looked like getting a 100 in the fourth Test as well when he was 60-odd runs before he got out. And thank God for that!

But it was amazing to see this man play such long innings. Just a year and a half before it looked very unlikely that this man would like to be kept quiet but here in this series there were periods when he went scoreless for 15 to 20 minutes, but it didn't seem to bother him. In the series in India in '74, if more than a couple of overs were bowled without him having scored you could bet he would try and play a funny shot and try and get some runs. But all that had vanished and he was looking more solid than ever before. We came to know that he had taken some hypno-therapy in Australia which enabled him to gain confidence and crack almost 250 runs in the last two Test matches that he played including one hundred and another near hundred and he had caught on the century habit. This was evident because after our series he went to England immediately and plundered over 800 runs in just four Test matches. Over there, being sick and therefore not being able to play the Lord's Test in 1976. 800 runs in England is certainly a tremendous achievement because the Englishmen don't make things easy at all for you. They are professional bowlers, they pride themselves on their professionalism, and when they know that they can't get you out they trv to see that you don't score too many runs off them and try and keep you tied so that you lose your patience and get out playing a foolish shot. The fact that Viv was not only able to keep scoring runs, and score them in such a big volume, indicates his complete mastery over their attack.

The summer was one of the best summers they have ever had. There was hardly a day in the entire summer when it rained, when a match was interrupted because of rain, and for the West Indians, who, like the Indians, are used to having the sun on their backs, this was, indeed, a God send. How they managed to make use of this freak weather in England is well chronicled and the outstanding performances of the tour were by Viv Richards in the batting department and by Michael Holding and Andy Roberts in the bowling department.

The side was superbly led by Clive Lloyd and they just did not give England a chance at all. They just completely cleaned up the series and they seemed to have been spurred on by the comments of Tony Greig who, before the West Indian team arrived in England, said that the West Indians were susceptible to pressure and that he would make them grovel. Now grovel is a word which we all know is derogatory particularly to the West Indian race and this seemed to make the West Indians try all that harder. It's no wonder then that Viv Richards was not happy with just 230 in the first Test but went on to score 291 and I think getting out at 291 must not have been as painful to him as the fact that he got out bowled to Tony Greig.

Whenever Tony Greig came out to bat Michael Holding, Andy Roberts and all the big bowlers would find extra strength and bowl yards faster at this man who had uttered those words. Many times in that series one found Greig's stumps were sent flying away before his bat came down, so quick were the balls delivered by the West Indian fast bowlers. Yet, for the West Indian fast bowler, to be able to bowl consistently, with attacking fields, one needed that the West Indians would boast big totals and this was where the genius of Viv Richards came into play. He missed out on the Lord's Test but scored runs in just about every other Test match with two double centuries and a century and an innings of 60 in the Headingley Test where on a whole day's play the West Indians plundered almost 400 runs. Something unique as far as today's Test match scoring rates are concerned.

Viv Richards was the one man that the English team had to get rid of, and Viv never really gave them the pleasure unless he was well past his hundred and the West Indies were well established on their way to a big score. Although he missed out on the Lord's Test because of a virus he made up for this absence by scoring a hundred the next time he played at Lord's in a Test match and that was in 1980 when his 145 was a superlative innings and was one of the best innings that England has seen in recent years. But Viv Richards, like all great players had to go through a fairly lean patch by his own standards, and that came about in 1977 when the Pakistan team was touring the West Indies. Now after all his big scores the previous season, everybody expected him to plunder the Pakistan bowling on the West Indian wickets but in fact Viv's highest score in the series was a 90-odd and he failed to touch a hundred which was remarkable because at no stage did he look as if he was batting badly. But the old impatience seemed to have crept in and with it the desire to try and dominate the bowler from the first ball. The papers also said that he had become a little over-confident, but who wouldn't become over-confident after having scored almost 1,800 runs in the whole of the previous year? But this was just one of those phases which every batsman goes through and Viv went through that although he had a harrowing time at the hands of the West Indian spectators who expected their champion to just blast the Pakistan attack and were therefore disappointed, and some were pretty vocal in showing their disappointment. The pressure on Viv was therefore increased and he wasn't happy with the way the West Indian public had received his efforts against Pakistan

It was during this time that the famous Packer episode took place and the entire West Indian team signed up to play for Packer This in effect meant that Viv missed out on a few Test matches. For example, the West Indian team that toured India in 1978-79. I'm sure, he would have scored a packet of runs. India, at that stage, were going through a phase when their spinners were on their way out and Kapil Dev was just making his mark, it was just the kind of attack that Viv would have loved and unfortunately for the Indian spectators but fortunately for the Indian team, Viv was not there because of his commitment to World Series Cricket. He was playing in Australia and was scoring a lot of runs against the Australian teams on wickets which were hard, lively and bouncy, just the kind of wicket he likes.

When the Australian team came to West Indies in 1978, the West Indian Board had decided to accept the World Series Cricket players and Viv, along with the West Indian colleagues, was back in the West Indian side. His duel with Thompson in the first Test was memorable and it was mainly because Thompson was inspired with a batsman of Viv Richards' class at the other end, to bowl some of the fastest overs he bowled ever since his unfortunate accident where he damaged his shoulder.

Viv did not come out of the battle unscarred though one shot of his, a parallel hook into the stands, proved how he was unafraid of the fastest deliveries. When a bowler like Thompson is firing on all cylinders even great batsmen like Viv Richards find him difficult to handle. This was one of the Tests where Thompson got the better of Viv Richards. However, after a couple of Tests, the old problem of the World Series Cricket surfaced when the players refused to give in writing that they would be available for the Indian tour later on in the year and which meant that the West Indian Selection Committee had no option but to try other players who would be available for the tour of India later on in the winter. So Viv and company were out after playing the first two Test matches and this was quite a blow to the West Indian spectators who showed what they thought of the series by attending in very few numbers the remaining three Test matches. The series was won by the West Indies by the margin of 3-1 and the last three Test matches were much closer because the West Indians did not have their full strength side.

In the winter Viv went away again to Australia and played another season of World Series Cricket. Another exciting season where the West Indians dominated the Australian team, but the matches were much closer than the previous season.

In 1979 after the West Indies had a fairly ineffective tour of India it was decided to call all the WSC players back into the fold for the World Cup, the inaugural World Cup in 1975 having been won by the West Indies, the West Indian Board and the West Indian public wanted the best West Indian side sent across so that the World Cup be retained.

In the final in 1975 Viv Richards had not contributed a great deal with the bat but his brilliant fielding had accounted for the Chappell brothers being run out when both were looking dangerous for the West Indies team. And in 1979 Viv Richards was already the best batsman in the world and what a place to prove that once more and with emphasis. He scored a brilliant 138 and those who have seen that innings will never forget the last two shots which he played. He flicked a six off the last ball of the 60 overs. He moved away to the off stump and as Mike Hendrick banged down the inevitable yorker, Viv was quickly into position, he converted it into a full toss and flicked it over the square leg boundary for a six.

That was one incredible shot, but even more incredible shots had been seen during Viv's earlier part of the innings and in his partnership with Collis King. The ball was regularly beaten against the boundary boards of the Lord's cricket ground. It was West Indian batting at its exciting best and Collis King and Viv Richards, in spite of the fact that West Indians were under pressure at that stage, proved that strokes could be played and played without any nervousness. Both of them played the kind of innings the West Indian public have been privileged to see and what the rest of the world hears about. This was the kind of approach that has made the West

Indians so popular all over the world and that's how they won the World Cup

In '79, of course, the West Indians had the formidable fast bowling quartet of Roberts, Holding, Croft and Garner and they weren't let down at all by these four who saw to it that not many runs were scored against them by any team.

And that is precisely what happened, they virtually ran away with the World Cup in '79, finding very little opposition from anybody In '75 they had a little problem with Pakistan which they scraped through thanks to Derek Murray and Andy Roberts for keeping their heads about But in 1979 they had very little opposition and they just ran through the World Cup.

That winter Viv was again in Australia, it almost seemed that he was due to go to Australia every winter And that winter he played official Tests because the previous two winters he'd been playing WSC which was not recognised by the international cricket boards. But here in this season organised after a settlement had been reached between the WSC authorities and the Australian Cricket Board a series was organised with the West Indian and England teams called to participate in a triangular tournament where the Australians would play three Tests against the West Indies and three against England along with a number of one-day matches which would be triangular matches played between the three teams.

The West Indies not only won the Benson and Hedges championship for the one-day cricket but they also won three Test matches that they played against the Australians and they never looked in any danger at all Viv was not fit having a problem with his back and his thigh but still managed to score a brilliant 140 virtually on one leg and then contributed his bit in the field by diving to his left and snapping up Allan Border. These were truly the efforts of a man who has the good of his side at heart and Viv has always been a man who has played for his side.

His innings of 140 included memorable shots again — a flat bat hook off Jeff Thompson at his fastest which went between mid on and mid wicket was the shot of the match, and so also a flick off Lillee when Lillee pitched the ball a shade up and bisected through mid on and mid wicket. The Australian bowlers thought that Viv was not so hot on the off side and fed him on the off stump. Viv was there with his cover drives and thumping straight drives and it was a lesson in batting for all the youngsters who were privileged to watch that innings.

Also memorable of Viv's efforts in Australia that year was a 153 he took off the Australian attack in a one-day game. To score a hundred in a limited-over-game is a very rare thing. Not, of course, for Viv, but for most batsmen. Viv not only topped a hundred but went on to score 50 more runs! And he and Greenidge just demolished the Australian attack and made the victory for the West Indians a mere formality.

By this time Viv had been appointed the vice-captain of the West Indian team, recognising the authority that he wielded with the bat and the respect and command he got from the West Indian players.

In 1980 when Clive Lloyd brought the West Indians over for a full Test series in England Viv got a chance to lead in the last Test after Lloyd had pulled a muscle in his leg, and Viv therefore captained his country for the first time. Lloyd was not always at his best in this series, suffering from muscular injuries though he scored a brilliant hundred in the Old Trafford Test, his second home, Lancashire. Viv was the man who set the crowds alight with his knock of 145 in the Lord's Test. It was a joy to behold the way he smashed Bob Willis. And he continued it in the next Test though he got out bowled to Ian Botham in his 60s. This was one of the inexplicable dismissals of Viv when he looked so much in command and completely in control. It was therefore a surprise to see him get out in that series for anything less than a hundred.

By this time he was universally acknowledged as the best batsman in the world and he proved it again when the England team went down to the West Indies in the winter by thrashing two hundreds off their attack. The second hundred being one made specially for the occasion of Antigua's first ever Test match. Viv hails from Antigua and the people of Antigua had only read about and maybe seen a little bit of Viv on film and television and were getting the opportunity to see their hero bat in a Test with their own eyes. And Viv did not let them down. He scored a hundred although it looked at one stage that the hundred would come in less than a hundred minutes. That was the way he started, he had seven fours in his first 28 runs and he looked in superb touch but suddenly he seemed to realise that too much of a good thing would not be the right way to try and get a hundred, maybe over-confidence might creep in and so he played a game which was different to his usual game. He waited and waited for the loose ball. It looked almost as if he was determined to see that he got out for nothing less than a hundred which he eventually did. He scored the hundred and whole of Antigua went wild.

Before that, of course, Antigua had another reason to celebrate when Viv married his childhood sweetheart Mirium and according to reports it looked as if the entire population of Antigua had turned up for the wedding though obviously not everyone could have been invited for the wedding! But nobody would have wanted to miss the wedding of their prince. That's how dear Viv is to the population of Antigua.

My only season in county cricket came about because Viv was going to be with the West Indies team in 1980 for the major part of the season and so I was required to play only for the time Viv would be away from the Somerset side. I enjoyed that period and even after Viv had returned I was with Somerset and one of my abiding memories is of sharing a flat with Joel Garner and the West Indian contingent in the Somerset side turning up religiously every evening for a meal cooked by Joel.

I have never been embarrassed about my being a very poor eater but the only time I really felt embarrassed was when Viv, Joel, Hugh Gore and Hallam Moseley used to come over to the flat and have their meals. The way they tucked into their food was a sight to be seen and in spite of the huge quantities they consumed they never seemed to put on weight, the waists seemed to be as narrow as ever and the quantity consumed did not seem to add on at all to their waists.

They would be joking and laughing all the time while eating and in typical West Indian style the laughter would not be just a static laughter but a laughter where the whole body had to take part and so while laughing either of them would go under the table, crumple under the table in fact, and while the person was thus crumpled under the table with laughter somebody would pick up the food from his plate and eat it himself. It was truly an incredible sight and something which I'll never forget.

I confined myself to toast and tea that time mainly to avoid being dubbed a poor eater by them because I would have really been embarrassed to eat or pick at my food which I normally do. Yet, I just couldn't help but admire the way they ate and it is something which amazes me because the effect of the eating would not tell on their waists at all. If I eat a little more than usual the effect is instantaneous and I can always feel the bulge coming over. But nothing seems to happen to

Viv whose waist seems to be the same as when one saw him in 1974. He's, of course, very deceptively strong. From a distance he doesn't look very big because when blokes like Clive Lloyd and Colin Croft and Holding are around he looks smaller than them but as you come closer to Viv you realise what a barrel chest he's got and those muscular arms stare at you straightaway.

Viv is also very fond of dressing well, he's got an incredible wardrobe and if I'm told correctly, he never wears the same shirt twice in a county season. That must mean that he must possess an unbelievable variety. It is very true to believe that because one sees him always immaculately dressed. A briefcase is his constant companion as he gets involved into the business aspect of being a cricketer and Viv today must have a few pounds saved up in the bank.

I know the Indian public is waiting anxiously to see this great player again and the opportunity will be there in 1983-84 when the West Indian team is due to tour India and I have a feeling that at that time Clive Lloyd will have called it a day and it will be Viv Richards who will be leading the side to India.

As we go to press we learn that Lloyd has been reappointed the captain and Viv is the vice-captain which perhaps is good because then Viv can concentrate on making runs and showing the Indian crowds why he is the best in the world.

31

Zaheer Abbas

My only Test wicket and probably the only Test wicket that will be credited to me is Zaheer Abbas. The great man was on 96 in the second innings, and was set for the second century of the match having scored 176 in the first innings in the first Test at Faisalabad between India and Pakistan on the 1978 tour. That wicket is still etched in my memory. It was more a moment of sorrow than a moment of joy for me.

Zaheer has been a personal friend since we toured together with the Rest of the World team in Australia. For me to get his wicket when he was just four short of a landmark was most painful. I still remember the ball. It was just an innocuous delivery. I am still surprised as to how Zaheer mishit that delivery. Earlier on with the match petering out into a draw, I had been fooling around a bit with different versions of a run-up. There was a bowler who used to bowl at the Hindu Gymkhana and I was trying to mimic him with his leg-breaks. Suddenly, in this over, I decided to bowl with my normal run-up and bowled one to which Zaheer came down the track to loft straight over the bowler's head, for the boundary which would have given him his hundred, but instead he managed to get an edge and the ball went to Chetan Chauhan at mid-on for a catch. Normally that ball would have been or should have been hit anywhere. Zaheer could have driven it along the ground or he could have flicked it past the mid-wicket or he could have still cover-driven it. But why he tried to lift it over my head is still a mystery to me. There was still time left for a few more overs during which he could have definitely got his hundred. Though he has not yet scored a century in each innings of a Test, he has the enviable record of scoring a double century and century in a match on four occasions. And this is a world record and I don't think anybody has got near this. His consistency is amazing. Today, he has over 100 hundreds in first class cricket to his credit and he is the first Asian to join the ranks of those who have scored a hundred hundreds. It was an achievement treated with pride in India and Pakistan. At last an Asian had joined the select band of those who have scored a hundred hundreds.

Zaheer Abbas came into prominence on the 1971 tour of England by Pakistan. In his first Test against England he hammered 274 runs and I have always asked him as to how he got out at 274 Was it out of fatigue or was it due to over confidence? He told me that he tried to sweep Illingworth and somehow the ball came a little slower than he had expected. It took an edge and he was caught at square-leg. Zaheer is very, very fond of setting up records and he had the record of 365 before his eyes when he got out. Because he is so energetic and his concentration so amazing, that it was not a surprise when in 1974 he went on to crack 240 against England and this time he again disappointed by not going on to a triple hundred by chopping a ball from Underwood on to his stumps. The next double hundred came against India when he scored 235 not out at Lahore. This was another brilliant, strokeful innings. And the declaration came as Pakistan were going for victory, the first Test having ended in a draw, Pakistan had to declare and give us some time before knocking us out. That they did it is now history and that is how the stalemate of draws was broken in this match at Lahore of the 1978 series.

I first met Zaheer when he was brought to our dressing room at the Oval in the 1971 Test by Abid Ali. Zaheer at that stage was much more thinner than what he is now. And everyone just wondered how this frail-looking man could have scored 274 runs that year. When you shook hands with him you could feel the strength in his wrists. When we saw clips of his 274 and saw those wristy shots we knew how those runs had come. We got along fairly well at that stage and we both found ourselves in the Rest of the World team that toured Australia in 1971 when the Australian Board withdrew the invitation to South Africa and the Rest team was hurriedly got through after the English season to replace the South Africans. Right from those days we got along well and even today we are very close friends.

Over in Australia, Zaheer dominated the initial matches with plenty of runs and the fastish Australian wickets seemed to suit his style of play. As the ball came up, he was able to deflect it over his hips or drive it on the up. He had a most peculiar looking flick shot to anything pitched on the legs at that stage, because he was committed on the front foot and therefore if he wanted to flick it he was a sort of hopping and jumping at the same time hitting the ball with enough punch past the square-leg umpire for a boundary. As far as his off-side strokes were concerned, they were mainly in the cover region and very seldom did he straight-drive or off-drive a ball. All the runs were scored from the extra-cover region onwards and he got most of his runs with that shot and the flick shots. He was not afraid to hook, though he employed that shot on rare occasions if the ball was really a short one and he was confident of hooking it.

In the first Test he did not get too many runs and in the second he was going on well when he was run out. In the early days his calling was not in the top drawer. His calling was not as precise as his batting was. In the third Test he was dismissed cheaply in the first innings as at that stage of his career he was found vulnerable to an outswinger pitched well up and he tried to drive without getting into proper position and edged the ball quite often to the slips or the wicketkeeper. But in the second innings of this Melbourne Test he was the one who took the sting out of Dennis Lillee's bowling making 86 before he was out to a wild-looking shot and was caught in the slips and thus missed a hundred. That was most unlike a Zaheer shot because when he gets near the magic figure, he seemed to concentrate more and has nc nerves in the nervous nineties. He used to get through that with just a few attacking shots to his hundred. In this case, though he was out for 86, and in the fourth Test he did not get many runs, but he got a fifty in the fifth Test but he showed another facet, his weakness, when he was talked out by the Australians. Keith Stackpole was giving him a bit of lip for the way Zaheer had played a few shots earlier on and Zaheer was trying to hit Stackpole out of the ground when he was bowled. Stackpole had won a tactical victory. Thereafter, Zaheer and I kept in touch whenever we were in England. But the most important point was when the 1971 tour was on, the third war between India and Pakistan broke out. A new nation, Bangladesh, was born and that was the time our friendship was put to test because we used to get conflicting reports from people as to the way the war was going. That was the time when we were tensed and as the eyes of the media were on us, our friendship was seen in its true colours. All of us, Asif Masood, Intikhab Alam, Bishan Bedi, myself and Zaheer used to go out together to a Pakistani restaurant for snacks and dinner and not once did we talk about the war though Bishan seemed to be understandably worried because Amritsar, where he lived, is very close to the border. Never was the topic of war ever discussed amongst us. At the end of the tour on a general discussion on politics, Zaheer had something to say about our leaders and I had to express my opinion about Pakistan. Of course, these were not opinions of any earth-shaking nature but opinions of individuals who were following the fortunes of both the countries and we were just expressing it in a manner of discussion.

Zaheer signed up for Gloucestershire for whom he has been playing for the last ten years with great success. On the 1974 tour of England the Pakistanis had a very strong side led by Mushtaq Mohammad. In addition to a strong batting line-up, they had a very good bowling side and though they did not have anybody of genuine speed, Imran had still to find his confidence of bowling genuinely quick, they had bowlers well enough for the English conditions. Well they did not win the series, despite scoring well in two of the Test matches. After not scoring well in the first two matches, Zaheer came with a bang in the last Test and thereby erasing all his previous failures. Thereafter, Zaheer seemed to go in a bit of decline as far as his batting form was concerned because he did not hit a century for a long, long time though he got very near that figure against the Australians in 1976. Against the West Indians too when the Pakistan team went there in 1976-77, he was not able to score too many runs. In fact, he was injured, he had a broken toe. He was also lucky that he was not drowned in a tragedy because he and Wasim

Bari while surfing had met with an accident. They were carried away by waves but fortunately rescued by the lifeguards. Otherwise, the world would not have seen the magnificence of Zaheer Abbas after that. When he came back to Pakistan, he had to play against the Indians. Scores of 176 and 96 in the first Test, 235 not out in the second was ample proof of the man's awesome ability. He scored over 500 runs in the three Test mini-series and he was the man responsible for destroying our fearful spinners.

In 1977, there was a bit of controversy when the Pakistanis were released by Kerry Packer from their contracts so as to enable them to assist Pakistan against England who were touring Pakistan. But the Englishmen did not want to play against the "deserters" of Test cricket so the Pakistani professionals were not included. In any case, Zaheer's arrival in Pakistan created a storm of protests though the Test eventually went on peacefully. The point was not lost on the Pakistan Board that they would have to invite their WSC players to play against India. Unfortunately for India, they all came and reinforced the team and saw that the Indian team had no real chance.

When the Pakistan team was due to play in India in 1979-80, the two players we were really worried of were Javed Miandad and Zaheer Abbas. While we could plan a bit of strategy for Zaheer Abbas, try and curb his run-making, it was almost impossible to think of such a plan for Javed Miandad. The plan to curb Zaheer's strokes succeeded in a large measure due to excellent bowling of Kapil Dev and Karsan Ghavri, supported by Dilip Doshi. The bowlers bowled to a plan and, fortunately for us, Zaheer fell in the trap so much so that the Zaheer Abbas we knew in Pakistan in 1978 was nowhere in evidence. We are told in the last Test he did not want to play and made way for another player. It was typical of Zaheer who had always kept the interest of the team before his personal interest. All cricketers who score profusely give an impression that they are worried only about their individual scores. That is not always the case and Zaheer Abbas is a prime example that comes to my mind of a player who plays for his side rather than for himself.

Thereafter, Zaheer had a wonderful season with Gloucestershire scoring ten hundreds and there was a period when he scored 1,500 runs in a month. This was an amazing sequence of run-making even by Zaheer's standard and his greed for runs does not seem to diminish at all. The Indian public was disappointed that they could not see this great player in action as much as they wanted to but the Indian players and the bowlers were very happy that Zaheer Abbas kept on getting out match after match.

The Indians returned the visit in 1982-83 and once again found "Ted" as he is known in the cricketing world, in great form. With a double hundred in the first Test he became the first Asian to hit a century of centuries. If we thought that he would stop there we were mistaken because with another two centuries Ted amassed over 600 runs and also became the first Pakistani to score 4,000 runs in Test cricket.

He has one ambition and that is to score a Test century in India. So come September Kapil and Co. will have to watch out for this gentle, smiling murderer.

REVIEWS OF SUNNY DAYS

"...The book should keep the reader engrossed throughout"

—Sportsweek

"...most interesting and full of anecdotes"

—The Statesman

"...an interesting and revealing book which every cricket lover will read with pleasure"

—Hindustan Times

"...a valuable book"

—Indian Express

"...this book will be of great value to all cricke - ters particularly the youngsters"

—Hindu

"...a best seller"

—Times of India

Rs. 20.00

OTHER Rupa PAPERBACKS

ADVENTURE

	: Modern Adventurers	15.00
	: World Adventurers	15.00
KENNETH ANDERSON	: Man-Eaters and Jungle Killers	16.00
	: Nine Man-Eaters and One Rogue	16.00
	: Jungles Long Ago	FC
	: The Black Panther of Sivanipalli	16.00
	: The Call of the Man-Eater	16.00
	: This is the Jungle	16 00
	: Tales from the Indian Jungle	FC
	: Tiger Roars	FC

ANTHROPOLOGY

MILES BURKITT	:The Old Stone Age	12.00

BUSINESS & MANAGEMENT

B.H. ELVY	: Marketing Made Simple	25.00
W.F. COVENTRY	: Management Made Simple	25.00
D. WAINWRIGHT	: Journalism Made Simple	25.00
K. HOYLE & G. WHITEHEAD	: Money & Banking Made Simple	25.00
PROF DUNCAN	: How to Conduct Meetings: Company, Club, Political and Social	8.00

J.B. DURYEA	: How to Solicit: A Must for all Insurance selling agents and Salesmen	10.00
MRITYUNJOY BANERJEE	: Essentials of Modern Marketing	23.00
P.K. GHOSH	: Government & Industry	12.00

CIVIL ENGINEERING

E.H. WILLIAMSON	: Data Book for Pipe Fitters and Pipe Welders	12.00
C.E. REYNOLDS	: Reinforced Concrete Designer's Handbook	125.00

COOKING

PREMILA LAL	: Indian Recipes	16.00

CRITICISM & ESSAYS

TARAKNATH SEN	: Three Essays on Shakespeare	12.00
BERTAND RUSSELL	: Mortals & Other Essays	12.00

DRAMA

OSCAR WILDE	: Complete Plays	20.00

EDUCATION

CHARLES & MARY LAMB	: Tales from Shakespeare	15.00
D. BOWSKILL	: Photography Made Simple	30.00
F. JEFKINS	: Advertising Made Simple	25.00
H.J.C. GRIERSON	: Shakeaspear's Macbeth	12.00
HUGH JARRETT	: How to Write English	9.00
IVAN ILLICH	: Energy & Equity	6.00
	: The Right to useful Unemployment	16.00

IVAN ILLICH & OTHERS	: Education Without Schools	10.00
W.R. GONDIN & E.W. MAMMEN	: The Art of Speaking Made Simple	25.00
PROF. DUNCAN	: How to Spell Correctly	8.00

FICTION (Classics)

ALEXANDER DUMAS	: The Man in the Iron Mask	FC
	: The Three Musketeers	30.00
CHARLES DICKENS	: A Tale of Two Cities	20.00
	: David Copperfield	30.00
	: Great Expectations	16.00
	: Hard Times	16.00
	: Oliver Twist	20.00
	: Pickwick Papers	30.00
CHARLOTTE BRONTE	: Jane Eyre	RP
DANIEL DEFOE	: Robinson Crusoe	FC
D.H. LAWRENCE	: Sons & Lovers	15.00
EMILY BRONTE	: Wuthering Heights	15.00
GEORGE ELIOT	: Adam Bede	FC
	: The Mill on the Floss	20.00
	: Silas Marner	RP
HENRY FIELDING	: Tom Jones	RP
JANE AUSTEN	: Emma	15.00
	: Pride and Prejudice	16.00
	: Sense and Sensibility	15.00
JEROME K JEROME	: Three Men in a Boat	12.00
JULES VERNES	: Around the World in Eighty Days	FC
JOHN BUNYAN	: The Pilgrim's Progress	16.00
JONATHAN SWIFT	: Gulliver's Travels	16.00
LEWIS CARROLL	: Alice in Wonderland & Through the Looking Glass	FC

MAUPASSANT	: A Woman's Life	12.00
MARK TWAIN	: Tom Sawyer and	
	: Huckleberry Finn	FC
RIDER HAGGARD	: She	15.00
ROBERT L STEVENSON	: Treasure Island	15.00
W.M. THACKERAY	: Vanity Fair	16.00
THOMAS HARDY	: Tess of the D'Urbervilles	20.00

FICTION (other Novels)

BIMAL JYOTI DAS	: The Rose and The Lily	7.00
J.C. POWYS	: All or Nothing	3.00

FICTION (Crime Detection and Mystery)

ALISTAIR MACLEAN	: Athabasca	12.00
	: Goodbye California	15.00
	: Partisans	12.00
	: River of Death	12.00
	: Floodgate	15.00
ALBERTO MORAVIA	: Time of Desecration	20.00
CZESLAW MILOSZ	: The Issa Valley	20.00
DESMOND BAGLEY	: Bahama Crisis	12.00
	: The Enemy	15.00
	: Flyaway	15.00
	: Windfall	15.00
EUGENE IONESCO	: The Hermit	12.00
HELEN MACINNES	: Agent in Place	10.00
JOHN LE CARRE	: The Little Drummer Girl	20.00
JACKIE COLLINS	: Hollywood Wives	30.00
JACK HIGGINS	: Touch the Devil	15.00
	: Exocet	15.00
JAMES JONES	: Whistle	18.00
ROBIN COOK	: Fever	20.00
	: Godplayer	20.00
SALMAN RUSHDIE	: Shame	30.00
SIDNEY SHELDON	: Master of the Game	25.00

HISTORY

A.L. BASHAM	: The Wonder That Was India	60.00
DR. B.N. PANDEY	: A Book of India	30.00
DURGA DAS	: India from Curzon to Nehru & After	25.00

HOBBY

	: The Big Book of Luck & Fortune	15.00
LAURENCE MALLORY	: The Rightway to Use a Camera	12.00

LANGUAGES

E. JACKSON & A. RUBIO	: French Made Simple	30,00
E. JACKSON & A. GEIGER	: German Made Simple	25.00

MEMOIRS

CZESLAW MILOSZ	: Native Realm	20.00

MEDICAL

DR WU WEI-P'ING	: Chinese Acupuncture	FC
D L WOOD & J L WOOD	: Acupuncture Handbook	15.00
J W. ARMSTRONG	: The Water of Life	10.00
MARGERY G. BLACKIE	: The Patient, Not the Cure: The Challenge of Homoeopathy	16.00
F.W. POWELL	: Biochemic Prescriber	9.00

PARAPSYCHOLOGY & RELIGION

DR. GOUR MOHON DAS DE	: Departed,Soul In The Land of Mystery	18.00

PARAPSYCHOLOGY & RELIGION

Author	Title	Price
CORNELIA DIMMITT & J.A.B. VAN BUITENEN	: Classical Hindu Mythology	30.00
JOHN DOWSON	: A Classical Dictionary of Hindu Mythology and Religion	30.00
W.J. WILKINS	: Hindu Mythology	30.00

POERTY

Author	Title	Price
E. FITZGERALD	: Rubaiyat of Omar Khayyam	15.00
PALGRAVE	: Palgrave's Golden Treasury	FC

REFERENCE

Author	Title	Price
PAIGE PALMER	: Travel Guide to North India	12.00
ALAN AND PALMER	: Quotations in History	16.00
	: Collins Gem English Dictionary	13.50
	: Collins Gem Thesaurus	15.00
	: Collins English Learner s Dictionary	49.80
ERIC NEAL	: A Sentence Dictionary	16.00
WILFRED D BEST	: The Student's Companion	15.00
MICHAEL J. WALLACE	: Collins Dictionary of English Idioms	10.00

SCIENCE & TECHNICAL

Author	Title	Price
ALBERT EINSTEIN	: Ideas and Opinions	20.00
H. JACOBOWITZ	: Electronics Made Simple	30.00
H. JACOBOWITZ	: Electornic Computers Made Simple	25.00
L. BASFORD	: Electricity Made Simple	25.00

SHORT STORIES

Author	Title	Price
AMRITA PRITAM	: The Aerial & Other Stories	8.00

JANE AUSTEN	: The Complete Novels of JANE AUSTEN	75.00
OSCAR WILDE	: Stories of Oscar Wilde	20.00
GOPINATH MOHANTY	: Ants and other Stories	8.00
MAUPASSANT	: The Complete Short Stories of DE MAUPASSANT	75.00
SUDHIN N. GHOSE	: Folk Tales and Fairy Stories from India	15.00
	: Folk Tales and Fairy Stories From Farther India	15.00

SOCIOLOGY

LUCY MAIR	: Marriage	12.00
JEFFREY MEYERS	: Married to Genius	16.00
ASHOK MITRA	: Calcutta Diary	18.00
	: Terms of Trade and Class Relations	18.00

SPORTS & PASTIME

	: Hand Book of Asian Games	12.00
	: Athletics Records of Asian Games	3.95
OSCAR HEIDENSTAM	: Muscle Building for Beginners	12.00
ARLOTT & TRUEMAN	: On Cricket	20.00
	: The MCC Cricket Coaching Book	15.00
CHESTER BARNES	: Table Tennis	15.00
DENNIS LILLEE	: The Art of Fast Bowling	20.00

DR. NAROTTAM PURI	: Portrait of Indian Captains	12.00
E.A.S. PRASANNA	: One More Over	12.00
ERIC MIDWINTER	: W.G. Grace—His Life and Times	16.00
FRANK TYSON	: Complete Cricket Coaching	RP
F.N.S. CREEK	: Teach yourself Cricket	FC
FRANK WORRELL	: Cricket Punch	10.00
GOPESH MEHRA	: Asian Games	15.00
KERSI MEHER-HOMJI	: Cricket's Great Families	20.00
MIHIR BOSE	: Keith Miller	15.00
SIR DONALD BRADMAN	: The Art of Cricket	60.00
SUNIL GAVASKAR	: Idols	20.00
	Sunny Days	20.00
SUDHIR VAIDYA	: Know Your Cricketers	15.00
S. MUSHTAQ ALI	: Cricket Delightful	15.00
TREVOR BAILEY	: Sir Gary	15.00
TONY COZIER	: The West Indies: Fifty Years of Test Cricket	15.00
VINOO MANKAD	: How to Play Cricket	9.00
VIJAY HAZARE	: A Long Innings	20.00